GILBOA

*New York's Quest for Water
and the Destruction of a Small Town*

Alexander R. Thomas

University Press of America,® Inc.
Lanham · Boulder · New York · Toronto · Oxford

Copyright © 2005 by
University Press of America,® Inc.
4501 Forbes Boulevard
Suite 200
Lanham, Maryland 20706
UPA Acquisitions Department (301) 459-3366

PO Box 317
Oxford
OX2 9RU, UK

Library of Congress Control Number: 2005921303
ISBN 0-7618-3070-7 (paperback : alk. ppr.)

For

Barbara Thomas,

who gave me life,

and

Polly Smith-Thomas,

who makes that life worth living

Table of Contents

List of Tables

List of Figures

List of Periodicals

Preface

I must confess a certain fascination with cities—it was born in my childhood. As a young child a trip to the "city" meant something very specific to me: a ride on a train into Penn Station, with my father upon our arrival combing the streets of his youth with my mother and I in tow. It was the 1970s, and my awe of Manhattan was marked by the contradictions of the times. A grungy streetscape pierced by gleaming office towers. Breasts peering through the windows of newspaper stands amid the modernistic promise of the lights of Times Square. Illegal entrepreneurship among the dealers in Bryant Park—behind the library. As I would later learn, the greatest city in the world was bankrupt at that time. However, the city revived during the 1980s and 1990s. There are more towers in the city, and I gleefully have lunch in Bryant Park unmolested by the Marijuana market. There is today an ESPN Zone where my mother would once cover my eyes in the car. And while I have long since lost that special view of the world granted only to children, I have never lost that sense of awe of the city.

But I spent most of my childhood in upstate New York. We lived in a small town with few urban graces, and so I swam in the creek behind my grandmother's trailer and ice-skated on a frozen pond at my cousin's log cabin a few miles away. Hiking was fun while at camp, but did not truly differ from the regular walks down the logging roads behind the town cemetery where most kids played. My parents, however, never quite gave up their metropolitan roots, and so we would periodically spend weekends with relatives still on Long Island and do our shopping in one of the local malls. By High School, even though I lived less than 30 miles from the Utica suburbs, I could have more easily explained how to get to Smithaven Mall or Northport Harbor than anywhere in the Mohawk Valley. It was with my driver's license and a cache of friends that I finally "discovered" the upstate cities. We would drive to Utica or Albany or Binghamton. We would cruise their main streets as if they were our own and frequent many of the businesses I knew only from the New York suburbs. And at the end of the night we would leave the city behind and drive back into the darkness of our own hometown.

I suppose, then, that my training in sociology, marked as it was by my experiences in Utica and Boston, has brought me to be neither an urban nor a rural scholar, but rather to the grey area that exists in between. My first book, *In Gotham's Shadow* (SUNY Press, 2003), compared the experience of the Utica Metropolitan Area to that of the rural hinterlands of Otsego County. *Gilboa*, however, should not be viewed as a follow up to that effort but rather as a different perspective on the same theme: how cities and their hinterlands relate to one another. Whereas *In Gotham's Shadow* seeks to *compare* differences and similarities of how urban and rural communities responded to the same trends in the global economy, this work seeks to *explain* the essence, to whatever degree I am capable, of the relationship between city and country. It is thus primarily a historical and theoretical work, augmented only slightly with interviews, statistics, and a survey.

Were it possible to conduct research on my own, it is debatable whether I would want to do so. The staff and students at Gilboa-Conesville Central School were friendly, insightful and honest, and this made the research an enjoyable experience. Their neighbors around the area, many of whom were willing to stop their chores of the moment and talk to a stranger from Oneonta, similarly made this an enjoyable study. Most of the research was historical, however, with several libraries and archives playing key roles in the collection of this data. For several months I was a familiar sight at the New York State Library and Archives in Albany, and I owe the staff a debt of gratitude. The vast collections of the New York Public Library—spanning several buildings in midtown Manhattan—were more easily navigated with the help of the professionals working with them every day. Likewise, the staff of the New York State Historical Association in Cooperstown have been friendly and helpful with this book, just as they were with my first book. At home, the staff at Milne Library at SUNY College at Oneonta have once again proven their unrivaled professionalism.

Polly Smith-Thomas, not only my fellow sociologist but, more importantly, my fellow traveler, has provided a sounding board and insights for the ideas contained in this book. Robert and Todd should be commended for once again enduring "the book" with no complaints. Alex Smith was a great help with the work in New York and Albany. Robert Smith has provided valuable feedback, as have the anonymous reviewers. Corinne Pollak has provided important resources in the past, for which I am grateful. The Sociology Department at SUNY Oneonta—Lisa Curch, Marilyn Helterline, Ho Hon Leung, Brian Lowe, and Fida Mohammad—makes arriving at work a pleasure. My students make the work itself pleasurable.

The research in this book was made possible by the generosity of a Walter B. Ford Research Grant from SUNY College at Oneonta.

Oneonta, N. Y.
9 August 2004

Introduction

This is not the book I wished to write. During the Fall of 1998 I was asked to teach a distance learning course. I taught Introduction to Sociology to fifteen students at the SUNY College at Oneonta campus and another dozen or so in a special room at Gilboa-Conesville High School approximately an hour away by car. I had never been to Gilboa, and so had no mental picture of what the community was like. During one class I asked students to describe their hometowns and was met with a chorus of, "we don't have a town" from the Gilboa students. I had recently completed my dissertation dealing with small towns and was in the process of writing my first book, and so I was accustomed to hearing children in small towns disparage their home communities. I assumed the students were exaggerating, that surely a place with a school must be amidst some kind of urban settlement—no matter the size. A then I drove to Gilboa to broadcast from their school.

I drove for many miles before turning onto New York 990V. The road descends into the ravine a little downstream of where the village once stood, crossing a frightening bridge (now replaced) to a post office amid the trees. A short distance further, carved into a hillside and surrounded by yet more trees was the school. I was greeted by a most dedicated staff, escorted to a small office and found myself transfixed by a photograph of the village overshadowed by a great dam. I was told of the village's condemnation by the City of New York in order to expand its water system. A company was to film the village's final end as the City burned the buildings in order to prepare the reservoir for water, but the villagers themselves burned the community the night before in order to deny New York the opportunity to profit from such destruction. I was, as many a sociologist might be, elated at the prospect of such a story of a community's resistance to its demolition. Alas, I found the story to be a myth developed later, and the bittersweet story I wished to bring to the world a rather depressing expose of the dynamics found between the greatest city on earth and its hinterland. Gilboa residents acted in much the same way as residents of the other—there were dozens—communities condemned by the City. A concerted campaign of resistance would make for a dramatic story, but perhaps instead an analysis of overall submission is a more accurate and ultimately helpful study. To refrain, this is not the book I wished to write.

. Nevertheless, my primary motivation was not to write a good story but rather to understand, not simply the building of a Catskill Mountain reservoir but the relationship between New York City and its

hinterland. With the drama of its events, Gilboa has provided a fascinating look into the dynamics found between great cities and the surrounding countryside. As a sociologist, it is my first instinct to examine the social context of any behavior, and as such I have examined the building of the dam as a form of institutional behavior. The raw facts of the project are compelling, but a deep understanding of why they occurred requires an examination of the *thick context* of events: the broad dynamics that have created the case over time. Hence, in order to explain the building of the Schoharie Reservoir, it is necessary to understand the significance of Iroquois power in upstate New York for the selection of Manhattan as the site for the city; of New York's founding as a trading center; and its dependence upon upstate infrastructure, such as the Erie Canal and the railroads, in its mercantile and industrial development. A discussion of British feudalism and its influence upon legal concepts such as land tenure and eminent domain, the significance of the decline of the Hapsburg Empire, and New York City's geology are all important foundations of New York's dominance. And of course, the influence of the reservoir on future relations between city and country shows that this historical event is not in the past but is very much a part of the present as well. The sociological significance of this moment in time is that there are social dynamics from which it arose and to which it leads. Indeed, the foundations of any moment of time are found deep in the past, in faraway lands among people who neither comprehend nor appreciate the gravity of their decisions. A greater desire on the part of the Dutch to stick to their first choice of settlement—modern day Albany—and all history would have been altered. A few votes cast differently by state legislators could have doomed the Erie Canal, thus also changing history. Yet other decisions that seemed so significant at the time, such as the founding of New Sweden in the Delaware Valley or the Dutch claim over Canomakers (the upper Susquehanna Valley near Cooperstown, New York), today are mere footnotes in history. Of course, they may somehow seem significant in years to come. To understand a unique historical moment, one must understand the totality of the moments leading to and from, not as a sequence of events but as the pulse of social dynamics streaming through time.

Once a work is to be understood in thick context, the urban sociologist must do the unthinkable: decenter the city as a unit of analysis. As discussed in chapter one, there is a great mythology embedded in the histories of New York and other great cities. This is the myth of urban self-sufficiency: that, somehow, a city grows of its own accord and momentum, attracting the best and the brightest because it is, in fact, so great. There is legitimacy in this idea as migrants from around the world have specifically chosen the city because of its greatness. But it is not a complete picture: New York, as all great cities, depends on the hinterland for nearly all of the basic human needs. Water for people to drink, food for people to eat, raw materials for factories to create the wares to be sold by the mercantilist class. A city's strength is thus its ability to maintain the networks of social interaction between themselves and the people in the hinterlands who control these resources. At times the means will be peaceful, at times exploitative. In order to explain how a city develops and operates, one must note not only the linkages to the outside world as they exist today—a project that forms much of the basis for studies of urban political economy—but also how these linkages have evolved over the full life of the city.

This work thus delves deep into the networks of social action, emerging as a complex history of the dynamic relationship found between New York and Gilboa. For all the complexity, I have endeavored to write a work that is readily understandable to those who wish to know the story. Although complex concepts do at times require some technical language, every attempt has been made to avoid unnecessary jargon. While I am sensitive to arguments suggesting that social science terminology should be as exact as humanly possible in order to convey meaning precisely, my belief is that the last half of the twentieth century has demonstrated remarkably well the futility of conveying precise meaning. While I may fail to convey my academic credentials as a result, I will derive great satisfaction with the knowledge that one need not be a social scientist to read this book.

1 Gilboa and the Goliath

October 18, 1925 was a typical autumn night in a not so typical small town. Stars peered through passing clouds as a deep chill settled into the Schoharie Valley. Moonlight cast a dim glow over the tiny Catskill Mountain hamlet of Gilboa, a strip of houses stretching along the road besides the bubbling of Schoharie Creek. At one end of a stretch of buildings that functioned as the village's downtown, the newly built Gilboa Dam loomed over the village, an omen of destruction in the Catskills and a beacon of progress for the great city that built it: New York. The village stood on the wrong side of the dam's brownstone façade, and as a result would soon be 150 feet under the waves of water soon to course through the mains ands veins of the greatest city on earth, allowing the rapid growth of the 1920s to continue unthreatened by draught. Most of the community's 400 residents had moved elsewhere—to Oneonta, to Cobleskill, to Afton—but some had remained to work on the dam along with thousands of immigrant laborers newly arrived in New York City and shipped upstate to help build the water supply. There were rumors swirling about town that the city had contracted with a Hollywood producer to film the burning of the village in order to make way for the new reservoir.

A little after 10:00, a foreman called "Wolf" strolled through the chasm of condemned downtown buildings. There was the murmur of conversations from various directions as some laborers laughed, and perhaps others gambled, as some grew intoxicated and others withdrew to their own dreams and memories. Something caught his attention—smoke, and the flicker of flames in the store of H. S. Slover. As the night wore on, the fire spread from building to building, from one side of the tightly packed street to the other, consuming 18 buildings in all. Fire companies from throughout the region arrived to fight the inferno in the valley as others drove their cars to the hilltops in order to watch the events unfold. The glow was visible in the night sky for miles in every direction. And in the morning, the heart of the hamlet lay in smoldering ruins.

Some residents—at the time and even decades later—would cite the resolve of Gilboa's residents to not allow the city to profit from their destruction by allowing a Hollywood producer to film the burning of the town. It is a difficult story to authenticate, as conflicting stories made the rounds of the newspapers at the time, and no document left behind by New York City officials claimed to have contracted with a film crew. Nevertheless, without the scene that night in Gilboa, as well as countless far less dramatic scenes of destruction in the hinterland, New York would have had insufficient water supplies and simply could not have functioned. Everything that New York City is today is the end product of its quest for water.

A New Rome

New York is the greatest city in the world. This is not a laudatory statement uttered by a lone individual strolling through the high peaks of midtown Manhattan. Nor is it praise showered by a politician with the anticipation of votes from a grateful populous. It is not an empirical statement, although some may choose to downplay the subjective nature of such a claim. It is, however, for the millions who have lived, worked, or visited New York, the most simplistic and articulate description of the city that can be offered.

New York City is a mammoth landscape, overwhelming in every dimension. Its streets offer up rows of twenty story plus buildings the way small towns proudly display two and three level structures. There are approximately 100 buildings over fifty stories tall. The shear breadth of the city overwhelms, stretching across five boroughs (in fact, counties) and spewing densely settled suburbs dozens of miles in every direction in three different states. The city alone has a population in excess of most states, and the homeless population of 100,000 exceeds that of the majority of cities nationwide. And if one cares to notice, the activity extends deep beneath the streets in tunnels for utility lines, subways, roadways, intercity trains, sewers, and, of course, water.

The city is home to many of the most powerful companies in the world, the wealthiest people in the world, the greatest diversity in the world. It is the greatest of all global cities, a beacon of freedom to millions if not billions around the world for decades. New York has the best and the brightest. Given such economic, political, and cultural brawn, its hinterland is not surprisingly absorbed, ignored, or expropriated for the great metropolis. Such presentations of the city as the Ric Burns (2001) documentary *New York* and Edwin Burrows' and Mike Wallace's (1999) book *Gotham* portray the city as self-made and self-sufficient. It is a familiar narrative: a city is founded and, due to the opportunity it offers, attracts the best and the brightest and so becomes even more great. But from where do the best and the brightest come? What effect does their emigration have on their home communities? And for that matter, how does a large urban environment provide the food, water, and raw materials necessary for the survival and employment of the best and brightest hordes? Examined more closely, the myth of New York's or any city's solitary greatness is a mere construction that conceals the reality of a necessary repression of the city's hinterland. And this is nowhere more apparent than in the water that throbs through the city's pipes beneath the streets.

Describing Cities

Like all cities, New York and Gilboa, a rural village in the Catskill Mountains, share in common a basic structure on which they are both constructed. This structure is based on the four major aspects of social life that any social organization must ultimately address and develop. These are, in no particular order or importance, polity, economy, culture, and environment (PECE). It is thus an appropriate starting point for an analysis of how cities function and, by extension, how New York and Gilboa function.

Polity, as discussed by Parsons (1951), is the institution by which collective decisions are made. Although it is theoretically possible for decisions to be made through consensus, collective decision-making is most often the result of the domination by some over the interests of others (Weber, 1986). The methods by which this takes place—which is to say power—will be discussed in detail later in this chapter.

Economy, as also discussed by Parsons (1951), is the institution responsible for the production and distribution of the necessities required for continued existence. Economies can be rather simple, as is the case with many Hunting and Gathering societies, or quite complex, as is the case in modern industrial societies. As will be discussed, this is ultimately dependent upon production.

Culture refers to the accumulated knowledge of the social organization (Parsons, 1951). Culture is constantly created through the social interaction of participants (Goffman, 1959; Blumer, 1990; Collins, 1975). Individuals reinforce each other's culturally learned ideas—norms, values, beliefs, etc.—through interaction with others. Bourdieu (1972) has referred to this store of cultural knowledge within the individual as *habitus*. Because of habitus, one's perception of reality is constructed through social interaction (Berger & Luckmann, 1968. Although culture has at times been understood as a kind of superstructure or collective conscience (see Durkheim, 1997), it is in fact a pattern of learned behaviors that is constantly recreated and reinforced through social interaction.

Environment refers to the external factors that affect an organism. This includes the physical environment, which includes all of the biotic (living, such as plants and animals) and abiotic (non-living, such as climate and soil) resources available to the organism or society. Also included is the social environment, which not only structures social interaction (Giddens, 1991) but access to physical resources as well. This is analogous to Bourdieu's (1972) concept of *field*.

These aspects of social life are constantly interacting with and changing one another. For instance, the political structure and the economy of a social organization are intractably linked to one another (Ormerod, 1994; Granovetter, 1985). In fact, as Phillips (2002) demonstrated well, the truly large fortunes of the past 1000 years have been accumulated due to either a dominant position in the power structure of a region or a proximity to those who hold such positions. There is frequently an appearance of reciprocity between the operation of such institutions. For instance, the culture is often utilized by the political elite to justify its domination (Weber, 1986; Marx, 1990), and this changes the culture such that the masses seldom seek to change the dominant political system (Herman & Chomsky, 1988). The environment is crucial in determining the type of economy possible—agriculture depends upon the availability of water, industry that of access to raw materials, and so on.

For example, in the ancient Greek city of Athens, the urban settlement was surrounded by what remained of its polis (Attica): the hinterland surrounding the urbanized area of the city (Connolly & Dodge, 2000; Hall, 1998). For the Greeks, the polis was not only the state but the definition of the city itself (Keller, 2003). Athens ended not at the outskirts of urbanization but rather included its hinterland as a necessary, if not in time unsatisfactory, adjunct to the city. It was from the hinterland that precious food was raised and grown, and the ideal pursuit of the Greek gentry was that of farming. In time, Athens grew so that the city necessarily looked elsewhere for food, trading the products of olives to pay for them. (Attica was well suited for olive cultivation, but little else). The city had outgrown the polis.

The economic structure of Athens was by necessity oriented toward providing at first food for the city and then toward raising agricultural goods for export in trade for, in many cases, food and other raw materials not readily available at appropriate levels in the polis. Landholdings of wealthy Athenians were scattered throughout the countryside but owned by urban dwellers who proffered supposed rights of private property as the moral mechanism for continuing their domination of agricultural land. This was supported by a political system that, contrary to modern conceptions of Athenian democracy, conferred citizenship to relatively few polis residents and favored among them the wealthiest members of the society. In fact, the definition of the polis as including the city and the countryside inherently favored the interests of the more populous urban population over the lower number of those who lived in rural areas. City claims of ownership of the surrounding territory is a common trait of urban cultures, and with it are overlapping dynamics of social class and other forms of social differentiation (race, ethnicity, etc.). The environment of the polis, as craggy and poorly soiled as it is, was best suited for the cultivation of olives, thus forcing the Athenians to trade rather early in their development.

The legitimacy of the system was upheld by the culture, both through the formalized culture produced in the city (such as plays, music, etc.) and the everyday interactions of residents, including between residents of rural areas and the urban patricians who maintained homes in their midst.

Much the same can be said of New York and countless other modern cities. The occasional community garden cannot supply the city with food. Any natural resources locked in the ground are buried deep beneath buildings and the people who dwell within. And water—a persistent challenge from the days of the Dutch—the water in the city, surrounded as it is by people and pollution, is best left in the ponds and fountains. A Goliath amid a sea of Davids, the city is dependent upon the resources of other places in order to secure its own survival. This is not an aberration, but rather a fundamental truth of urbanization.

The Urban Dependency Model

Athens provides an interesting archetype for later global cities. Peaking in population at only "about 40,000 citizens and perhaps 275,000 people in all" (Hall, 1998, 35), Athens was the largest and most powerful city in the Mediterranean world, peaking about 450 BC. It was not born into such greatness, but instead grew into a global (for the time) city. It is the process of that growth that is interesting, for it is similar to that of major cities in other time periods as well, save for locality and time specific variations. In the Athenian polis, the city formed around a center for trade and religious ritual. Well placed within the polis and a gateway to the Aegean Sea and the Mediterranean beyond, Athens grew through trade and conquest. The hinterland early on supplied the city with food and raw materials, as like other poleis Athens "was based not on trade but on a self-sufficient and self-governing group of villages, in a narrow and closed region lying around an urban centre" (Hall, 1998, 35). As the population grew, however, the hinterland could no longer adequately provide food and otherwise supply the city, and thus trade grew more important, even critical, over time. Trade, aided by a skilled military, brought wealth to the city and attracted immigrants from throughout the Greek world (Hall, 1998). In fact, some of the most notable figures of Athens were in fact *metoikoi* (resident aliens) and not native Athenians. At the time of Athens' golden age, agriculture for subsistence had been largely supplanted by agriculture for trade, notably in olives and olive oil. As the city and country were so linked in Athens, it is not surprising that similar relationships have existed and continue to do so between cities and their respective hinterlands today. Yet even in the great city of Athens, the population could see the linkages between agriculture and city life, between trade and prosperity, and their own nearby boundaries and the dependence upon other regions (Keller, 2003, 18). In the unimaginably large cities of today, such linkages are obscured behind the countless circuits of trade. Few today would consider the presence of corn syrup in their cola when passing a growing field. In order to understand not only Athens, but New York City and Gilboa as well, it is necessary to understand the distinction and interrelatedness of rural and urban production.

In Athens, in New York, in any number of different types of societies, people need to eat and drink, require clothing and shelter to keep them warm and dry, and desire interaction with others. The latter was met by the existence of social groups that predate the human species, but the others require some level of extraction from the environment. With a low population, a settlement may extract and produce for its needs with the resources from the immediate surroundings. Such economic activities oriented toward the extraction or production of food and raw materials (e.g., metal ore, stone, wood, etc.) can be called rural production.

Rural production has two major traits: 1) it is space extensive, and 2) it is labor extensive. All rural products are land extensive in that they either require a large amount of space and/or they are found only in specific places beyond the control of human intervention. For instance, most crops require considerable acreage to grow in amounts that can support a population. This is a characteristic of the plant itself: a single corn plant may require nearly a square foot to grow in a healthy and productive fashion, and there is little humans can do about it. With fertilizers and biotechnology the amount of space may be reduced, but only to a point. Similarly, cattle require considerable acreage for grazing when in a natural environment. Even confined to the unnatural environment of a barn, a large amount of land is required to grow the food for the animals. In some cases, the resource is not transplantable and thus requires that people travel to it for extraction. Metal ores, for example, are formed in place and cannot be created in a more convenient location—extraction must take place at the mine itself.

All rural products are, to one degree or another, non-transplantable. Plants can only grow in certain climates and landscapes, for instance. Due to the ability to build canals and other transport devices, water is more transplantable than minerals but, due to limitations imposed by gravity and other factors, is not as transplantable as agricultural products.

Rural production is labor extensive. This is not to suggest that there is no labor expended, as considerable time and technology is often expended on cultivating the right environment for some forms of rural production (e.g., farming). However, the production of the resource requires no human intervention. Minerals are created by geologic forces, not human labor. Similarly, the cow or sheep grows with no help from people—these processes occur naturally. In fact, human labor in rural production is devoted primarily to transplantation or extraction (harvest) of the resource, such as planting a field of crops and harvesting the grown plants. The transformative process that is at the heart of production (i.e., growth) itself, however, occurs naturally.

Rural production is a necessary precursor to all forms of production that seek to transform a raw material into a finished product, and thus may be thought of as the rural circuit of production. A second circuit, or urban circuit, revolves around the transformation of the extracted resource.

Urban production is generally space intensive. In most cases, once the necessary materials have been assembled urban production can take place nearly anywhere. It is thus highly transplantable and, not surprisingly, increasingly mobile with advances in transportation and communications technology (Harvey, 1999; see also Bluestone & Harrison, 1982). In contrast to rural production, urban production takes less space, although a factory can appear rather imposing in a densely settled urban environment. This space typically does not compare with the amount of space necessary for the extraction of the raw materials involved. Much of the space in modern factories is not utilized for production *per se*, but rather as a means for making mass production efficient and rapid. For instance, an automobile requires a considerable amount of raw materials extracted from an immense area, such as rubber for tires, cotton for cloth, and petroleum for plastics. Each of the raw materials are necessarily processed and the parts assembled in a factory for purposes of mass production, but could theoretically be produced in a much smaller area (a backyard, perhaps) once the component parts have been collected.

The actual production—the transformation from one or several objects into another—is labor intensive. There are no car seeds that grow to be a Buick, but rather considerable labor power that accounts for the transformation. It is likely that the earliest forms of urban production took place in order to streamline the process of rural production. *Homo habilis*, for instance, used stone tools as an aid to breaking apart the bones of animals in order to extract the marrow (Maryanski & Turner, 1992). Much more recently, the plow was developed as an aid to agriculture (Johnson & Earle, 1987). In both cases, however, the initial resource (stone and wood, respectively) was extracted from the environment (rural circuit) and then transformed into a final product (urban circuit). The end product could then be used as an aid to rural production (marrow extraction and agriculture).

Urban production varies in terms of degrees of separation from rural production. The assembly of an apple pie by a colonial farmer from materials grown on the farm has little if any separation: the rural circuit of production is immediately apparent. Consider the automobile, however: assembled as it is from a multitude of items already processed, e.g. tires, cloth, plastic, etc., which themselves are created with processed items, the degree of separation between the automobile and its roots in rural production is quite large.

The dynamics between city and country created by urban dependency often result in a discourse that favors trade over self-sufficiency as the city's own self-sufficiency wanes. Athens maintained an extensive trade network and exercised considerable control over the Hellenistic economy (Hall, 1998; see also Morley,

2002). Rome, too, expanded its sphere of influence in central Italy through trade and war, and in time the expansion of that influence through empire building became an end in itself (Hall, 1998). New York, as shown in chapters 2 and 3, is no different. Even though the city was settled to be a trading center, the resources of Manhattan were sufficient for decades, supporting not only New York but several other villages, such as Greenwich and Harlem. Over time, however, the burgeoning city needed to look further inland for basic resources, trading with upstate farmers for food and eventually extending the water system to areas closer to Albany and Binghamton than the city itself.

Within this complex of rural/urban dynamics was Gilboa, a rural town built along the banks of the Schoharie Creek. Schoharie Creek flows from the Catskill Mountains north to the Mohawk River near the industrial city of Amsterdam. The valley contains some of the oldest European settlements in New York State, as the initial wave of migration funneled settlers north through the Hudson Valley, west through the Mohawk Valley, and south through the Schoharie Valley. Although some settlements in the region date to the 1740s, Gilboa was first settled in the early nineteenth century. The relationship between Gilboa and its distant neighbor to the south has had dramatic consequences for its settlement space and the social construction of community.

Urban Domination

Given the dependency of large urban settlements, it is often easier for smaller settlements to support themselves with no assistance from other communities. As Heilbroner & Milberg (1998) have discussed:

> Communities numbering only a few hundred can live indefinitely. Indeed, a considerable percentage of the human race today lives in precisely such a fashion— in small, virtually self-contained peasant communities that provide for their own survival with a minimum of contact with the outside world. (2)

Gilboa was for most of its history quite capable of providing food, water, and shelter for its residents. Settled in the fertile Schoharie Valley, there were no real problems finding water and growing crops. The heavily wooded countryside provided material for shelter. Had the villagers sought a thoroughly non-urban existence similar to, for example, the Amish of Pennsylvania, they could have prospered. Alas, they did not.

As urban communities become larger, they must by necessity enlarge their sphere of influence over the rural hinterland. And if the rural hinterland contains another rural village, the village itself must by necessity be in some way brought under the control of the larger community. A failure to do so would bring about starvation in the larger community until its population fell in line with the carrying capacity of its own hinterland. New York had been capable of self-sufficiency early in its history under Dutch and British colonial rule. Based on its trade economy, New York grew ever larger and eventually consumed other communities on Manhattan Island and eventually in other counties as well.

In Marx' (1990 [1867]) view, it is in the interest of capitalists to keep wages low as the costs associated with buildings and machines are fixed. But even as wages paid for labor are more flexible, there is a fixed component to labor cost as well: the workers must be paid enough to feed themselves and reproduce more laborers. However, the costs associated with the reproduction of labor are not entirely fixed. Variations in the cost of food and other rural products influence the costs of keeping a worker alive, and therefore it is in the interests of capitalists to control the cost of rural production (Thomas, 2003). It is thus over the costs associated with rural production that capitalism most sharply comes into conflict with rural producers. Or more precisely here, how New York City came into conflict with its upstate neighbors.

When there is a balance between the amount of food that can be produced in a region and the number of people living in a given city, prices over agricultural products will tend to remain stable over time. In a capitalist system, however, one way of lowering wages below the level required to purchase food is to lower the cost of food itself. One way of lowering food prices is to lower the cost of agricultural production itself through mechanization, which often generates an oversupply of agricultural products available to urban producers (i.e. food processing companies) and consumers and thus results in depressed prices. There is also the added benefit that capital can sell urban products to rural producers, thus bringing them into the money system and subjecting rural production to capitalist forces. Just as often, urban capitalists may expand the sphere of influence they hold over rural producers in order to insure an oversupply of farms, and thus, an oversupply of agricultural products. In both cases, prices of agricultural products are lowered and with them the "fixed" costs associated with the reproduction of labor. Capitalist producers are thus able to lower wages and in so doing the surplus labor of not only the worker but the farmer as well is transferred to the capitalist.

Similarly, the costs associated with acquiring raw materials must also be lowered in order to maximize the profits of the capitalists. As with food, this seemingly fixed cost in the circuitry of urban production can be lowered by either increasing the supply of the products through mechanization or by simply expanding the sphere of influence (and hence the trade network) of the capitalist city. Again, the oversupply lowers the market value of rural goods and thus transfers the surplus labor of the rural producer to the Capitalist.

The need to maintain prices of agricultural products and other raw materials needed for urban production at a relatively low level translates into an objective need for any city to enlarge its sphere of influence beyond its own hinterland

and into other areas. Marx (1985 [1848]) discussed this necessity in the following terms:

> The bourgeoisie has subjected the country to the rule of the towns. It has created enormous cities, has greatly increased the urban population as compared to the rural, and has thus rescued a considerable part of the population from the idiocy of rural life. (84)

Marx recognized that cities exercise power over rural areas and even considered such dominance as positive. However, Marx failed to adequately analyze the fact that rural production is a necessary precursor to urban production, and thus the rural population was not simply the feudal equivalent of the proletariat in the outgoing economic era but rather a necessary component of capitalism as well. This is perhaps why he concentrated primarily on the political and economic relations involved with urban production.

Modern capitalism further exacerbates urban/rural dynamics by favoring urban producers in large urban settings over urban producers in smaller communities. Cities have grown not only because of the capitalist need for labor and their potential replacements, but because of the economies of scale produced by bringing ever larger populations into a small geographic area. The population of a large city represents a mass market for an array of goods and services within short proximity of the producer. In addition, access to credit, research, and governmental services give many urban locales a decided advantage over smaller towns that lack many of these attributes. The result is that urban producers in larger cities are able to utilize the economies of scale of their respective cities to produce a greater supply of a given product at a lower cost than possible by companies in smaller towns. The lower production costs and higher profits available to larger producers allow them to undercut the pricing of companies in smaller communities, leading to businesses in smaller towns closing or being bought by larger companies. Accordingly, the evolution of modern capitalism has been accompanied by trends toward increased concentration of urban production in larger urban settings and the relative immiseration of smaller villages and the rural hinterland—the essence of combined and uneven development (O'Connor, 1998). It is thus important to recognize that global cities are the beneficiaries of the increased concentration of the world economy precisely because they are in fact so large—their corporations have used their city's size and location as a vehicle for growth that eventually allows them to take over the corporations of smaller communities (see also Sassen, 1991). Not surprisingly, the relationship of the near hinterland thus changes over time as its own institutions and productive capacity is first absorbed into the city and gradually surpassed by the lower labor costs found in more distant locales.

During the nineteenth century, New York became increasingly dependent upon trade with the interior for food and other rural products. A great trading center, the city handled much of the goods coming into and leaving the northeast, especially along the corridor of the Erie Canal in upstate New York. By forming alliances with the elites of the lesser cities upstate, New York was able to control many of the decisions regarding its future in state government in Albany. Smaller communities were, in a sense, at the mercy of the state when confronting the great metropolis, and the results were not always favorable to rural towns. Such was the case in Gilboa, increasingly brought into the trade system during the nineteenth century and finally, between 1916 and 1925, burned and flooded to make way for the Schoharie Reservoir. New York needed the water for its burgeoning population, but it was the state that granted the city the power to destroy any community that dared challenge the right of Gotham to grow.

The Role of the State

It might be successfully argued that the rise of the state in the ancient world was a function of rural/urban dynamics. The ruling elites of growing cities, as elites everywhere, needed to maintain an appearance of legitimacy or risk losing the ability to rule (Weber, 1986). As food, water, and raw materials are vitally important to the social and economic life of the city, a failure to secure a reliable supply could bring about a crisis of legitimacy. As the city grew, the elite necessarily looked elsewhere for a steady supply of rural products.

In some cases, ruling elites could increase the supply of rural products by attracting additional laborers. In Babylon, for instance, the sacking of Jerusalem in AD 70 resulted in additional slaves for the Babylonian Empire who could be used in the production of food and the maintenance of the urban infrastructure. Athens also attracted outside labor through both force in the form of slavery and voluntary immigration by residents of other cities.

Ruling elites also have the option of expanding the sovereignty of the city. For instance, Rome initially sought to assimilate the population of other communities in central Italy, simply considering them to be Roman as well. This worked only to the point that the Romans shared significant cultural similarities, and in time found it necessary to conquer neighbors by force, beginning with the Etruscans to the north.

The growth of the city and the enlargement of the city's sphere of influence necessitates the beginning of the state. The state functions as an instrument of integration among the elites of the disparate communities involved. In addition, the state serves as an intermediary between city and hinterland and, in the case of states with multiple cities, between competing cities as well. However, the intermediary function is not entirely balanced as the city can exercise considerable power on its behalf, and so often the state operates as an instrument of the dominant city. In addition, the existence of the state functions to obscure the domination of rural interests by the urban elite. The urban elite gains legitimacy in exchange for a forum in which the dominated hinterland can address their concerns.

For Max Weber (1986), the existence of the state symbolized the monopolized use of power. The most obvious mode of exercising power is through coercive means, and it is of this that most people think upon hearing the word. It may be defined as the use or threat of use of force in order to achieve a given objective. Force or the threat of force can be utilized to convince rural producers in other areas of the need to trade with the city. This has been true in pre-capitalistic times as well, as the Roman Empire was (initially, at least) created and maintained through these means. Similarly, the British utilized force to create a worldwide network of rural producers for the benefit of their own urban enterprises (e.g., mercantilist traders; textile mills).

As force often requires a considerable outlay of resources, it is generally more efficient to use cultural means to broaden the sphere of influence of the city. The United States, for instance, serves as a large free market that strongly benefits urban producers but was formed through primarily peaceful means (although not entirely so). Power is gained by the urban culture offering its products to rural consumers, thus cultivating allegiance. The relationship is normally one-sided, however, as cities have greater populations and economic power. Typically, cities are the center of cultural production in their respective regions, and as such the opinions and perspectives presented are based on an assumption of urban superiority while rural interests, tastes, and perspectives are by and large ignored (Thomas, 2003). Such exercise of power can be understood as hegemonic. Mann (1986) considered such a source of power as ideological, but I argue here that ideology is not so much a source of power as an exercise of power.

Both coercive and hegemonic power is normally used by the state in order to control a given population, both those within the city and those who live outside its borders. Power may be exercised in a multitude of ways, but these techniques fall into three broad categories: military, political, and economic (Mann, 1986). In each form of power, both coercive and hegemonic control is utilized to varying degrees as a continuum.

Military power is specifically the ability to utilize force against a population. The obvious practitioners of military force are, of course, the military. Not so obvious are the many non-military forces that exist in a society, such as the police, private security forces, etc. In an exercise of hegemonic control, such institutions as the police are defined as being "non-military" despite their essential role as an enforcer of "peace" within the society. Military power typically extends beyond simple coercive control in other ways as well. For instance, in many militarized societies the military or its internal analogs are portrayed in exalted roles, such as the savior of children, protector of the innocent, and keeper of social order. In many cases, the military agents themselves assume such duties, such as the DARE (Drug Abuse Resistance Education) programs that proliferated throughout American schools during the 1980s and 1990s. In essence, military power threatens the safety and security of individuals, and such a threat must necessarily be either concealed or portrayed as beneficial.

Political power is the ability to exercise control over policy through personal or party characteristics. Although such power is often reinforced by military power, it ultimately lies on the ability to control actors through charisma or personal loyalty. Similarly, the effect of such considerations on others can encourage a wayward political actor to tow the line of the organization. Hence, a political machine in a major city may control the votes of elected officials by an appeal to party loyalty (hegemonic control) or by threatening to withhold electoral support (coercion). Political power is essentially the ability to have others alter their own course of action in line with someone else's wishes.

Economic power is the ability to exercise control over and with the processes and institutions related to production. At its heart, economic power involves a threat to an individual's or party's ability to feed, clothe, and shelter themselves. Economic power can be utilized in a coercive manner, as when companies threaten to leave communities unless granted a tax break. However, economic power is perhaps best utilized as hegemonic power, such as convincing individuals that their own economic interests are identical to that of the economic elite, e.g., the odd American Constitutional notion that corporations are legally constituted people and thus deserving of the same rights as actual living beings (Hartmann, 2002).

In each case, power is dynamically enhanced by the existence of other forms of power. Thus, military power enables economic exploitation, which leads to more investment in military power and hence enhanced military power, which contributes to political power which similarly enhances both military and economic power. In the case of the New York City water supply, the tremendous economic resources of the city enabled it to buy off much opposition in the form of relatively high wages. The city also had considerable political power in Albany, and in fact state government acted very much as a mouthpiece for city interests during this time period. Both the city and the state sent police forces into the area in order to ensure that any remaining opposition could not mount a successful defense of the region.

Theory & Practice

To reiterate, the basic contours of the relationship between New York City and Gilboa are to be understood as bounded by environmental factors evident in both communities and the territory in between. New York was blessed by its environment for trade, holding a strategic position on an island at the terminus of the Hudson-Mohawk River system and within a bay guarded from the Atlantic Ocean. It was not particularly well situated in regard to natural resources, certainly not for the seemingly boundless population who would move to Manhattan. The city needed its hinterland to grow, and Gilboa was (and is) merely a part of that vast hinterland.

The environment specified an economy based on trade and, later, manufacturing and service industries. Trade was the path to wealth, but it was first the path to mere survival. As New York grew due to its trade economy, the city became increasingly dependent upon its hinterland not only for food and raw materials but other goods to trade as well. After the (1825) opening of the Erie Canal, New York State became the most urbanized state in the country and New York City traded nearly all of its wares with the rest of the world. In a sense, even the upstate cities were part of an "urban hinterland" that supplied an array of goods that enriched themselves and the great metropolis.

New York City was able to utilize the state government for a variety of chores, from the incorporation of the Manhattan Company—an early attempt at building a water system—to the ability to use the power of eminent domain to condemn and destroy entire communities in the way of its water system. The state was, in a sense, an instrument of City power, but with a great tradeoff: New York needed to listen to the concerns of others. That the state acted as an arbitrator between New York and other regions was evident to many, as upstate residents at times grew resentful of the city's power in state government. New York City itself, in an acknowledgement of the utility of state government mechanisms, at one point rejected a plan to tap water in western New England and instead built the more costly "Catskill" water system because of its ability to influence state government. In many cases, the City acted in concert with legislative delegations from other major cities who shared interests common to urban areas.

The culture of New York State thus came to be dominated by urban interests. Contrary to the popular misconception of an "urban" downstate and a "rural" upstate, New York is better characterized by a southern tip containing one of the largest cities in the world, an upstate urban corridor of four million residents, and a handful of smaller cities scattered throughout the remainder of the state. Of the state's 1.5 million residents not living in a metropolitan area, nearly all are within an hour's drive of a metropolitan area. In short, New York's culture is urban and reflects the interests and views of city life. Not surprisingly, there has traditionally been little controversy about the need and supposed right of New York City, or any of the state's other major cities, to condemn property in order to meet its needs. Such controversies as there were related to the specific properties involved and not the right of the government to do so.

In reality, the tidy parameters of Polity, Economy, Culture, and Environment are interlaced and dissectible only with great effort. The environment of 1920s Gilboa included the power relations that favored New York and other cities over small towns. The culture reinforced such dominance by providing the intellectual justifications: that the needs of the many outweigh the needs of the few (apologies to *Star Trek*), that cities are the key feature of "civilization," etc.. Perhaps more important, the culture included for some the knowledge that fighting the City over the building of Gilboa Dam would be difficult at best and quite possibly fruitless. For others, the culture concealed the reality that this was so by constant allusion to "democracy" and "representation." As for most rural areas, "representation" belongs to cities with their high populations and the tyrannical powers that reside with the majority. For Gilboans, this was a simple, if unrecognized by many, political fact. Even without the power afforded by representative democracy—representative by population and not space—New York City and the larger urban-based political economic system of which it was the most central part had the economic resources to sway other politicians, divide the resident population into factions, and ultimately build the dam.

Such power, infused as it is throughout the basic functioning of a society, has the potential, although not the certainty, of breeding in its practitioners perceptions of infallibility, permanency, and even virtue. Such a perception propagates notions of unquestionable morality even when such treatment fails to reach even the most basic of ethical guidelines. (Indeed, it is the simple ethical guidelines that are most difficult to follow). No New Yorker would ever suggest the demolition of the great city if it were for the betterment of our society as a whole—nor would I. But city engineers not only proposed but followed through on a plan for the Schoharie Reservoir that included building of the Gilboa Dam through the middle of what was downtown Gilboa, scattering the village's 400 residents to the winds, for the betterment of New York City.

The tarnish on the Golden Rule is not the focus of this book. It is an ever-present feature, as it is in much of history, but the challenge of social science research is not to decry but to understand. The destruction of Gilboa was not an isolated event but rather was rooted in an ongoing relationship between New York and its hinterland. The relationship was in place long before the Schoharie Reservoir, and it continues today.

2   Foundation

It was not a *fait accompli* that the people of New York and Gilboa would share such a legacy as the Schoharie Reservoir. New York is a coastal city and Gilboa was a mountain village, the former turning to the sea as the latter was surrounded by crude trails through dense forest. Culturally, pre-colonial New York belonged primarily to Algonquian Lenapes, whereas Gilboa was more familiar to the Algonquian Mohicans and later the Iroquois Mohawks. In numerous other ways, the territory of each future community was a world apart from the other even before Europeans took an interest in the Hudson River watershed.

The First War

As perhaps every proud middle schooler knows, Columbus did not truly "discover" America. There is the obvious consideration that since the Americas supported an indigenous population for over ten thousand years (Fagan, 2000); it is rather presumptuous to suggest that Columbus discovered anything. Rather, Columbus was a European discoverer of America. Even here, however, Columbus was not the first. Norse sailors had found and even settled the coast of New Foundland centuries before Columbus—a tale recounted in the Norse Sagas (Magnusson, 1965) and proven with an archeological site at L'Anse aux Meadows. More properly, then, is the proposition that Columbus' discovery set in motion events that changed the course of world history.

By 1492, the Americas, just as Europe, had witnessed the rise and fall of empires and cultures. To the south of New York, Spanish explorers following the example of Columbus stumbled upon several prosperous civilizations as well as those subject to or in fear of their power. In the imperial centers, the cities rivaled the greatest of Europe. Perhaps the most elaborate was Tenochtitlan, the capital of the powerful Aztec Empire today buried beneath the streets of Mexico City. To the south, the Inca Empire stretched for thousands of miles along the spine of the Andes Mountains in western South America. Its capital, Cuzco, was fabulously wealthy with numerous buildings clad with gold (Fagan, 2000). As the sixteenth century wore on, the Spanish Empire and their ruling family, the Habsburgs, grew wealthy through the plunder of their conquests in the Americas.

The Habsburg Empire included not only the Iberian Peninsula but a stretch of territory between France and modern Germany in the north of Europe as well. Far from the halls of power in Spain, these "Netherlands" contained some of the most important trading centers in Europe, such as Amsterdam and Rotterdam. The Dutch merchants in what is today known alternatively as both Holland and The Netherlands commanded much of the trade from the new world[1]. What they did not have was a strong sense of loyalty to the Habsburgs, a fact that became all the more crucial to Dutch and American history as a result of the Protestant Reformation.

It was on October 31, 1517 that Martin Luther nailed his famous proclamation to the doors of Wittenberg Cathedral and the Protestant Reformation began its sweep through northern Europe. Earlier incarnations, in particular the Lutheran and (later) Anglican branches, are best characterized as demands for reform of the existing structures of Christendom (Smith, 1989). To varying degrees, much of the rebellion was directed at the Catholic power structure, especially the Pope, with relatively minor theological changes. In later years, however, the Reformation took a far more radical turn with the teaching of John Calvin. Calvin taught that not only was the hierarchy of the Catholic Church invalid, but that those Protestant Denominations that failed to shed themselves of a dedicated priesthood were still guilty of "papalism." Moreover, Calvinists believed that, as God is a timeless entity, all events that would occur had, from the vantage point of God, already occurred. It of course followed that those "saved" during the events described in the biblical book of Revelation had already been chosen (Johnstone, 2001). Such a belief in predestination rested squarely in contradiction to Catholic teaching that stressed a continual struggle with sin requiring regular cleansing through mass and confession. Calvinism taught that believers, by virtue of having been called to the fold, were saved. In a region remote from Rome and under the thumb of the Habsburgs, such a message of predetermined salvation spread quickly. As the Catholic Habsburgs sought to quell religious and, ultimately, political dissent, the cause of freedom and Protestantism spread ever more rapidly. By the late 1500s, the Netherlands was in open revolt against their Spanish overlords (Hooker, 1999). Faced with civil war in the north and increasing competition for economic and military domination, the Spanish Empire began to rot away from the inside out (Kennedy, 1989).

For the future New York, it was not the Dutch who first found the Hudson Valley of interest. Under contract with French King Francis I and a group of Lyons silk merchants, the Florentine sailor Giovanni da Verrazano explored

---

1. Technically, Holland is the largest of several provinces in The Netherlands.

New York Harbor in 1524. However, it was not until 1609 when Henry Hudson led his Dutch ship *Halve Maen* (Half Moon) to a site near present day Albany on his namesake river that a colony seemed both possible and desirable.

With the Union of Utrecht the Dutch "Netherlands" formed the Dutch Republic in 1579, fortified their navy and fought wave after wave of Spanish invaders intent on maintaining Catholic spirit and Habsburg power in the region (Israel, 1998). At the same time, Dutch ships raided Spanish ports and shipping throughout the new world and thus signaled Spanish vulnerability to the up and coming British and French. When the Spanish assembled the largest naval armada ever to sail the English Channel in 1588, the Dutch aided the British in ultimately defeating them. It is thus no surprise that 1609 has a significance that extends beyond Hudson's exploration of their future colony: it was also the year that Spain finally relented and offered the Dutch a cease-fire. Although it would be another forty years before the arrangement was final, the Dutch had won independence.

The Dutch West India Company

The Dutch West India Company was formed in order to emulate the success of the Dutch East India Company. Founded in 1621, the Dutch West India Company was granted rights to trade in the new world. From the beginning, the company favored its more profitable operations in the Caribbean and South America. As the cease-fire with Spain came to an end, the Company found piracy among its most profitable ventures, sacking and looting Spanish strongholds and shipping throughout the Americas. In sum, the company was organized for strict purposes of making a profit through whatever means possible.

One such profitable enterprise involved the trade for animal furs. The discovery of the new world allowed western Europeans the opportunity to develop new sources of furs (Bachman, 1969). Prior, many furs were harvested in Russia and commanded high prices in such cities as Amsterdam and Paris. The French were the first to develop a vibrant trade in furs by establishing outposts in the Saint Lawrence River valley and developing trade networks with native tribes. The Dutch turned their attention to their south, to an area first explored by an agent of the Dutch East India Company: British explorer Henry Hudson. Hudson had in fact been looking for a passage to the East Indies during his explorations of 1609, but his ultimate goal was a failure, as one did not exist. The Hudson River valley could be valuable to the Dutch West India Company as an avenue for the fur trade.

The Dutch claimed all territory between the Delaware and Connecticut Rivers. Some early maps also show the territory of the upper Susquehanna Valley—a region the Dutch called Canomakers—as well. The central focus of the colony, however, was on the Hudson Valley. The Dutch West India Company set up *factories*—not the industrial variety known today, but rather trading posts. The earliest outpost was on Castleton Island less than ten miles from modern Albany in 1617 (Burrows & Wallace, 1999). The first serious attempt at settlement, however, was attempted at Fort Orange (today called Albany) in 1624. When thirty families arrived in the new colony they called New Netherlands, the company sent a handful to factories throughout the territory, but the greatest number went to Fort Orange.

Fort Orange would remain an important factory and settlement in the colony, eventually being renamed Albany and made the state capital in 1797. But not during the Dutch tenure. In one of those moments when fate intervenes, a complex set of events forced the population south to the tip of Manhattan Island. Due to French incursions in the Saint Lawrence valley, the Iroquois Mohawk Indians were forced south into what became eastern New York. The region was already home to the Algonquian Mohikans, and thus a war ensued for the territory. The conflict was not a balanced one, however. In the late sixteenth century, the Mohawks had joined with other Iroquois tribes to become the League of the Five Nations.[2] Also known as the Iroquois Confederacy, it was formed so that it "might be effective in restoring sanity and peace to their nations" (Kehoe, 1992, 245). As with many nations, the subtleties of defense and offense were blurred and the Confederacy fought a number of clearly offensive wars, including the one to conquer the Mohicans.

Within this context, the Dutch made two fateful and wise decisions. After some initial study, they chose to involve themselves as little as possible in the conflict, siding if forced to make a decision with the more powerful Mohawks. Faced with both Iroquoian and European invaders, the Mohicans had little chance to maintain their sovereignty and this fact was not lost on the Dutch. Not only did the Iroquois represent a formidable force in the Hudson and Mohawk River valleys, their territory stretched to the territory of the Senecas by Lake Erie and thus presented the potential for trade for items throughout the Great Lakes. In short, the Iroquois could bring furs from thousands of miles away whereas the Mohicans could not.

The other fateful decision was the 1625 relocation of most of the residents of Fort Orange to the settlement of New Amsterdam—future New York City. Although today a comparison between Albany and New York would appear to many to be an obvious and lopsided choice, in 1625 the choice of major settlement was not nearly so apparent. New Amsterdam was recognized as a fine port even before Dutch settlement, but the Hudson is in actuality a tidal estuary as far north as Albany and thus the ocean going ships of the time could sail to either port. In Pennsylvania in later years, ships made a similar journey up the

---

2. Technically, the League of the Five Nations became the League of the Six Nations when they were joined by the Tuscarora in 1720.

Delaware River to Philadelphia. In addition, Fort Orange was more easily defended against ocean-going European powers—a primary reason for the selection of Kingston (60 miles south) and then Albany for the state capital. It's location along the Hudson and several creeks (or kills, as called by the Dutch) meant that fresh water was plentiful, whereas Manhattan is surrounded by salt water on all sides. Not surprisingly, complaints about water quality and quantity were persistent for New York's first 200 years. And of course, Fort Orange was closer to the Iroquois and the Great Lakes fur trade. Due to the escalating war between the Mohawks and the Mohicans, however, the Dutch saw fit to maintain only a small settlement and move most residents to New Amsterdam (Burrows & Wallace, 1999).

Company Town

By the end of the 1620s, the Dutch had established a modestly profitable trading colony. Within the overall organization, the profits gained were less impressive than those that came from the company's other ventures, especially piracy. In comparison to the fortunes gained by the Dutch East India Company, the Dutch West India Company and New Netherlands were rather meek. Still, New Netherlands gave the Dutch a foothold in North America and as such was a source of national pride. The primary purpose remained constant: to make money. Within a few short years, an efficient mechanism—perhaps the only efficient aspect of New Netherlands—had developed to do just that.

At first, trade took the form of barter. Given that the Dutch were trading with societies that found little utility with the European medium of exchange—primarily gold and silver coinage—there was little recourse beyond barter. It was not the first time that Europeans found the economic values of the new world to be at odds with their own. As the Spanish toppled the Aztecs and the Inca, they transported thousands of pieces of gold artifacts, artistically crafted and spiritually significant, back to Spain so they could be melted into coins and bars.[3] In time, however, the trade arrangement grew more complex.

Wampum

It was noted in chapter one that rural production is a circuit of production that occurs prior to urban production. That is to say that the harvest of rural products such as food, mineral ore, and lumber, etc., is a necessary precursor to the transformation of such materials into finished products through the expense

---

3. This is not to say that some artifacts were not kept in tact or melted for use in new artifacts, but rather that much was turned to coinage.

of labor. It is thus no surprise that the accumulation of wealth takes different forms. In rural production, wealth is obtained through the control of given resources, especially land but not necessarily always so. It is based ultimately on use values—the accumulated resources are in some way valuable for their utility, such as physical, aesthetic, or spiritual purposes. If an economic unit (e.g., individual, family, tribe, etc.) controls enough for its survival and no more, it is a subsistence economy and little or no wealth is accumulated. Wealth is generated only when there is an abundance of resources—use values are met and there is a surplus of resources available for trade. Such surplus value can be traded for other items that, in theory, are useful to the economic unit. Based as it is on over-production or natural abundance, the level of surplus varies with an array of conditions, such as the number of plants nursed or climatological conditions. Thus, the exchange value of rural products is subject to basic laws of supply and demand.

On the shores of Long Island Sound and Narragansett Bay existed an array of seashells that washed up on beaches in mind-boggling numbers. Local Algonquian tribes, such as the various Lenape tribes on Long Island, harvested these materials and created wampum: strings of shells and other objects that were traded with inland tribes (Martien, 1996; see also Pena, 2001). Wampum was used as ceremonial objects and a form of proto-writing that recorded events and treaties. The actual creation of wampum relied on urban production—once harvested, the raw materials for wampum could, in theory though often not in practice, be assembled anywhere. Though the raw materials for wampum represented a source of surplus value for the populations living in those areas, the transformation of those items into finished products (wampum) through the exertion of labor added further value to what was already in existence. In other words, value came not from the exertion of labor power but rather was supplemented by it—ultimately, value is borne of the surplus of useful products beyond the use values necessary for subsistence.

As the Dutch initially traded with the Mohawks near Fort Orange and the Lenape near New Amsterdam, the trade relationship was one of barter. Most often, barter relies on notions of use value as the guiding principle to the transaction. Thus, the Dutch initially traded items of aesthetic and practical import, such as glass and tools and weapons, for furs. By the 1630s, they discovered that the Mohawks desired wampum from the coastal Lenape and a new trade relationship resulted. Prior to this discovery, the barter system was binary—consisted of two parties—and thus hypothetically had a relationship that balanced the use values of the items involved, as in figure 2.1.

Fig. 2.1: Binary Barter

100 Muskets, axes, and caps ←→ 100 beaver and raccoon furs

With the discovery of the Iroquois desire for Wampum, an additional circuit of trade developed. The Dutch traded goods with the Lenape for wampum, which they could then in turn trade for furs with the Iroquois. Because the Iroquois had a great desire for wampum, it could be used as a medium of exchange, but the use of a medium of exchange itself allowed for a distortion to be introduced in terms of the use values of the various items, as in figure 2.2.

Fig. 2.2: Tertiary Barter

100 muskets, ←→ 100 wampum ←→ 120 beaver & raccoon pelts
axes, cups   strings

Through the use of wampum as a medium of exchange, the Dutch clearly profited. However, the source of the profit rested not in the use value of the European goods nor of the pelts, but rather in the use of the medium of exchange itself.

Collins (1975) discussed power relations in terms of chains of social interaction across social networks that he referred to as Interaction Ritual (IR) chains. Collins' point was to show that what seemed to be macrological forces or power was in fact the result of numerous interactions of order-givers and order-takers across the network (see also Collins, 1982). Each interaction within the network encapsulates the power relations between all of the individuals across the network and thus constantly reproduces the power structure. Similarly, economic transactions take place between individuals within the context of a wider social network. Each transaction represents and reproduces the political economic order and the culturally ascribed preferences of each participant. Thus, as the exchange value of an item may be quite independent of its use value, the distortion comes into being. Such was the case with the Dutch use of wampum. The Dutch traded items to the Lenape that the natives found useful and in exchange received wampum. For the Dutch, wampum had little if any value besides its exchange value, but for the inland tribes there was its use value grounded in ceremony and record keeping. As such, the Dutch could demand a greater amount of furs in exchange for wampum as one party (the Mohawks) perceived a great need and the other (the Dutch) did not, and used this knowledge to demand a higher price. However, had the Mohawks fully comprehended the lack of value wampum commanded in the Dutch homeland, they would have been capable of demanding more favorable terms from the Europeans. In brief, the medium of exchange allows one party (the one with the exchange medium) to exercise power over another and thus demand more favorable terms from the other party (the one trading for use value and thus more emotionally involved). However, this interaction of power is highly dependent upon one party having knowledge the other does not. In this case, the Dutch knew of the Mohawk's desire for wampum, but the Iroquois had little comprehension of the tenuous position of the Dutch by trading with such a valueless item in their home country.

Both the Iroquois and the Lenapes were agricultural societies living in settled villages. Unlike the Dutch and other European societies, they had not developed economies based largely on exchange values. The great Mediterranean and Middle Eastern civilizations of Mesopotamia, Egypt, Greece and Rome had all developed highly sophisticated mediums of exchange in the form of coinage. Precious metals, such as gold and silver, were cast in predetermined weights and sizes for use as money. Unlike the money of today, coinage had some element of use value: a coin could be melted down for jewelry for example, although it is unlikely that this was a common practice. In contrast, currency in most modern societies often takes the form of paper currency and numbers on a computer hard drive and thus has no use value whatsoever. By the seventeenth century these ancient monetary customs were dominant in Europe but unknown to Native Americans. For the Lenapes and Mohawks, at least in the beginning, trade was meant to acquire items with use value and not merely as speculation to get more items.

For the Dutch, the trade circuitry was very complex. Individual investors bought shares in the Dutch West India Company using coinage (money), which then financed the purchase of items for trade with Native Americans. These items were traded for wampum with the Lenape, which was then traded for furs with the Iroquois (who, in many cases, had similar trade circuitries throughout upstate New York), which was then traded for money back in Europe. The proceeds from the trade were then distributed to investors in the form of dividends. The investors then traded their new wealth for food and, assuming a surplus of funds after paying for food, shelter, etc., could then be reinvested in the Dutch West India Company or some similar venture.[4] If at any point in the network of interactions the exchange value had fallen, the system would collapse. For example, had the Mohawk simply refused to trade from wampum—a real possibility given the lack of exchange value in Europe—the Dutch would have been forced to severely cut their rate of exchange (i.e., prices). This knowledge, or the lack thereof, is central to the transaction.

Due to unequal power relations and levels of knowledge in the social interaction at each circuit of trade, the potential for the distortion between use and exchange values exists and, over time, becomes the basis for profit.

---

4. Often, this money was simply held back from investors as seed money for new trade when dividends were paid.

Kindred Spirits from a Rival Nation

Throughout the 1620s, different factions within the Dutch West India Company debated the merits of settlement versus non-settlement. Some believed that settlement was not only a chief purpose of colonization but an effective way of dispelling possible conquerors. Others believed that the colony would be most useful as a relative wilderness within which furs and other such goods could be harvested by the native inhabitants and then traded with the Dutch. As the colony was owned outright by the Dutch West India Company[5], it is not surprising that the emphasis remained on making money and that relatively little effort was expended on settling the region. In fact, the fear that settlers could be perceived as a threat by native tribes encouraged company managers to keep settlement to a minimum. But the 1620s began with the Pilgrims in Plymouth and ended with still more puritans in Boston in 1630. They were fellow Calvinist Protestants in search of religious freedom, many of whom were Pilgrims who had lived in the Netherlands prior to moving to the new world. Nevertheless, the two groups were on divergent paths spiritually and a collision course politically.

The Calvinist settlers of New England were British in search of escape from the power of the Anglican Church. They sought a place to live a particularly strict form of Christianity, and not surprisingly the New England colonies attracted the most zealous of Calvinists. In time, religious schisms lead to still more colonies, such as Connecticut, Rhode Island, and settlement on eastern Long Island. The puritans of New England were attracted to the new world for reasons of religious purity and piety and exercised a strict version of their faith (Johnstone, 2001).

The Dutch, in contrast, had a roaring economy at home and, far from being a minority, had a Calvinist church (Dutch Reformed) that dominated religious life. When offered the chance to freeze in New Netherlands, many Dutch shied away and so the Company had to entice the few settlers who did come. From the beginning, New Netherlands was a haven for settlers of all faiths as the colony had a *de facto* policy of religious freedom.

By mid-century, New Netherlands was squeezed between the northern British colonies in New England and those to the south and west. In order to retain its possession, the Dutch West India Company more actively pursued a policy to settle the colony. They turned to the system they had known for centuries under Habsburg rule: feudalism. Beginning in the 1629, Killiaen van Rensselaer and others argued for the establishment of Patroons, or manors, subject to a quit rent payable to the company and the ability to improve the land in a set period of time. Fearing a British takeover of the colony if more settlers

---

5. At least from the European perspective. The native tribes, of course, did not recognize this claim.

did not arrive, the Dutch West India Company acquiesced and numerous patroonships were granted throughout the colony. By the time of the British takeover of New Netherlands in 1664, only the van Rensselaer patroonship still existed, the others having failed and been dissolved. Nevertheless, a pattern had been established.

The British are Coming

It was possibly the most uninspired defense of a city in American history. In 1664, British King Charles II granted his younger brother, James, Duke of York, the territory between the Delaware and Connecticut Rivers. In short, New Netherlands. All that was left for the Duke to do was to send Colonel Richard Nicolls with four ships and two thousand men to take the colony from the Dutch.

Peter Stuyvesant had at that time been governor of New Netherlands for eighteen years. During that time he had infuriated settlers by attempting to impose the Dutch Reformed Church on members of diverse faiths, failed to compete against the growing English colonies to the east and west, and acquired a reputation for corruption. Although he had successfully conquered the colony of New Sweden in the Delaware Valley, attempts to win settlers for New Netherlands had by and large failed. Several new villages relied heavily on English settlers and all but the patroonship of the van Rensellaers (Rensellaerwyck) had failed. To make matters worse, the Mohawk Iroquois had by and large taken the fur trade from the Mohicans and were now playing the three major European powers—Dutch, British, and French—against each other (Aquila, 1977). Faced with increasingly angry settlers at home and Amsterdam backers who spent as little as possible, Stuyvesant governed a colony without the fortifications, guns, or will to defend itself. When Colonel Nicolls moved his ships within firing distance of New Amsterdam, Stuyvesant ascended the bastion of the battery ready to open fire only to be lead down again by his trusted minister. On September 8, 1664, New Netherlands was given over to the British[6].

The Dutch period in New York history was relatively short-lived, but nevertheless set the stage for the future. Chief among the dynamics set in motion by the end of the Dutch period was the accommodation of the significant power of the Iroquois Confederacy, the dominance of trade as the primary generator of wealth in New York City, and the organization of rural production under feudalistic social arrangements. Each of these dynamics grew under British rule as royal governors either continued or expanded upon Dutch practices.

---

6. The Dutch did retake New Netherlands for a brief period in 1673, only to lose the colony again in 1674.

A Great Power

Despite Dutch claims and attempts to make New Netherlands a sizable colony extending from the Connecticut River in the east to the Delaware and Susquehanna Rivers in the west, in reality the colony failed to venture far from the banks of the Hudson. For instance, in the face of British claims that extended west of the Connecticut, the territory was ceded with little resistance. Only in the northern-most reaches of the colony did the claim hold, and a sizable chunk of that became Vermont after the American Revolution. The Dutch did wrest the inland colony of New Sweden—a blip in American colonial history—from Sweden, but Sweden was never truly a major power in the region. The maps of the Europeans gave New Sweden a legitimacy never truly deserved, as they did much of New Netherlands as well. In reality, the British controlled almost all of the territory east of the Hudson, allowing only a thin ribbon of Dutch presence and influence through the valley. To the west, a power greater than the Dutch but minimized in stature on the maps prevented the Dutch from pushing too far west: the Iroquois.

The myth, as many myths, features a spiritual leader and inspiration. Deganawidah, a Huron, experienced a vision in which he learned of the potential strength and security that all Iroquoian tribes could share if they stopped warring themselves and banded together. Deganawidah, however, had a lisp, and so needed the assistance of someone with fine skills of oratory to spread his message. That assistance came in the form of Hiawatha, a Mohawk, who preached his message of peace and security among all the Iroquois tribes. Their goal was only partially realized in the birth of the League of the Five Nations formed by the alliance of the Seneca, Cayuga, Onondaga, Oneida, and Mohawk tribes along the southern coast of Lake Ontario. Other Iroquois tribes in southern Canada, such as the Erie, Neutrals, and (ironically) the Hurons did not join. In time, Confederacy military actions against their Iroquois cousins precluded the eventual fulfillment of Deganowidah's dream of uniting all the Iroquois into the League, most likely to eventual European advantage (Kehoe, 1992).

The dream of Iroquoian unification has been repeated often in world history. Egypt thousand of years before, in Italy and Germany in the nineteenth and twentieth centuries, in Macedonia and Kurdistan today. Iroquoian agriculture, while distinctly different from that of their European counterparts, was finely tuned to the season and soil conditions of the Great Lakes. As Kehoe (1992) commented:

> Fields of maize, beans, squashes, and sunflowers (raised for the edible seeds) surrounded the town, on the hill slopes as well as the flood plains. These fields were cleared by the slash-and-burn method of killing trees by girdling and then burning off the dried brush and trees, a method that returns valuable nutrients to the soil in the form of ashes. (234)

Instead of growing food in fields dedicated to a single crop, Iroquoian farmers typically grew a variety of products in natural settings, thus eliminating the need for field rotation (Kehoe, 1992).

Each tribal region had administrative villages of meeting places referred to as "castles" by the Europeans. The towns themselves were often fortified with earthworks and logs and contained as many as fifty longhouses, which typically were home to an extended family and centered on an elder woman. By law, elder women elected male chiefs and representatives to the grand council of the confederacy, and thus held considerable sway in tribal politics. In addition, women had veto power over any action that could lead to war.

The birth of the Confederacy itself is evidence of recognition of cultural similarity that extended beyond the village or the tribe to a level that can only be described as nationalism. In time—perhaps only a few more centuries— Iroquoian civilization would likely have vaguely resembled other American civilizations, such as the Mississippian Culture of the upper Mississippi watershed and perhaps the Aztecs and Inca so recently destroyed by the Spanish Conquistadors. Not in terms of language or culture, but certainly in terms of military, political, and economic power. One can see in the "castles" future provincial cities, and perhaps somewhere a gleaming woodland imperial capital. It is of course mere speculation as to what might have evolved without European intervention, but such was the course of Iroquois civilization when the colonizers arrived. They arrived to find a fully functioning Confederacy, and needed to deal with that power. If the maps did not show the Confederacy as a valid power, it was through no fault of the Iroquois.

The reality of Deganowidah's dream was that, in time, the Confederacy used its considerable resources and military might to control much of the fur trade (Aquila, 1972; Kehoe, 1992; Burrows & Wallace, 1999). With the stability and support afforded by the League, the Mohawks dogged the Mohicans—who had no similar power to whom to turn for help—for decades. As noted earlier, Mohawk ferocity convinced the Dutch to largely vacate the settlers of Fort Orange to New Amsterdam. If pushed, the Dutch sided with the Mohawks, preferring to trade and not to risk annihilation by the more numerous Iroquois (Burrows & Wallace, 1999). Dutch activities west of the Hudson were by and large limited to hunting, trapping, and trading. Settlements remained south of Iroquois territory in what is today the New York metropolitan area and New Jersey. Simply stated, the Dutch foothold in New Netherlands was tenuous.

The British thus took over a colony that meshed well with New England to the east but was bound by the threat of the Iroquois to the west. Despite the most powerful navy in the world, the mother country and her resources were thousands of miles (read: months) away. Even over one hundred years later, the British lost the American Revolution against the rag-tag Americans despite vastly superior resources across the ocean. In 1664, the low and sparse population was capable of securing territory already gained in a time of peace, but hardly capable of launching a credible campaign of invasion and occupation against the Iroquois. Besides, the Dutch approach seemed to work best: trade with the Iroquois and place your settlements in the territory of the more easily defeated Algonquian tribes.

The continuity of New York's policy toward the Iroquois was all the more important precisely because of the British takeover. With only two European powers remaining (England and France), the Iroquois constituted one corner in a triad of diplomacy—and the favorable one at that. As over-trapping reduced the supply of fur in the eastern Great Lakes, the Confederacy found themselves in the role of middleman between the tribes of the western Great Lakes and the European powers. This gave the Iroquois considerable bargaining power in the twenty years before and after 1700. Aquila (1972) compares the diplomatic efforts of the League to the American policy of détente in handling the Soviet Union and China during the 1970s. The Iroquois played the British against the French in regard to trade, settlements, and an array of local situations. It was not until after the Europeans had established outposts west of Iroquois territory that their power began to wane, and it was not until after the American Revolution that the colonists were finally able to dominate the Confederacy.

A Center of Trade

The Dutch West India Company was formed for the sole purpose of making money through trade and, of less relevance for New Amsterdam, piracy. The purpose of New Netherlands in particular was as a source of furs for the fur trade. This was ultimately the reason for the desire to remain out of the fray in the wars between the Mohawks and the Mohicans. The establishment of Fort Orange was meant to facilitate trade between the Dutch and the local tribes. The settlement of New Amsterdam at the tip of Manhattan Island, despite the distinct disadvantage of being surrounded by salt water, was the perfect port in one of the world's best natural harbors.

The orientation of early New York was always to the sea. Early illustrations and maps were most often drawn from the vantage point of the sea, spreading as a triangle from the tip of the island. Much of the labor force, such as longshoremen, fur traders, bankers, and administrators, were involved directly with trade—often the payroll of the West India Company itself. The government of the colony was responsible not to the Dutch government but to the Company. There were farms near the city, but much food also came from farmers farther upstream and even from the Netherlands. Simply stated, the early culture of New Amsterdam inherited by British New York was one that looked to the sea for sustenance.

With such an orientation toward trade, the actual settlement of the colony was quite a failure. The patroonships established in the 1630s had mostly failed due to a lack of settlers. The few villages that did survive were relatively autonomous and close to New Amsterdam. Devoted to farming or trade with natives, they were linked directly to the economy of New Amsterdam by either providing additional food or items for shipment to Europe (such as furs). Dutch New Amsterdam thus looked to its hinterland as a region to be exploited, the settlements in those hinterlands as agents of the city in the exploitation of the great interior. The city by necessity traded with Europe for sustenance, and the interior provided the commodities that allowed it to do so.

The colony the British took over thus relied on an economic network that was highly interdependent. A typical fur might be trapped by a member of a tribe neighboring the Senecas near modern day Buffalo on Lake Erie, work its way through the territory of the Iroquois, and then be traded to a Dutch trader operating from modern day Albany on the Hudson. The fur would then travel down the Hudson to New York, where it would again change hands for transport to Europe. In return, manufactured goods from Europe would filter back through the network. The British were familiar with such an economic system due to the operation of the New England colonies to the east. Similar networks could be found around such cities as Newport, New London, and Boston. If there was a difference, it was that New England colonies were founded by Puritans seeking to escape the clutches of Europe and thus sought a large degree of economic autonomy. New York was different: the culture of the entire colony perceived the hinterland as mere extensions of the trading city. There was no real attempt at autonomy beyond what was deemed necessary for survival, no religious zealots seeking to create their own homes. The lack of such a population deprived New Netherlands of a significant level of development, but also insured the purity of the trade ethic in the development of early New York.

The Feudal Order

By the British takeover in 1664, all but one of the patroonships established by the Dutch had failed. They are today remembered primarily by name, in places like Pelham Manor and Briarcliff Manor, but they were abject failures. One did survive: Rensellaerwyck, the estate of the van Rensellaers that comprised much of modern-day Albany and Rensellaer Counties. Among the terms of the British takeover was that it be mainly a change in administration— social and economic life would remain largely unchanged. This resulted in the retention of the van Rensellaer charter and the application of British Manor Law to its governance.

In England as in other European countries, the fall of the Roman Empire witnessed the evolution of feudalism as the dominant economic and political system. Even in regions not directly under the control of the Romans, such as Scotland and Ireland, feudalism became the dominant system (Ganshof, 1996).

In England, the origins of feudal order in existence during the seventeenth century began with the conquest of England by William the Conqueror in 1066. William rewarded his supporters with grants of land referred to as feudal baronies (Cannon & Griffiths, 2000). Each Baron in exchange gave the king (William and his descendants) an annual tribute, usually in the form of agricultural products raised in the territory, the service of armed knights, and in later years some form of money. In principle, a hierarchy existed with God as the ultimate authority. The king derived authority (and land) directly from God, although there is no record of God as an actual cosigner to this arrangement, but rather the blessings of his supposed representative on Earth, the Pope. (After the Protestant Reformation, English kings instead looked to the Arch-Bishop of Canterbury for proof of God's blessing). With the blessing of the Almighty, the king thus delegated authority over territory to the nobility through the feudal hierarchy—a system of which there is ample documentation. Baronies were ultimately divided into manors presided over by Lords of the Manor. A lord of the manor was considered to be landed gentry but not a member of the nobility like barons and the ranks above them. Lords were required to pay tributes to the barons above them in the social hierarchy (Ganshof, 1996; Reynolds, 1996). By the seventeenth century, England had also developed a system of noble rank based on monetary payment for service rather than grants of land today called "bastard feudalism" (Hicks, 1995). It was within this context that the feudal system of New York would take form.

Feudalism in New York involved the same legal principles, but without the embedded relations of British nobility took a different form. As in the mother country, the King retained the right of eminent domain. Eminent domain was a legal concept that held all British territory as ultimately belonging to God and thus to be administered by his earthly agent, the King. The right to administer a territory was thus derived ultimately from God and simply transferred down through the hierarchy. As such, the New York colony ultimately belonged to God, who in theory granted the territory to the British king (at least according to the Arch-Bishop of Canterbury). The king granted the territory to the Duke of York, but it was the king who appointed the royal governors of the colony. The governors were responsible for the overall operations of the colony, including the collection of tribute from the colonists for the benefit of the Duke and the King. Of the proceeds, the governor could retain a portion for himself. Tribute most often came in the form of quitrents on royal property—the predecessor of property taxes—and taxes on commerce. With the British takeover of New York, Rensselaerwyck thus became a manor whose lord was directly responsible to the Duke of York and with none of the intervening hierarchy found in England. Although officially belonging to the Duke of York, in practice New York was administered by the King and his agents. As lords of the manor, the van Rensselaers were not considered to be nobility, but they were considered to be landed gentry. Similarly, the governor, as an agent of the king, was also not considered to be part of the nobility. Technically, according to British law, New York had no nobility. In practice, the landed gentry filled the same niche in colonial society.

With the precedent of feudalism established by the existence of Rensselaerwyck, succeeding governors began to sell off the king's lands as new estates or "patents." Although there were episodes of royal disagreements (Ellis, 1946), in general the recommendation of the governor for a royal charter resulted in the land grant requested. The favored land was that along the banks of the Hudson due to the "civilized" environs and potential for trade. By the 1760s, the Hudson and Mohawk valleys had been doled out and the governors were well on their way to granting the wilderness west of the Hudson Valley to aspiring aristocrats. In some cases, the lords sought something akin to the puritan utopianism found in New England. The Hartwick Patent, south of modern Utica, for instance, was granted in 1761 to John Christopher Hartwick for the express purpose of founding a "'New Jerusalem' based on piety, hierarchy, and feudalistic social arrangements" (Thomas, 2003). In most cases, however, the goal was quite conventional: settle the property and collect the rents on the farms. The van Rensselaers, for instance, collected quit rents from tenant farmers, a portion of which was passed to the royal governors as rents for the grant. Such a pattern was called "land-lease" as the tenants of the property were not the "owners" of the land. Typically, leases were written in very long terms, such as "the lifetime of John Smith, his oldest son, and in turn his oldest son" in a typical "three lifetime lease." The tenant had the option of "selling" his lease in much the same way as a modern sublet on a rented apartment.

"Freehold" arrangements prior to the American Revolution took away the middleman. The freeholder paid a quitrent directly to the governor or his agent. If the property was in a chartered city, such as Albany or New York, this was in addition to fees for city administration and contributions (physical and financial) for the upkeep of city services. For instance, New Yorkers were required to help in the maintenance of their particular section of street in terms of paving, sanitation, and other necessary chores.

Many large landholders, especially those who owned parcels at a distance from the Hudson, found that there was an insufficient demand for their property. After the American Revolution, many sold their property under the "freehold" system. Large tracts of land were subdivided and sold under this system, the former owners gaining almost instant capital with which to speculate in more land. The Cosby Manor, for instance, was sold in such a way and became not only the city of Utica but a number of its suburbs as well (Clarke, 1952; Ellis & Preston, 1982). In contrast, those that chose to cling to the land-lease system found that their property was less attractive to potential settlers. This was aided by a particular outcome of the Revolution.

The American Revolution freed New York from Great Britain, but much of manor law and the estates themselves remained in tact. The major change was the repeal of primogeniture. Primogeniture mandated that a manor pass from the lord to his eldest son upon the lord's death, thus maintaining the integrity of the entire patent. With its repeal, large landholders could subdivide their property and freehold arrangements became more numerous. A wave of speculation ensued as enterprising land developers bought land grants and sold them under the freehold system. With so much land available under the freehold system, traditional land-lease became less attractive to settlers and in time either attracted primarily the poor or was sold under freehold arrangements (Taylor, 1995).

Revolution

The American Revolution did more than just free New Yorkers from British rule and the bounds of primogeniture. The ideals of democracy and equality began to sweep through the former colonies. Equality was understood as a freedom from the remnants of European feudalism and a meritocratic ideal. As has been noted by numerous authors, early American culture did not always fully realize these ideals (Zinn, 2003; Nash, 1999). African-American slaves, for instance, were defined as two-thirds human for purposes of representation in the Constitution. Similarly, a belief in equality did not address socioeconomic status, and the landed gentry in New York as in other states remained in place. However, equality understood humans to be equal before the law, and thus represented a change from earlier beliefs. Democracy was the outward political expression of this equality; it was collective decision making conducted by an entire populace favored by God.

Democratic government itself was perceived to be entirely different from that which preceded it. Freeholders and lords no longer paid quit rents to the colonial government and the nobility, but there remained a state government independent of the King that needed revenue in order to operate. With the authority of the people, they would instead pay taxes. In theory, the people were collectively granted authority by God and thus granted such authority to the state. In practice, the names changed but the basic structure remained very similar. In the end, the people maintained eminent domain over their territory, but it was the state that could wield the power that eminent domain represented.

New York entered the nineteenth century poised for world trade and new projects at home. New York City was the largest city in the newly formed United States, one-third larger than Philadelphia, the nation's next largest city, and its hinterland would soon benefit from the very success of New England that cost the Dutch their colony.

3   The Empire State

The period after the American Revolution was a pivotal one for New York City. It is at this point that numerous histories would address the unique features of the city: the geography, the location, the diversity, the money. It is a "great man" theory of history scaled to the level of cities. But such is not the story of New York's greatness, but rather it is the relationship of the city to its hinterland that made the high peaks of Manhattan possible. A complete history, which this is not, would examine New York's relationship with all its hinterland: in New York, New Jersey, Connecticut, and Long Island. As the future chapters will concentrate on the relationship between New York and Gilboa, a more limited discussion is appropriate. However, it is the development of eastern New York as a whole, of which Gilboa is part, which is so important to the growth of the metropolis.

Washington's Conquistadors

The American Revolution had begun with a strong, albeit declining, Iroquois Confederacy. The French and Indian War, known in Europe as the Seven Years War and a truly global confrontation, had resulted in the withdrawal of the French from Canada in 1763. Faced with the British as the only Europeans in their midst, the Iroquois sought certain guarantees of their sovereignty. They were not alone, and the British responded by proclaiming that no white settlement could be west of the Appalachian Mountains. The local superintendent for the British—Sir William Johnson—negotiated a formal treaty line with the Iroquois along a line that ran from Fort Stanwix in modern day Rome to the headwaters of and along the Unadilla River (National Archives, 1998). As the treaty placed a westward boundary on European settlement, it was not entirely popular with many New Yorkers. As the treaty cut through the heart of Iroquois territory, thus representing a considerable ceding of territory, there were Iroquois detractors as well. In the treaty the interests of the two sides were well advertised: the Iroquois desired to maintain sovereignty and thus were determined to be a barrier to European settlement in their territory, and the

Americans showed in their disgust their desire to encroach further on Iroquois lands.

It is not surprising that the American Revolution brought about the very circumstance that Deganowidah had warned the Iroquois to avoid above all else: the League was divided. The simple way to understand the split is to say that the Oneida fought with the Americans and the other tribes fought with the British, but such generalizations are overly reductionist (Graymont, 1990). Even within the tribes, there was conflict. The Americans were the actual neighbors of the Iroquois tribes, and if they won the Revolution they would surely take vengeance on the League. In contrast, the British were the stronger of the two sides and seemed more willing than the Americans to guarantee a border. As a result, Iroquois warriors fought on both sides of the Revolution.

In what was then the western frontier of the state, settlers loyal to the crown and Iroquois warriors carried out a number of successful and brutal raids on communities near the border. During the early years of the Revolution, native Americans and British loyalists carried out a series of raids on the frontier, in such places as German Flats, Stone Arabia, and Cobleskill. In 1778, the most devastating of the raids occurred at Cherry Valley, south of the Mohawk River and less than 30 miles from the border at the Unadilla River, resulting in the death of 48 soldiers and civilians. By the end of 1778, most settlers still alive sought safety in Albany and General Washington was forced to act.

The orders were delivered to Generals Clinton and Sullivan in May 1779, directing them to focus their attention on the native population, the Iroquois in particular. Sullivan was to march his troops from Baltimore through the Susquehanna Valley, whereas Clinton was to march through the Mohawk Valley and then south through the Susquehanna Valley until he met with Sullivan's forces near present day Elmira in mid-summer. Washington's orders were simple: "destroy the Iroquois ability to sustain themselves and their warriors by targeting their settlements and fields so that the country may not be merely *overrun* but *destroyed*" (U. S. Library of Congress, 31 May 1779; emphasis in original). Under no circumstances were the generals to accept an Iroquois surrender "before the total ruin of their settlements (was) effected" (USLOC, 31 May 1779). The soldiers zealously followed their orders, devastating "the villages of the Indians, slaughtering their livestock, and burning their fields" (Ellis et al, 1957, 116). They flooded the valley at the site of present-day Cooperstown and swept away crops at the river's edge and targeted large game animals in order to deprive the natives of sustenance. They swept through the Susquehanna, Tioga, and Genesee River Valleys and scorched a large portion of modern upstate New York (Graymont, 1990). The results exceeded the stated purposes as outlined by Washington: not only did the campaign effectively stop the border raids, it crippled the Confederacy to such a degree that American settlement, especially from New England, flooded the region in the decades after the Revolution. Many Iroquois became refugees in Canada, while those who remained could only pretend to the greatness of this civilization as the settlers cleared their land with near impunity. The Iroquois were defeated.

The Yankees are Coming

Upstate New York is a conglomerate of regions that are ultimately part of somewhere else. Western New York is at heart a great lakes region, culturally more similar to the Midwest than the hustle and bustle of Manhattan. Rochester and Buffalo are aesthetically more similar to Cleveland and Indianapolis than anything in eastern New York, and some of the earliest European movements in the region were French—not Dutch, British, or even Swedish! Eastern New York is, in contrast, the east coast. Cities like Albany and Schenectady are in appearance more like the neighborhoods of New York City and Boston than the big cities in the west. Only Utica, at the head of the Mohawk River, seems to have elements of both regions, and thus may be called the quintessential New York City. That such regional differences are noticeable in the state today is testimony to the sheer diversity of the state in the early nineteenth century.

The end of the American Revolution resulted in a flurry of land speculation in upstate New York. The former colonies of New England were, for the time, becoming heavily populated, and what little land was left for the enterprising farmer was often mountainous or otherwise undesirable. Given the sheer population, demand was high for even this land and thus prices were relatively high. In contrast, speculators were rapidly selling the fertile valleys of upstate New York at prices that most farmers could afford. Terms generally involved the extension of credit on the part of the speculator, and over a period of several years many farmers could own their piece of land. For example, William Cooper sold the land of the former Croghan Patent south of the Mohawk Valley for a percent down payment and regular payments that stretched over a period of ten years (Taylor, 1995). As noted in chapter two, such terms of the freehold system helped to make the land-lease system less attractive to many potential buyers, although it did not entirely kill the system (Ellis, 1946). The result of these two trends was a flood of settlers from New England to upstate New York bringing with them the customs, religious fervor, and place names of their homeland.

In western counties, this flood of Yankees became the defining feature of the early cultural development of the region. In eastern New York, however, it was met with residents who had been there for years. The Mohawk Valley, for instance, had for generations attracted the settlement of Palatine Germans. Some of them had cleared farms and even small villages in the northern reaches of the Schoharie Creek Valley north of Gilboa, and over the years the Palatine presence and influence was apparent in eastern New York. In some cases, these earlier settlers became part of the power structures of numerous Mohawk and Schoharie Valley towns.

The influx of New England Yankees did, however, overwhelm the local population. The small numbers of Palatines had dwindled as a result of the American Revolution as many settlers sought safety in Albany. In the Schoharie Valley, many did not return to the waiting obligations of their land-lease farms on the patroonships, preferring to seek out freehold arrangements to the west (Ellis, 1946). Thus, when the campaign against the Iroquois is factored in, the Schoharie Valley underwent a tremendous demographic change during the forty years after the American Revolution. Many, although not all, Iroquois and Palatine Germans left the region either by choice or by forced circumstance. In their wake, Yankees from New England and a small population of African Americans, primarily freed slaves seeking a livelihood on the patroonships, inundated the region (Morey, 1991; Daniels, 2000). It was this demographic transition that established the major cultural patterns of life in the valley for the next two hundred years.

For many of the new settlers, the goal of settlement was an independent and reasonably prosperous existence. Sheriff (1997) explained:

> (When) farmers did exchange goods and services with neighbors, those transactions rarely involved cash—not because cash was in short supply, but rather because they saw no use for assigning monetary values. Instead, they calculated value in terms of social worth, and simply kept accounts of what they owed and were owed. A farmer, for example, might work two days in his neighbor's cornfield in exchange for two chickens, since that was what it would take to feed his family during the time he spent away from his own farm duties. Or he might simply hold the neighbor accountable for two days' labor at some later time. These farmers sought, not to accumulate wealth, but to secure a "competency" that would allow their families to live a comfortable and independent existence in a community limited in geographic reach. (11)

The Yankees were fiercely independent, industrious, and prided themselves on being hard workers. Work was viewed as an end in itself, and Yankee children were raised with such values. Taylor (1995) described the values James Averell Jr. sought to instill in his own children:

> Averell stressed the bourgeois values of frugality, industry, and the constant calculation of economic advantage; . . . (he) trained his sons as businessmen first and as gentlemen as a distant second. Instead of encouraging his sons to consume money gracefully, Averell taught them to delay gratification in favor of accumulating even more capital. (403)

This pattern of self-sacrifice, thrift, and moral piety was partly a result of the religious beliefs, however liberalized from the Puritan founders of New England, called the "protestant ethic" by Max Weber (1992). A certain optimism permeated the early settlers: left to its own devices, nature itself will ensure that things work out in the end. It was believed that misfortune is the result of humans' interference in the natural order, and so "if it ain't broke, don't fix it." These are all themes that continue to be strong beliefs today.

Highways and Byways

By 1800, the former territory of the Iroquois was rapidly being filled. Over forty miles from the former international border with the Iroquois at the Unadilla River, the Schoharie Valley had a head start over the region to the west, but nevertheless was undergoing intense change with the influx of settlers from New England. The valley's main attraction was its location near the Mohawk River— as close to "civilization" as the frontier afforded at that time. Travelers could negotiate through the relatively flat Schoharie Valley north to the Mohawk River, which was navigable, near Amsterdam. From Amsterdam, it was only 15 miles to Schenectady or 30 to Albany. In contrast, early settlers in western New York were typically hundreds of miles from the nearest city or major trading post. But such an advantage was faced with numerous disadvantages.

The Schoharie Valley ran from its headwaters in the south to the creek's outlet in the north. Settlers, however, looked not to the south but to the west as the "land of opportunity." Combined with a mixture of freehold and land-lease arrangements, such a cultural trait among the migrants predisposed many against the Schoharie Valley. In addition, the topography of the region was less well suited for farming than it was for the trapping of furs. At its northern end, the Schoharie Valley offers a relatively wide and fertile valley floor ideal for agriculture. As one travels upstream, the valley narrows and becomes hillier. By the time one reached the site of Gilboa, the terrain was decidedly mountainous. The future village, in fact, would stand in what could be alternatively called a narrow valley or a wide ravine. The hilltops were relatively fertile, but also presented the farmer with considerable obstacles in terms of the number of rocks in the soil and the climbing involved.

To the west, New York seemed a farmer's dream. At the western end of the Mohawk Valley, the land opens onto the Great Lakes plain and continues for hundreds of miles. The land was, in contrast to the Catskill Mountains, relatively flat and very fertile. At the present-day site of Rome, Fort Stanwix stood between the eastward Mohawk and westward Woods Creek, forming a flat, lowland corridor for those traveling west. Fifteen miles east of Rome, at the point where the valley widens onto the plain, the future city of Utica began its history as a hotel standing by a fording spot in the Mohawk River. From these two cities, a network of transportation routes would move settlers to the west and away from the Schoharie Creek.

Although the Iroquois had left a network of trails throughout eastern New York, they were typically not appropriate for the wagons and coaches that many settlers took to the west. Shortly after the Revolution, a number of private companies proposed improving the existing trails and charging a toll for the upkeep (Klein & Majewski, 1992). Beginning in the 1790s, the state granted turnpike companies the right to build the roads. The Turnpike Movement resulted in many roads being built, one less than ten miles south of Gilboa. The preferred routes, however, were to the north of the future village. The Western Turnpike, today US 20, pushed through the woods along the crest of the Mohawk Valley in the northern part of what became Schoharie County. In Otsego County to the west, it split into a southern branch (today's NY 80) at Cherry Valley and again into the Skaneateles Turnpike in Richfield Springs. The Western Turnpike Company faced competition from companies operating in the Mohawk Valley that offered routes filled with fewer hills and more towns. As the rush of Yankees flowed into upstate New York, the vast majority came nowhere near the future Gilboa, and as a result much of the settlement occurred far to the north along the more established turnpikes. But the turnpikes would soon face competition of their own.

From the American Revolution on, there was discussion of making the Mohawk more navigable by building canals around its major rapids, especially at Little Falls and Cohoes, and creating a water link between that river and Wood's Creek. The result would be a continuous water route from New York City to Lake Ontario. There were some early attempts, but it took the urging of the state, specifically Governor DeWitt Clinton, to build a canal that would work. The plans were grand, as the Erie Canal would be built not simply to Lake Ontario near Oswego along the obvious route, but to Lake Erie at modern day Buffalo. In 1817, work started on the Erie Canal in Rome along the flatlands near the meandering Mohawk to Utica fifteen miles away. Much of the land was marsh and very fertile, and not surprisingly the work went quickly. Still faced with detractors, work continued on the section between Rome and the cluster of settlements that became Syracuse along the flatlands of the Great Lakes plain, and again the work went smoothly. By the early 1820s, many of the detractors had been disarmed and the hard work was due. Workers were slowed down in the veritable quicksand of Montezuma Swamp between Syracuse and modern day Rochester, the cliffs of present day Lockport, and the more rocky soils in the Mohawk Valley. Work continued, however, and in 1825 the Erie Canal was opened. For the opening ceremony, a bucket of Lake Erie water filled in Buffalo was transported to New York City via the canal and the Hudson River and dumped in the harbor.

The canal was conceived as a generator of economic development from the start, especially in regard to trade. Despite its upstate location, it was as much a project for the benefit of New York City as it was for the cities along its route. As a result of the canal, western New York grew some of the largest cities in the United States during the nineteenth century, such as Buffalo, Rochester, and Syracuse. Smaller cities, such as Albany, Schenectady, and Utica, benefited not only from the growth within the city but began to foster strings of suburbs along the route of the canal. In Albany, for instance, where the canal ran alongside the Hudson River for several miles before meeting the Mohawk at Cohoes, such industrial suburbs as Menands, Watervliet, and Cohoes grew into small but independent cities. Similarly, strings of small towns extended for miles east and west of Utica along the route of the canal. In the east, for example, the canal followed a route south of the Mohawk River through Frankfort, Ilion, and Mohawk. In Utica itself, development concentrated along the route of the Erie Canal as well as the later Chenango Canal, ignoring the floodplain of the river entirely. (The area is today a wildlife refuge in the center of the city). As the cities grew, so did their economies as each developed profitable industries: salt in Syracuse, textiles in Utica, and photographic equipment in Rochester. Buffalo grew to the status of a global city by 1900 as its status as the major port of the eastern great lakes attracted numerous industries and major corporations. But even as the canal spawned one of the most urbanized corridors in the United States, nothing compared with its impact on New York City.

Prior to 1800, New York City faced stiff competition for the title of busiest seaport in the nation. Philadelphia, an inland harbor on the Delaware River, boasted of good water, admirable public services, and a rich trading economy. Boston, located on a neck of land between Boston Harbor and a briny swamp called the "Back Bay" had the advantage of a direct line with Europe and a large sphere of influence from which to acquire goods to trade with the Europeans. New York was a major port, but its dominance in foreign trade was yet to be determined. With the opening of the Erie Canal, however, New York now had access to an immense area for the accumulation of inexpensively shipped trade goods. It was not just that the city had easy access to much of its hinterland in upstate New York, but due to the port city of Buffalo on Lake Erie, the entire Great Lakes basin was also within easy reach. Goods produced in Michigan or even as far away as Illinois had a water route, and thus an inexpensive route, to the foreign trade port of New York. The catchment area of trade for New York—all of upstate New York and the entire Great Lakes basin—encompassed nearly a quarter of the present area of the contiguous 48 states. Such cities as Philadelphia and Boston had more limited options, such as overland wagons and trains, and a smaller catchment area as a result. In a fundamental way, the Erie Canal and its various spurs made New York City the great port it eventually became.

The canals of New York faced competition very soon after their development in the form of the railroad. The major railroad was the New York Central and Hudson River Railroad. The New York Central, as it was called, was initially a series of short line railroads that was consolidated later in the nineteenth century by Cornelius Vanderbilt and his son, William Henry Vanderbilt. The main line went to Chicago by way of the route of the Erie Canal and the Great Lakes plain. The canal cities of the state all had the presence of the canal and the New York Central, as well as numerous spurs off the main line and competitors, such as the West Shore Railroad. As a result, the major cities of the state were major transportation hubs where canal, rail, and stagecoach lines all met. In general, rail lines were the choice of passengers and time-sensitive goods, such as many agricultural products, due to the speed of the trains, whereas the slower canals were better for durable goods, such as lumber and stones. Simply stated, the corridor that ran north through the mountains from New York along the Hudson, west through the Mohawk Valley and along the Great Lakes plain to Buffalo did not simply have the canal, but an array of competing transportation options in regard to speed and price.

New York State thus developed as a highly accessible region with the richest port in the country. However, it developed not as a whole but rather along its transportation corridors. Not surprisingly, the busiest corridors attracted the largest number of people and created the largest cities. The Erie Canal corridor itself spawned five metropolitan areas each roughly an hour from each other. At about 300 thousand residents today, the Utica metropolitan area is the smallest; both the Buffalo and Rochester metropolitan areas have over a million residents. Metropolitan Albany and Syracuse both have in excess of 750 thousand residents. Every metropolitan area outside of this Hudson River—Erie Canal corridor is smaller than metropolitan Utica. At the southern terminus of the Chenango Canal is Binghamton and at Glens Falls is the Champlain Canal. Only two of the state's metropolitan areas, Elmira and Jamestown, did not have a canal that linked directly into the Erie.

The uneven development of the state evolved such that major industries were concentrated in the urbanized corridors along the transportation routes. These were centers of urban production. In the urbanized region centered on Utica, for instance, the number of textile mills was so high that prospective workers immigrated to the city by the thousands. Many of the immigrants were from the surrounding rural areas not directly in the corridor. For instance, from 1840—the beginning of the steam age in Utica—through 1940, the population of the city of Utica increased from 12,782 to 100,518, and Oneida County (of which Utica is part) grew from 85,310 to 203,636 (Shupe et al, 1987). In surrounding counties, however, the population remained steady or even declined despite birth rates that without emigration would have insured very rapid growth rates. The population of Otsego County, for instance, hovered between 47 thousand and 52 thousand during the same time period, illustrative of a general pattern in other nearby rural counties near both Utica and other major upstate cities (Shupe et al, 1987). The emigrants from New York's rural counties moved to the cities in order to work in the growing industrial sectors. They were often met by immigrants from around the world, in many cases also displaced former residents of rural areas, who similarly worked in the industrial economies of the cities[1].

---

1. See Chapter 6 for a more detailed analysis of these trends.

The relative population stability of New York's rural counties is due to several factors. In fact, many rural counties lost population after 1840. One factor was the emigration of many residents to the cities. Most often, residents would emigrate due the limits imposed by rural production. As rural production is space intensive, it typically requires a considerable amount of land. Land is, of course, a finite commodity, and when the land is expended to various families more cannot be created. By the 1840s, much of the arable land in upstate New York had been brought into production, and thus a potential farmer could not easily find new land for development. As a result, as the children of farm families came of age they often could not find a farm of their own. Because a farm needs a certain amount of land in order to be productive, it was common for only one child to inherit the farm. This left the other children, and there were often several, to fend for themselves. Some could perform services in the local towns but, as with the farms, there were only so many ministers and doctors (for example) necessary for a community anyway. The result was that many moved to the cities out of necessity. In addition, such counties often failed to attract large numbers of newcomers because of the same lack of opportunity that forced so many of their young to move away.

Rural counties did have a certain amount of urban production, but found that they faced basic economic limitations when compared to the cities. For instance, northern Otsego County was well south of the Hudson-Erie Canal corridor and did develop a degree of urban production in the textile industry. Faced with a difficult trip to bring the products to market towns along the canal for shipment, their products were typically more expensive than those of companies that produced directly along the canal. In time, several of the mills in the county were bought by Utica area firms who within a generation closed them. Besides the inefficient shipping, the flood of immigrants to Utica made for a less expensive and more reliable workforce when compared to the young farm girls who typically operated the factories in Otsego County. The city itself also provided its own market for products that rural Otsego simply did not have, and so by 1900 much of the industry had consolidated in the metropolitan area (Thomas, 2003; Bohls, 1991).

Typically, rural communities grew when they had a unique institution: an institution that functioned to integrate the community with the larger urban economy (Thomas, 2003). Unique institutions varied, but they functioned to attract the interest and/or tutelage of the larger urban society. In many cases, they were industrial. In the village of Canajoharie along the Erie Canal, for instance, the Beech Nut Company produced goods, such as baby food and breath mints, that were marketable in the urban economy and thus funneled income into the community from outside markets. This was possible, of course, because of the access to larger markets as a result of the canal. In contrast, a small county seat also typically attracted some investment and a wide array of services. Schoharie, the Schoharie County seat located over twenty-five miles downstream from Gilboa, featured a sizable shopping district for the region and a population that included doctors, lawyers, and other upper middle class occupations.

The general pattern throughout upstate New York was ultimately based on this relationship between rural and urban production. From the perspective of the landscape, the vast majority of territory was reserved for rural production. This began with the reserve of most of the territory for the harvest of furs during the Dutch period, but by the nineteenth century much of the land was given over to agriculture. More marginal land was often non-developed and thus functioned as hunting grounds for the population, often on steep inclines and marshy areas. Although the beginning of the nineteenth century is marked by the arrival of reasonably self-sufficient farmers, as the century wore on and the lure of goods produced in urban factories became more prevalent, even the most self-sufficient farmer by necessity was 1) brought into the money economy, and 2) increasingly dependent upon the goods and services found in the villages. The dependence of farmers on the money economy meant that trade with urban buyers became increasingly important; newspapers and books from the period reflect an increasing concern with the production of agricultural products for export rather than for food and raw materials. The availability of money made it easier for farmers to purchase finished products, which in turn made them even more entrenched in the money system. Such products were most often found in village business districts, but it was those villages that offered some degree of urban services that prospered the most. Villages with lumber mills, courthouses, and other unique institutions tended to attract a higher number of potential buyers from the hinterland and thus increased the economies of scale for the business district. The enlarged business districts were in some ways the malls of the nineteenth century, attracting shoppers from throughout the sphere of influence. Other settlements struggled with the increased competition of the villages and in many cases atrophied. The typical pattern for a rural community was thus a primary village surrounded by a hinterland by and large devoted to rural production, often farming. In some cases, farming was not the dominant product. For instance, the Adirondack Mountain region in northern New York was best known for lumber and relatively little farming for export was found. These rural community systems were scattered throughout the rural areas of the state.

In the busier transportation corridors, urbanized areas became quite large, often with a major city becoming the major hub of several different corridors. The enlarged population of the region often provided a market for a variety of local goods and services, and the efficiency that resulted from the high economies of scale translated into a distinct advantage for urban firms over those in smaller communities. In time, urban production became concentrated in the cities and larger villages, and the rural areas were, in most cases, left with rural production for export as their primary economies. This system would only change with the dominance of more flexible transportation systems, especially the automobile, in the twentieth century.[2]

The cities were, for the most part, dependent upon the production of agricultural goods taking place in the hinterlands. As most cities grew, their populations became too large for the surrounding landscape to support. In time, the cities imported food and other rural goods by necessity. This in turn meant that the cities not only needed farmers to be committed to money system, but that there would be an ever increasing number of rural producers willing to produce goods for trade or that the existing producers would be more efficient. The mechanization of agriculture succeeded in increasing not only the productivity of farms, but the amount of rural goods flooding into the city. As farmers became decreasingly likely to barter the food themselves, traders in the city could typically skim some of the money off from the trade as profit. As the amount of agricultural goods in most cities increased relative to the population of the cities, the amount of money offered farmers fell. As the products were produced not for need (use value) but for trade (exchange value), the farmer typically had little recourse but to sell for the lower prices. The lower prices for food translated, after some increased profit for the middlemen, into lower prices for the workers in urban factories which enabled owners to keep wages in check.

The dynamics of urban and rural production not only impacted the geography and economy of the state, but the politics as well. Given the democratic system of state government that existed, cities became attractors of power due to their high populations of voters. During the middle to late 1800s, most cities developed political machines that concentrated power in the hands of a few "bosses." The most famous of these was New York's Tammany Hall, whose organization was similar to that of other cities across the state. Leaders of the machine assembled and anointed potential politicians as "machine candidates." In most cases, the machine candidate ran as a Democrat, although in some upstate cities, most notably Rochester and, for a time, Utica, ran as Republicans. In Utica, in fact, a period during the 1880s witnessed machine domination of both parties (Bean, 1994). Once chosen, the organization would spring into action.

In each neighborhood, a block captain organized support for the machine through a variety of mechanisms. The block captain was at once a good neighbor, attending weddings and funerals and other major life events conveying the warmth and good will of himself and the organization. While it seems likely that many block captains were truly concerned with the state of the

---

2. By the end of the twentieth century, even most rural communities found that manufacturing was the primary driver of the economy. This was due to the influence of the automobile, the mechanization of agriculture that released large numbers of farm workers to find other sources of revenue, and the eventual decline of agriculture in the region.

neighborhood and the concerns of the neighbors, the organization was ultimately reimbursing them to do so. Part of being a good neighbor involved the doling out of patronage. A factory lay off or a death in the family might often spark a looming fiscal crisis for the family, and it was often the machine-backed block captain who came with temporary aid for the family. Perhaps more important was the block captain's ability to find work for his constituents in city government, often through the police and fire departments. By 1900, the ranks of the New York City police department had swelled so much with Irish-Americans that the stereotype of the "Irish Cop" began to compete with earlier stereotypes of the "drunken Irishman." A block captain might also be able to help local businesses get contracts with the city, such as street paving and the provision of coal. In many ways, it is difficult to sort out the distinction between the legitimate desire of New York cities to expand their infrastructure and the more nefarious question as to how many projects were completed in order to line the pockets of the machines' more wealthy supporters. Not surprisingly, the majority of supporters who were not wealthy, but rather were the millions of immigrants to New York's cities who voted for the candidates willing to speak to their issues and seemed to understand their collective predicament (Allen, 1993; see also Witt, 1963).

By the end of the nineteenth century, the various cities in the state constituted a system of control over state government that by and large promoted urban interests. Although a candidate for statewide office could, on paper, win an election by simply courting the New York City vote, in practice this has never been a workable strategy due to the number of uncertainties involved. Courting the urban vote statewide was a more sure strategy. It avoided the issues of putting all of the electoral eggs in one basket by spreading the message across the state, thereby minimizing the impact of regional variations. It also targeted the New Yorkers who lived in cities and large towns who were now the majority at the end of the century. Despite variations in size, the state's six largest cities (New York, Buffalo, Rochester, Syracuse, Albany, & Utica) were all impacted by similar transportation policies regarding the Hudson-Erie Canal corridor, state funding for infrastructure, and immigration issues, among others. Typically, these urban interests were understood as "downstate" issues because of the dominance of New York City, as the state's largest city, in promoting them. "Upstate" issues, by way of contrast, were more "rural" in that they frequently dealt with, among other things, agriculture and morality. There were legitimate conflicts between the New York City delegation and those of upstate New York, but the primary conflicts that developed in the state—over the provision of services, transportation, worker safety and wage issues, and water resource management—pitted not upstaters against downstaters but rural residents against urban dwellers.

As the nineteenth century wore on, places like Gilboa, indeed, the entire Schoharie Valley, were increasingly marginal to the overall operation of state government and the regional economy. With poor transportation and relatively little industry, the area welcomed few immigrants and bid good-bye to a fair share of its young. As the century continued, Gilboa's farmers worked less for their own subsistence and more for their exportable crops. They became more entrenched in the money system as they desired more urban goods. But as not only New York City sought food but the other major cities of the state as well, Gilboa was only one of thousands of communities throughout the northeast willing to supply it to them.

The century had begun with an entrenched feudal aristocracy that controlled much of the arable land throughout eastern New York, and that included the lands around Gilboa. New urban goods lured local farmers to sell crops for money. By the 1830s, many Schoharie Valley farmers recognized that the system of quit-rents built into their leases appropriated much of their income, and in many cases the ultimate beneficiary of their labor was the landowner who received not only a portion of the crops to sell on the market but a portion of the farmer's profit as well. For the urban system to develop as it did, and for rural producers to benefit from their own labor, the aristocracy had to go. As was happening in Europe at the same time, the outmoded system of feudalism was coming under attack.

A Most Unfortunate Death

His name was Stephen van Rensselaer, and he was a direct descendent of the original patroons of his land on either bank of the Hudson. He was a stately man with tailored clothes and an upper class gait, and debt. As it turns out, few of the people who performed services for van Rensselaer would, as they would for any other individual, insult the landed aristocrat by demanding immediate payment for goods or services rendered. Over time, much of his life in fact, van Rensselaer accumulated an enormous debt that would only become payable upon his death. At the same time, the Albany patroon had become rather lax in his collection of quit-rents from his tenants, who had enjoyed the benefits of a nearly "freehold" arrangement for years. Alas, the property was not settled by freeholders but rather remained a large tract of leaseholders. Van Rensselaerwyck was, in fact, a time bomb.

The great patroon died on January 26, 1839. Faced with debts, van Rensselaer opted not to release his tenants from their past obligations (as did some other aristocrats) because they represented a significant counterweight to his debts (Cheyney, 1887). Upon his death, those who performed services seemed to emerge from the woods seeking collection of what was owed them, and in order to settle the estate the debts owed van Rensselaer by his tenants came due immediately. The situation was made all the more critical as van Rensselaer, no longer restricted by the law of primogeniture, sought to divide his lands between his two sons. This necessitated a clear title to the land, and thus the farmers of van Rensselaerwyck would have to pay up.

By the fall of 1839, discontent rumbled throughout eastern New York as tenant farmers decried the high rents due the landlords, the taxes due the state and county, and the perceived minimization of their own labor during the preceding generations. Much had changed since poor farmers in search of land came to the region. The tenant farmers had transformed the wilderness into a checkerboard of field and pasture, interspersed with forests and small market towns. They had cleared the land without the efforts or assistance of the landlords, yet paid his taxes on the land and paid him for the privilege of remaining on what most considered their own land. Many had no rights of sale, and those who did were required to cede up to a third or even half of the proceeds to the landlord. From the perspective of the tenants, the landlord was nothing more than a middleman between themselves and the government, a leach that grew wealthy because of the efforts of the farmers. The settlers of the 1790s and early 1800s may have considered tenancy a fair, albeit undesirable, option. Their children, now subject to two and three lifetime leases signed by their fathers, perceived it as an old world remnant that lost its purpose at the close of the Revolution. There had been a growing discontent, and even a few incidences of resistance, prior to 1839 (Christman, 1945). But it was the fates of the van Rensselaer tenants that galvanized a movement to seek a solution once and for all.

For the rebels, the desired outcome of the conflict was the sale of the farms to the tenants. In spring, a committee of tenants from the hills of western Albany County—Bern, Knox, and Rensselaerville—traveled to discuss the situation with Stephen van Rensselaer (the son) in person. The meeting did not go well:

> Mr. Van Rensselaer . . . refused to speak to them or to acknowledge their presence, even by a nod. He went, instead, into an inner office, occupied by his agent, Mr. D. B. Lansing, and held a long and confidential conversation with him. The latter then came out and said that Mr. Van Rensselaer would communicate with them in writing. (Cheyney, 1887)

When the letter came, the tenants learned that their farms were not for sale.

By the middle of the summer of 1839, the courts had issued a number of writs seeking payment of past rents and threatening eviction. In order to enforce the court's orders, Albany County sheriff Amos Adams made his way to the western portions of the county. Traveling alone, he found his horse and wagon damaged at the end of his first night of serving notices. A month later, similar writs were to be delivered and similar troubles ensued. Several men had threatened the life of undersheriff Daniel Leonard, and in time he was being followed by a small crowd of Anti-Rent agitators. As the months went on, it became increasingly difficult for the sheriff's department to serve papers as the farmers and their sympathizers turned out in greater numbers, setting tar barrels afire in the road and generally making the sheriff's life miserable. On December 2, 1839, the sheriff finally resorted to forming a posse of about 500 men only to be turned back by an even greater number of rioters at Reidsville (Christman, 1945).

Throughout 1840, violence spread throughout the region as tenants of other manors saw an opportunity to overturn the inequities of the patroon system. What developed is today known as the "Anti-Rent Wars," an apt term that almost was not. Had the troubles remained on Rensselaerwyck, the incident would be remembered as only a second rate rebellion by tenant farmers against their lords. But other tenants in other estates recognized their own fates entwined with those of the farmers of western Albany County, and thus the violence spread over distance and in duration.

In Schoharie County, almost eighty percent of the land had originally been acquired through the sale of large tracts. The two largest tracts, Scott's Patent (56,000 acres) and Blenheim Patent (40,000 acres) became feudal estates. It was on the Blenheim Patent that Gilboa was settled, many of its residents tenants of one John Weatherfield (Cheyney, 1887). In contrast to the terms that were found in many of the older estates, the Schoharie County patents did not exact rent in the form of crops or service to the manor, but rather in money. The farmers were to sell their goods on the open market, a practice that enabled cities to grow, and pay a monetary rent to the landlord. On the Scott tract, leases ran for the lifetime of the first tenant and his son (two lifetimes) for $14.00 per one hundred acres; in Blenheim, the leases ran in perpetuity (all descendants) for $15.00 per one hundred acres. The use of money for the payment of rent changed the relationship of the tenant to the land. Under the former system, a tenant was expected to use the land to help support the manor in terms of food and trade items (hence, payment in crops) and service. Under the money system, the tenant by necessity sold goods to (primarily) urban middlemen who in turn sold to consumers. This required that the tenant produce enough crops to support the family and sell for cash to pay the landlord. This likely contributed to the increase in productivity in upstate New York (Ellis, 1946) and aided in the rise of a consumer culture (Ryan, 1981).

To call the rebellion a "war" might be overstating the animus of the campaign. In counties throughout eastern New York, as well as in manors established in western New York after the American Revolution, many tenants organized themselves into paramilitary organizations in order to fight the injustices of the system. In order to avoid prosecution, the paramilitaries swore their members to absolute secrecy and wore disguises when in operation. The symbol chosen was the "Indian" to allude to the patriots of the Boston Tea Party who had vandalized British tea imports under the disguise of "Indians" (Christman, 1945). Writing in 1887, Edward Cheyney described the disguise as follows:

> The "Indian" costume was made up of a sheepskin covering for the head and face, apertures being left for the eyes, nose and mouth, and the outside sometimes decorated with a pair of horns or a horse's tail. It also included a calico dress to cover the body, and a belt ornamented with tassels. Besides these, there was often, unfortunately, a rifle or musket. (39-40)

Such oaths of secrecy and disguises were not altogether uncommon among other fraternal societies of the nineteenth century, such as the Masonic Lodge and, more ominously, the Ku Klux Klan. However, the "war" is probably best understood as a series of confrontations between law enforcement and local activists.

There were considerable anti-rent agitations in the area, including a major incident called the Battle of Blenheim Hill. The local sheriff had sent a posse to arrest several area anti-rent leaders, but when they were not found the sheriff satisfied himself to a number of teenage boys who shared apparent anti-rent sympathies but had done nothing overtly illegal. They were jailed in a makeshift sheriff's headquarters at Ira Rose's tavern in Gilboa. Several people were fired upon by sheriff's deputies, but a full assault on the tavern by the "Indians" was discouraged by the more moderate anti-renters who favored legal means. An out-of-town attorney was called in by the anti-rent association who pointed out that the boys had in fact done nothing illegal and should be released. Such was one of the major battles of the rebellion (Mayham, 1906).

What was missing was blatant animosity toward the state. Though there were bands of "Indians," many others spoke of reforming the laws to be more favorable toward tenants by essentially forcing the lords to sell. There were anti-rent organizations that sought to change the system through legal means, although it seems likely that there was some contact between them and the paramilitary "Indians." Throughout the early 1840s, the Anti-Rent leagues supported candidates for public office who supported their views, and it is thus not surprising that by 1845 the state legislature was willing to act against the interests of the landlords. In 1846, a convention to rewrite New York's constitution convened to level the death knell to feudalism by, among other reforms, abolishing all feudal tenures, setting a limit of twelve years on leases, and making the taxes of the estates the sole responsibility of the owners and not the tenants (Cheyney, 1887; Christman, 1945). Within only two decades, the majority of the land in the feudal estates had been transferred to the farmers living there, and the feudal period was over (Christman, 1945).

The overall functioning of the regional economy, centered as it was on New York City and the network of upstate cities reliant upon the metropolis, set the parameters for growth of both New York City and Gilboa. With feudalism over, the urban system was free to become dominant.

4

A Tale of Two Cities
(Sort of. . .)

It is only within the context of the economic and political system of New York State that the growth or lack thereof of its constituent communities can be understood. New York City was, through the benefit of both trade and population, at the center of the system despite the official center of power in Albany. In fact, the location of the state capital in Albany was more than simply a defensive action; by locating the capital upstate, the appearance of the city's dominance in state affairs was mitigated. Such a gesture implied a unity of purpose in state government that extended beyond the southern counties, an inclusiveness that helped even the "Indians" on Blenheim Hill identify not the state but rather individual landlords as the problem they faced.

The Urban System

The urban system may be defined as a system of cities linked to one another through political and economic relations. It requires the development of an urban core that spreads influence through trade and/or conquest, and thus is not simply a network of proximate cities.

Urban production in and of itself does not lead to cities. The members of hunting and gathering societies regularly produce urban products necessary for their way of life: spears, cookware, clothing, etc., are all manufactured of rural products in the form of branches, mud or clay, and animal skins (Maryanski & Turner, 1992). Such societies can and often do maintain nomadic lifestyles that defy urban settlement. Nor is urban production necessarily restricted to humans: Chimpanzees have been shown to fashion tools for extracting termites from their mounds with sticks (Linden, 1992). Past research has shown that cities are ultimately the product of the agricultural revolution (Cauvin, 2000).

An urban settlement pattern does thus not automatically lead to the rise of an urban system. A small agricultural village such as that which may have been found in the Levant (particularly the Jordan River and Dead Sea Valley region) ten thousand years ago would likely have exhibited a familiar settlement pattern of dense settlement surrounded by hinterland, but in and of itself would not have constituted a system of urban areas linked to one another through political and economic relations (Johnson & Earle, 1987). However, the existence of a dense settlement pattern concentrates economies of scale in that geographic space, in turn acting as an attractor point for further development. The development takes place as increased population, both from natural increase and migration from the hinterland, concentrates power, capital, and talent (see chapter one). Due to the potential thus created, a city attracts traders from other cities. The traders constitute a network of individuals linked to one another through trade even though not every member of the network interacts with people in other cities. It is these networks that evolve into the urban system as elites from the various cities in the system recognize common interests.

As urban systems are based upon trade networks, they are inherently urban in character. Since the traders are attracted to cities, the populations in the hinterland often must utilize the urban merchants as intermediaries with the system. A rural farmer, for instance, often does not sell goods to populations in distant cities, but rather to a local merchant in the nearest city who then trades with those more distant merchants. Each city thus claims a sphere of influence over which the city is dominant. In most cases the hinterland is also the source of food and other raw materials for the city, and as such the transition from the hinterland as source of food to source of materials for trade is rather flawless.

The hinterland is perceived by urban dwellers as a possession of the city. This is not particularly the result of urban imperialism *per se*, but rather a byproduct of the earlier relationship between the city and the country. Small agricultural villages—tiny cities in form—often utilize the area surrounding the village for agricultural production as urban production takes place in the village. As population grows, this cultural attitude does not change; as the space required for rural production increases with population, the perceived area of ownership expands accordingly. As discussed in chapter one, the perceived hinterland eventually overtakes smaller villages and the urban system comes into being. As the size of the largest cities in the system increases, the size of vassal cities also grow. The urban system expands the city's hinterland by co-opting the use of other cities' hinterlands for their own use through trade. Due to the power of the largest cities, they are normally dominant in the system.

As New York State developed after the fall of feudalism in the 1840s, the urban system centered on New York City was the ultimate beneficiary of state largesse. Such a system is the reason for the fall of feudalism in New York: as the money system began to dominate in rural areas, urban merchants could directly trade with tenant farmers. The existence of the landed aristocracy was an unnecessary appendage to the system, even political competition to the up and coming capitalists. By the 1840s, a mix of democratic ideals and the fact that the new Capitalist class would soon eclipse the power of the aristocracy made it possible to overthrow the old order. It thus signified not only the victory of tenants over landlords but of the new (Capitalist) elite over the gentry.

An Imperial City

New York City was a mere "factory" during the Dutch period, capital of a fledgling colony of fur traders and aspiring New World aristocrats. Under British control, New York grew steadily but was often outcompeted for political and economic dominance by Philadelphia and Boston. The city's merchants traded with those in Europe and the West Indies, and of course with their competitors up and down the east coast. Even after the American Revolution, New York faced stiff competition from the two other east coast cities. In large measure, this was due to the relative hinterlands available to the respective cities. Boston had at its disposal much of New England, and even today is counted as the cultural capital of the region (Garreau, 1981). Boston had competition as well, such as the south coast cities of Newport and New London, but by 1800 benefited as the major city in the region (Albion, 1984). Similarly, Philadelphia benefited from the wares found in much of the Delaware River basin and from the fostering of trade networks in the interior of Pennsylvania (Burrows & Wallace, 1999). New York benefited from the same hinterland as their Dutch forebears, but it was more sparsely settled clear into the nineteenth century than either New England or Pennsylvania.

As discussed in chapter three, it was the building of the Erie Canal that dramatically expanded the hinterland and the population contained therein after 1825 (see also Shaw, 1990; Sheriff, 1997). The canal was built with the backing of New York State, but it is the composure of state government that is interesting. Built prior to the Anti-Rent Wars, many of the proponents of the canal were those who would benefit directly from its construction. Land speculators, such as the two military figures of Philip Schuyler and George Washington, both of whom owned property in the region. Landed gentry, the most famous of which was Stephen van Rensselaer. Merchant class politicians, in particular from New York City, such as DeWitt Clinton, three times mayor of New York and twice governor of the state. Clinton was so strongly identified with the project that detractors referred to the canal as "Clinton's Ditch" (Shaw, 1990). DeWitt Clinton's motives were consciously imperialistic, making the case for the canal on the basis of both the commercial benefits for New York City if given easy access to the Midwest as well as the boon to upstate farmers who would have access not only to the New York City market but those around the world (Cornog, 2000). Of course, a large number of those farmers were in fact tenants living on the feudal estates of the aristocracy. Many landlords, in contrast, followed the lead of Stephen van Rensselaer by choosing to live much of the time in the state's cities, in particular Albany and New York (Ellis, 1946). Such fixtures of the state power structure were joined by many merchants and community boosters along the proposed route of the canal.

The existence of the canal actually reinforced the relationship between the city and the hinterland that had been forged by the Dutch and evolving ever since. New York City's population had been growing steadily since its founding, and by 1825 had already absorbed its neighboring village of Greenwich and continued its climb up Manhattan Island. Moreover, other villages, such as Harlem and Washington Heights, were growing more slowly but steadily, and the city had spawned suburbs accessible by ferry, such as Brooklyn Heights (Jackson, 1985). The region that would become known as New York was growing, although much of what is today considered New York was then independent of the city's formal political structure. This growing metropolitan region created a demand for agricultural goods that the Erie Canal could deliver at low cost. In fact, goods shipped from the western districts of the state were often less expensive than goods shipped overland from much closer locales (Larkin, 1998).

But the Dutch conception of the hinterland was one of extraction of resources for trade, and the canal enabled city merchants to do just that. Upstate agriculture found its way up and down the Atlantic Coast, although the lack of refrigeration and modern preservatives placed temporal limits on the trade of such products. Other items, such as alcohol, maple syrup, and other processed foods could be more easily shipped great distances and thus found their way to more distant locales, such as Europe and the West Indies. But the greatest export products to flow through the Port of New York were also rural products extracted from the environment. Lumber was shipped through the Erie Canal and its various feeder canals (spurs off the main line) to Albany, from where it was shipped to New York and from there to Europe, where centuries of building and burning wood for fuel had created a shortage in some regions of the continent. Similarly, furs continued through New York Harbor, although by now the fur trade had moved to the western Great Lakes, and on to European markets. In time, New York began to trade not only in rural products but the many urban products that were produced in the state.

New York State began its industrialization in lockstep with its settlement. The ideals of independence pursued by the Yankee settlers in upstate New York caused them to desire, for both ideological and practical reasons, the ability to create certain finished products in their own vicinity. In the histories of villages in Schoharie, Otsego, and Delaware Counties in upstate New York, local historians typically trace the village's founding to the building of such a mill: a grist mill for processing grains, a lumber mill, etc. Such industries were typically oriented to serving the local communities, and as such surplus often translated into free time rather than trade goods for the world market. In time, increased access to markets favored some mills over others. For instance, due to the large local market and the access to global markets available to Utica area textile mills in the late nineteenth century, area firms were able to out compete and in some cases buy textile mills in the less accessible hills of northern Otsego County. By World War I, two of the largest textile companies in the world were headquartered in Utica (Thomas, 2003). The initial advantage for the Utica area firms came from the market built into the city itself, but the access to non-local markets provided by the canal for both westbound traffic (toward the Great Lakes) and eastbound traffic (toward New York City and the world) grew the companies to extraordinarily large proportions. As upstate New York industrialized, New York merchants were again beneficiaries.

As the various cities and towns of upstate New York industrialized, urban products were shipped throughout the various transportation systems to the major points of exit from the state: New York and Buffalo. There were of course other port cities throughout the state, such as canal junctions as found in Rome with the Black River Canal and smaller lake ports like Oswego on Lake Ontario, but it was in New York and Buffalo that the system accessed markets external to New York State. Due in part to its status as gateway city to and from the Great Lakes, Buffalo grew to be a global city by 1900, hosting the 1901 Pan-American Exposition, and building a world class infrastructure of museums, parks, and commercial institutions. Despite its diminished status due to the deindustrialization of the city during the late twentieth century, Buffalo today continues as one of the major centers of the nearly contiguous urbanization that stretches along the entire western end of Lake Ontario to Toronto, Canada. But Buffalo's success, as was the case with that of most American cities, paled in comparison to New York. New York grew rapidly throughout the nineteenth century as wave after wave of immigrants sailed for the premier harbor in the New World. The success of both cities rested in large part on the trade that occurred in them for the manufactured goods of the interior, especially in the smaller cities spawned by the canal. Textiles from Utica, salt from Syracuse, photographic equipment from Rochester and electrical components from Schenectady all passed through the terminus cities and enriched their merchant class.

As a major trading port, New York collected a disproportionate share of the goods produced in its hinterland, stretching from the New York suburbs to the westernmost Great Lakes, and traded them to the world. In effect, New York presided over an "urban hinterland" in which manufactured goods from throughout the region were traded in its own markets and throughout the world. In exchange, New York merchants had the opportunity to sell various goods from global markets back to its own hinterland by passing them through the corridor created by the Erie Canal. Due to growth in the Great Lakes as well as in New York state itself, by the time of the Civil War perhaps no other city in the world held so pivotal a position in so large a hinterland. Not surprisingly, New York City grew faster than every other city in the world during the nineteenth century (Gibson, 1998).

Such emphasis on trade in New York attracted more than simply people; it attracted capital investment in the form of financial houses (banks, insurance, stock exchange, etc.), manufacturing firms, and other forms of economic activity. Population not only moved to the city, but to various other communities in the region. Newark, the largest city in New Jersey, is less than ten miles from New York. Similarly, Brooklyn grew to be the fourth largest city in the nation as its suburban status eventually gave way to industrialization as people and companies sought less expensive locales with easy access to the city. As New York expanded up Manhattan Island, it absorbed several prosperous formerly independent villages along the way. Finally, in 1899, the state of New York attempted to consolidate the multiple jurisdictions in the region into the greater city of New York, which annexed all of Richmond and Kings Counties (Staten Island and Brooklyn) and parts of Westchester County (the Bronx) and Queens County. The newly formed boroughs each contained independent cities and towns that were rapidly being absorbed in more than just name by the spreading metropolis, such as Jamaica and Flushing in Queens, Fordham in the Bronx, and numerous smaller communities. Despite this incorporation of the region, the New York metropolitan area would continue to spread for dozens of miles in every direction. As the city grew, the area required to support it in terms of food and raw materials also grew, and by the turn of the twentieth century farmers throughout the region gleefully traded with the city that relied upon their products so heavily. In much of upstate New York, the cabins and small houses that dominated the landscape gave way to large additions and larger homes as even the rural regions experienced a considerable level of prosperity.

Growth in the counties that would become the New York Metropolitan area by the early twenty-first century is shown in table 4.1. The counties that were incorporated as New York City in 1899 all show high rates of growth between 1820 and 1910. Two counties (now boroughs) experienced their rapid growth later: Richmond (Staten Island) and Queens. In both cases, growth was found primarily in independent towns, such as Flushing and Jamaica, and then absorbed by the waves of urbanization as the city grew to overtake them, just as it had the Manhattan villages of Greenwich and Harlem. Upstate suburban counties show a similar pattern to their cousins further upstream. The counties with independent cities, such as Dutchess (Poughkeepsie) and Orange (Newburgh and Middletown) grew more rapidly than predominantly rural Putnam County.

A Peasant Village

By the late nineteenth century, newspapers up and down the Schoharie Creek Valley, such as the Middleburgh *News* and the Gilboa *Monitor*, included weekly features aimed at the commercial farmer. Gone were the days of a farm family seeking a "'competency' that would allow their families to live a

Table 4.1: New York Metropolitan Area Growth by County, 1820-1910

City:	1820	1850	% Change 1820-1850	1880	% Change 1850-1880	1910	% Change 1850-1910
Bronx[1]	--	--	--	--	--	--	--
Kings	11187	138882	1141.46	599495	331.66	1634350	172.62
New York[2]	123706	515547	316.75	1206300	133.98	2762520	129.01
Queens[3]	21519	36833	71.17	90574	145.90	284041	213.60
Richmond	6135	15061	145.49	38991	158.89	85969	120.48
Suburban:							
Dutchess	46615	58992	26.55	79184	34.23	87661	10.71
Nassau[3]	--	--	--	--	--	83930	NA
Orange	41213	57145	38.66	88220	54.38	116001	31.49
Putnam	11268	14138	25.47	15181	7.38	14665	-3.40
Rockland	8837	16962	91.94	27690	63.25	46873	69.28
Suffolk	24272	36922	52.12	53888	45.95	96138	78.40
Westchester[2]	32638	58263	78.51	108988	87.06	283055	159.71

1. Bronx County not formed until 1914
2. New York County annexed part of Westchester County in 1873 & 1895, which were later included in the Bronx in 1914
3. Nassau County formed from part of Queens in 1899
SOURCE: New York State Department of Economic Development, 2000

comfortable and independent existence" (Sheriff, 1997, 11). The independence afforded by subsistence farming offered an attractive puritan ideal, but commercial farming offered cash with which could be bought the array of urban products built by the very people for whom the food was grown. Like hundreds of similar villages throughout upstate New York, Gilboa provided these commercial farmers the goods of urban society in their own community.

The community system found in Gilboa was familiar to nearly anyone from a small rural community. The village functioned as the economic center of the surrounding area. Farmers would travel to the village along the region's rocky and mountainous roads until reaching the village nestled along a narrow plain by Schoharie Creek. The village itself was quite densely settled. Commercial buildings were placed such that their storefronts were close to the road (Main Street) so that passersby could view the contents of the windows. Residences and non-commercial public buildings were set farther back from the street to allow for a small lawn and, in the case of many residences, a front porch on which to keep cool and dry during the summer. Almost the entire village stretched along Main Street as there were no side streets and no apparent village plan. In the central business district, most storekeepers sold items that avoided direct competition with other merchants in the village, although there was some overlap. There was a three-story hotel—the tallest in town—called Gilboa House that also served as a restaurant and meeting place. There were also several stores that sold specialized foodstuffs that could not be produced at home, clothing and, perhaps as important, cloth. Near downtown, a small set of waterfalls in the creek were a minor tourist attraction, and the villagers had constructed a set of stairs down the embankment to get to them. Several businesses were scattered through the village that catered directly to other basic needs: a blacksmith shop, various small artisans, and of course, churches.

Surrounding the village was a particularly rough hinterland. The Catskill Mountains rise up to 1,000 feet above the valley floor, often at sharp inclines and at times with rock-face cliffs. Much of the soil itself is quite rocky, as one local farmer commented in 2002:

> Ya take a shovel, ya drive it in there, and you'll hit rocks. Big ones, little ones, every single time. You dig down as far as ya want, and that's what you'll find. We got equipment that'll just tear right through it (the soil) today, but ya gotta wonder about those poor bastards a hundred years ago.

Prior to the Anti-Rent Wars, some local farmers opted out of their leases and migrated west to the Great Lakes plain or further because of the combination of poor soil and feudal rental agreements. Located 45 miles south of the Erie Canal and near only minor highways, local farmers had rather poor access to distant markets. It seems likely that this hindrance delayed Gilboa's participation in the global economy by some time, but there is no reliable evidence to this point.

What is certain is that by the turn of the twentieth century Gilboa area farmers were fully participating in such trade and the older notion of independence through subsistence farming was as dead as the ancestors who had settled the region. Still, many local residents were poorer than their counterparts closer to the Hudson and Mohawk Valleys—a trait that remains today (see chapter 12).

In contrast to the great metropolis to which much of their farm goods went, Gilboa remained remarkably stable throughout much of the nineteenth century (see chapter five). If New York was at the center of a vast empire of trade and influence, Gilboa was an outpost of that civilization. New York was in a constant state of flux as millions of new residents arrived in the city and those that surrounded it; Gilboa was a bastion of stability. New York teemed with traders and tourists from around the world; Gilboa offered its residents the comfort of "everybody knowing everybody." New York was all that poets and reformers both loved and hated about urban life; Gilboa was all that ministers and anguished youth loved and hated about rural life.

Relating To Others

The differences between New York and Gilboa extended far beyond population and relative position in the urban-rural political economy. The position of each community within the overall urban system influenced how those who lived and worked in each related to and experienced other communities. In fact, the urban system posits a stratification of community interests that are often unstated but nonetheless understood. It is found and experienced differently at the local level, within state and national politics, and ultimately at the global level.

As discussed in chapter two, New York was the dominant community in the state within a few years of Dutch settlement. Such dominance at the state level translated into much of the state being understood as a vast hinterland from which to extract trade items for the prosperity of the city's merchant class, and as such many of the local communities were founded as outposts designed either to hold territory or provide food for the growing city at the tip of Manhattan Island.

Since the middle of the sixteenth century the defining dynamic present between New York City and its immediate neighbors was one of expansion. In the early eighteenth century, Greenwich was the first of the autonomous communities to discover this fact as its once proud village was engulfed and made indistinguishable from the expanding New York. Home today to New York University, the neighborhood is today known more for its eclectic population rather than its status as a once independent city. Similarly, much of the current city of New York is a conglomeration of once independent villages that progressed from being small farming villages to larger farm towns, then to commercial towns, growing suburbs, and thence to city neighborhoods. The history of each neighborhood is unique, but each is bound to one another by its absorption into the larger metropolitan entity. Two examples of New York's expansion illustrate only part of the local phenomenon: Brooklyn Heights and Bedford.

Brooklyn Heights is today an enclave of affluent urbanites seeking comparatively low rents and a commanding view of lower Manhattan. Filled with brownstones and rowhouses, the neighborhood evokes images of anything but suburbia. But Brooklyn Heights may be one of the oldest suburbs in the nation. The area is today accessible by subway under the East River, but in absence of such transportation in the early nineteenth century the ferry functioned in much the same way. Beginning initially with a sole ferry to the city, land developers recognized the relative bucolic charm of the area away from the filth that, like all cities of the time, permeated New York. A ferry ride to New York could land a commuter at work in less than half an hour after leaving home, and the community grew quickly as a result (Jackson, 1985). The town of Brooklyn grew from a population of 2,378 in 1800 to 806, 343 in 1890 (Jackson, 1985, 27). By the time that New York was consolidated in its current form in 1899, Brooklyn itself was the fourth largest city in the United States and was considered synonymous with Kings County. As a suburban community, the settlement of Brooklyn Heights was dominated by New York from the very beginning. New York was, for all intents and purposes, the justification for the community's existence.

Also in what is now the borough of Brooklyn is Bedford, today part of the Bedford-Stuyvesant neighborhood. Through much of the early nineteenth century, Bedford resembled Gilboa more than it did New York or its growing neighbor, Brooklyn. Bedford was originally settled by the Dutch in 1663, and for much of its history remained primarily an agricultural village. Gilman (1971) showed that as of 1850, Bedford had an occupational structure much like that of any rural village, with a variety of occupations represented among the population. It was primarily the middle class—merchants and doctors, ministers and teachers—who composed the upper crust of the village. Trades people and skilled labor were also found in the village, as well as unskilled laborers who did much of the physical labor. Surrounding the village—indeed, even within the village—were numerous farmers who worked the land in order to sell its wares to the great metropolis at the village's doorstep and spend the money earned in village shops. As early as 1836, the Brooklyn and Jamaica Railroad had pushed through the area, and even by 1850 some change had already begun. By 1880, the area had become home to thousands of Irish, German, and African-American immigrants (Gilman, 1971; Bedstuyonline.com, 2002). With this demographic change came an occupational and, likely, a social class change as well. Jackson (1985) relates that when Bedford, "had become part of the expanding metropolis, very few laborers remained, and the farmers had disappeared" (29; see also Gilman, 1971).

Bedford is today part of Bedford-Stuyvesant, the largest African-American neighborhood in the United States, and Gilboa lies destroyed at the bottom of Schoharie Reservoir. Both rural villages experienced the city's growth, but in different ways. Bedford was absorbed into the sprawling metropolis, whereas Gilboa was destroyed for it. In either case, it was the result of New York's expansion.

In contrast to being dominant in a local system of communities, Gilboa was at best competitive and at worst mildly dependent upon its local neighbors. There were several other villages nearby, all roughly the same size. To the south, Grand Gorge was a small crossroads village no larger than Gilboa. Slightly upstream (to the southeast) was Prattsville, also of like size. Prattsville was originally to be the village over which the Schoharie Reservoir would be built, but the city moved the site to Gilboa when it was discovered that the downstream location would yield more water. Ten miles west was Stamford, the largest community in the area and the only one to have over a thousand residents. Gilboa residents might travel to one of these villages when in need of a specific item not available in Gilboa, but residents of those communities would occasionally come to Gilboa for the same purpose. Most often, however, residents stayed near home—Gilboa afforded most of the necessities of life, and there were numerous traveling salespeople who could bring the rest. In contrast to the relationship between New York and her neighbors, Gilboa was neither dominant nor subordinate.

The dominance of New York was evident not only in the local area where its influence was primarily found in expansion, but at the state level as well. The existence of the state of New York is in some ways a historical anomaly. Founded as a colony, it was originally conceived as an administrative unit within the Dutch Republic under the control of the Dutch West India Company, and not as an independent country. The state has thus never acted as a sovereign country, although it was reasonably independent of other states under the Articles of Confederation (federal) government during the 1780s. New York City's elites have thus always had the challenge of leveraging decisions at both the state and federal level. Further, New York's capital had been in Albany since 1797, and this has required that the city's elite at least symbolically appease those in the rest of the state. City elites often sparred with state officials in regard to the formation of corporations (a state level prerogative), basic infrastructure, and state aid for city services, such as schools and public transit. Once such an appeal to the state was made, the city's legislative delegation by necessity had to negotiate with legislators from upstate communities in order to get the necessary votes. This process at the state level has historically acted as a check on city power over its history, but has also at times fueled resentment on both sides of the legislative debates. That said, New York's elite has also been able to utilize state government as both a source of additional funds and an institution that could confer legitimacy to the city's plans that the city government lacked.

New York has always contained over a third of the state's population, but nevertheless there have been projects needed by the city that, due to their expense, city elites would rather have the costs spread over a larger population. This is particularly evident with social welfare costs today, although such subsidization of the city comes primarily not from upstate communities but rather from the city's own suburbs to the north and on Long Island. In most such cases, however, the needs of the city's elite did coincide with the needs of certain areas outside the city that required a modicum of regional planning that the state provided. The building of the Erie Canal, for instance, required state assistance both in planning and financing the canal. More recently, the construction of the New York State Thruway and other highway projects were similarly designed with the express purpose of connecting cities, and there are countless small towns along its route that have no exits off the highways. In some communities, such as the village of Fort Plain in the Mohawk Valley, the Thruway slashes its way through the heart of the village, cutting the community off from the riverfront, and offers no entrance onto the highway. This is so because, like the canal itself, the Thruway was built due to a coalition of the elites of the old canal corridor cities who desired to built the road in order to serve cities, and not surprisingly the needs of the rural population in between was considered too expensive to satisfy.

Such coalitions of New York elites with those of other cities were found on the national level as well. Home to numerous multinational corporations, the elite structure of the national urban system often worked to influence national policy as well. The Interstate Highway System, for instance, was built in order to make it easier to cross the country in an automobile. Built under the auspices of the Defense Department (Kay, 1998), a primary concern was the mobility of troops and equipment. Bridge dimensions, for instance, are designed to allow the passage of trucks carrying missiles underneath. Another major factor, however, was the ability of trucking companies to transport goods across the country, a concern that benefited primarily urban elites. Indeed, there are more interstates built in metropolitan centers than in rural states, and the expressways themselves often aided in land speculation in the growing suburbs by deconcentrating the metropolitan population. Such a pattern was in actuality a continuation of the pattern found in transportation policy since colonial times (Jackson, 1985).

The interests of New York's elites and those of other cities have historically been given an air of legitimacy when forwarded at the state and federal level. The Erie Canal was not sold only as a means of turning New York into the world's most important port, but rather as a boon for settling upstate and helping upstate farmers and merchants (Larkin, 1998). Similarly, the idea that most of the Interstate highway System should be free was presented as a tax issue when in fact it transferred costs of maintaining the system from those who use it, primarily suburban commuters and trucking companies, to the population as a whole (Kay, 1998).

Not surprisingly, Gilboa had and continues to have a very different relationship with state and federal government. The dominant feature of Gilboa's relationship with the state and federal level has historically been one of passivity. Passivity is not meant to connote a lack of participation in state and federal government, for the region does have a proud history of government participation. However, as state and federal representatives have historically and continue to represent extremely large geographic areas, the influence of any one small town has tended to be minimal. In fact, it was typically the larger communities that received the attention of politicians if for no other reason that they had the most votes. As a result, Gilboa has tended to be at the receiving end of government policy. At various times in the area's history, government intervention in the area has had a positive effect. For instance, the Rural Electrification Administration (REA) electrified parts of the region that had not been electrified when the matter was left simply to private industry. The pattern of electrification had been left primarily to private companies, and as a result electric service was spotty. A similar pattern is evident today in regard to cell phone coverage—left to their own devices, cellular phone companies have provided only sporadic service to the region. Service is so poor that one local resident quipped in 2002 that, "cell companies shouldn't be allowed to sell phones here—it's false advertising to say you get service here." In the 1930s, REA electrified farms that were similarly left out of the modern world of electricity.

Government intervention has proved a mixed bag for the area, however. To a populace that settled the region in hope of a proud and independent existence, the Anti-Rent Wars showed a particularly ugly side of government. In the name of defending the rights of the landed aristocracy, government troops were conscripted from some regions of the state to fight against those engaged in the uprising. An admittedly odd occurrence for New Yorkers to suffer, the Schoharie Valley met an even more heinous fate in the 1920s. Under the auspices of the state, the City of New York destroyed the village of Gilboa in order to build the Schoharie Reservoir. To the quenched New Yorkers, the sacrifice of a small Catskill Mountain town was an unfortunate necessity. For the villagers of Gilboa at the time, the reservoir was an unspeakable horror, an atrocity for which other regimes are bombed when they force their own populations to move from their homes. If the good people of Gilboa and other rural towns choose to pursue a politics that calls on their representatives to leave them alone, it must be acknowledged that the state has not always been the friend of rural America. It need not be a reservoir—it has included urban bureaucrats drawing a line on a map for a new railroad that cuts through a farmer's field, or finding a location in "the middle of nowhere" for a garbage dump to accept urban trash, or simply building big box stores that devastate the small business communities for miles in every direction. Not surprisingly, despite the good government has done at times, many local residents would prefer to be left alone.

New York City justifiably bills itself as a global city. By any standard, New York qualifies as one of the cities of true global importance. Sassen (1991) showed that New York is one of a collection of cities, along with London, Paris, Tokyo, and others, that constitute a class of elite cities in which the great majority of the world's large corporations are headquartered. Such an economic landscape in the city encourages a truly global perception of the world—in essence, the world is New York's hinterland. New York's peers are other global cities, and the space between them is simply territory that can and often is divided among the elites of the great cities. This is, of course, not carried out in the name of the urban elites but rather in the name of national governments that often cater to their needs. The elites of such global cities often work in concert and conduct business in concert with one another, and thus this first tier of global cities constitutes a network of urban elites. As home to the largest number of corporate headquarters, New York is also extremely powerful even within the system of global cities. However, because other cities are also of primary importance in their respective nations and regions, it is only at the level of global cities that New York encounters significant competition for global dominance.

If passivity characterized Gilboa's relationship with state and local power, it is only heightened in its relationship with global cities. The economic and political power found in global cities, including New York, is a cultural icon for the rural residents of the region and always has been. This is characterized by social distance—rural residents are exposed to, bombarded really, by urban norms and values that are forged by the urban environment. The city as cultural icon is strangely distant, its customs presented as mainstream culture and replicated in the country. In return, the countryside is presented alternatively as a heaven or a hell. Urban dwellers across the nation aspire to have a "country kitchen" in their homes, but the reality of those who actually live in the country often does not resemble such quaint and pastoral imagery. Urban dwellers travel to idyllic small towns like Cooperstown, Lake George, and even nearby Stamford in search of a feeling of community that was lost with suburbanization, and such villages have transformed themselves into the stereotypes the urbanites expect (Thomas, 2003). The global economy and networks of urban elites is recognized by many, but is so distant and aloof that its significance in one's life is barely acknowledged.

Foundation Established

The events of the three hundred years preceding the building of the Schoharie Reservoir established both the cultural environment and the dynamics that would determine Gilboa's fate. New York was in the early twentieth century the largest city on the planet and rapidly becoming the most important political and economic entity in the world. The rapid rate of growth, both of population and of business, necessitated a stable water supply. It was the interaction of the city and the larger urban system of which it was part that guided decisions in the particular directions they took, and it was the temporal dynamics created by those decisions that eventually lead to the flooding of Gilboa. With an understanding of the history of the region and of the emergence of the urban system, the context in which such decisions were made can be better understood. Events, however, rarely begin at a relative identifiable time, but rather are rooted within the thick context of social dynamics that predispose particular decisions and deemphasize other possible alternatives as unpopular or impractical. As New York built its water system, it was its position in the urban system that ultimately guided its growth.

5   Quenching the Thirst

It is tempting to believe that a city that boasts the "best of everything" has always been able to make such a claim. In regard to water, however, New York has not only survived periods of inferior water service, but has at various stages in history been rather infamous for its poor water. The history of water in the city is fraught with scams, obstinacy, and sheer lack of imagination.

Isle of Abundance

New York is, of course, a coastal city founded at the tip of Manhattan Island. Surrounded by water, it is ironic that New York has spent half its history in a quest for drinkable water. New York Harbor and both the Hudson and East Rivers are salt water along the shores of Manhattan, and as such early New Yorkers necessarily looked to the island itself for fresh water.

It is difficult to imagine Manhattan Island in its natural state. The last farm was developed in the 1920s, and most of the island is subject to the droning regularity of the gridiron street system. Yet to the early Dutch settlers of the seventeenth century, Manhattan was a land of plenty, even in regard to water. Animals of all descriptions, some of which are extinct in not only New York City but New York State as a whole, roamed the island in abundance. The numerous birds flocked in the sky and both the fresh water streams and the salt water rivers abounded with fish, mollusks, and any other sustenance to be taken from the clean waters. It is safe to say that, when Dutch settlement began and for years afterward, city residents had little reason to fear that they would be short on water.

The problem with New Amsterdam, however, was that the abundant waters of Manhattan Island were found north of the defensive fortification that became Wall Street. Within the city itself, there was little fresh water to be found. The triangular city was bounded on two sides by salt water, and a long canal called Heere Gracht and the shorter Bevers Gracht cut into the center of the town. Fresh water was found in wells found behind private homes and particularly behind breweries. Due to their reliance on water, breweries typically required their own reliable source. The wells were "typically shallow, and, given the geological conditions, provided water best drunk after the boiling with requisite ingredients into beer" (Koeppel, 2000, 14). So close to the rivers and the canals, the quality of the well water was questionable. Beer was thus less of an evening diversion than an essential substance for the city—the process of boiling the water and the presence of alcohol made beer purer and healthier than the untreated water.

In addition to the private wells, there were some private cisterns. Cisterns collected rainwater and snow during wet periods. A good source of water during periods of high precipitation, the use of cisterns became more problematic during dry periods.

The Dutch Governor, Peter Stuyvesant, had on several occasions refused a request to build the city's only public well (Galusha, 1999, 11). Proposed for sites in and near the battery at the tip of the island, such a well could theoretically help in the defense of the city in case of a siege. Stuyvesant, of course, met such a day in 1664 when the British did in fact surround the city and present terms of surrender. One wonders of what Stuyvesant thought about his fateful decision as he was lead from the battery by his minister, but he did cite the lack of water at the fort in his report to the West India Company explaining why the city fell so quickly. In any case, the directors of the company were hardly impressed, stating that the excuse "sounds very strange to the Company" (Koeppel, 2000, 16).

The fact that the takeover of New Netherlands by the British was a positive development for England is evident, but the transfer of the city was positive for New Yorkers as well. The major British concern was not the city and colony itself but rather the elimination of the Dutch as a competitor in North America. It also created a solid block of British colonies from the border with the Spanish in the south (Florida) and the French in the north (Canada). For New Yorkers, however, the British brought a leadership that was more concerned with settlement than the Dutch had been, and this translated into more than just the continuation of feudal relations in the colony. New York was to be a major port city, and the British were willing to support the city's leaders in their commercial ambitions. Chief among those was water (Galusha, 1999).

Within two years of the British takeover of the city, the British Governor, Richard Nicolls, became the first to order the digging of a public well. Completed in 1666, it was located in the fort at the tip of the island so that the British could, if necessary, withstand a siege. Even though the Dutch had surrendered the city so painlessly, the reemergence of Dutch warships in New York Harbor was still a possibility. Indeed, Stuyvesant claimed that the West India Company would have an easier time of recapturing the city than defending it against siege, and it was this consideration that ultimately encouraged him to surrender the city (Koeppel, 2000; Burrows & Wallace, 1999). Such a calculus was evident to the British as well, and so it is not surprising that the first public well was located within the fort. Other wells followed. One was built in 1671 behind City Hall, and in 1677 a concerted effort was made to provide drinking water for the city's growing population. A decade of British rule had grown the population to over two thousand residents, and it was apparent that the growth would continue (Koeppel, 2000, 18). There were problems with the first public well system, but by 1686 the system was well underway. Specific neighborhoods were required to "pay" for their own wells both financially and through the provision of labor to build and maintain the well. Caretakers were assigned for each well, and in time they became center of community life and identity (Koeppel, 2000). Wells were generally dug in the middle of public streets, which were at the time the center of neighborhood life (Jackson, 1985).

British rule brought not only new wells but a most unwelcome new fact of life. In 1668, disease, most likely Typhoid or Malaria, spread thought the city's population (Burrows & Wallace, 1999; Koeppel, 2000). In ensuing years, epidemics would become a regular part of life, sweeping through the city primarily during the summer months when the island's swamps nurtured the local mosquito population and the filth of the city's streets encouraged a proliferating rat, and thus flea, population. It is likely that the city's growth accounted for the epidemics more than the sudden emergence of the British, as it was the traditions started by the Dutch in terms of sanitation that were unfortunately followed by the British. Street sweeping was required by law, as was proper disposal of privies and household garbage in the rivers. Such minor provisions could have only a minimal impact on the sanitary conditions of the city, but as the population was low (below 2000) during the Dutch period such laws were adequate. Even so, the Dutch governors were uneven in their enforcement of such laws, and New York was considered filthy by many of the visitors who passed through the city (Burrows & Wallace, 1999; Koeppel, 2000). The growth experienced under British rule rather quickly strained what little sanitation there was, and as such the epidemics began.

Population growth also brought pollution, and pollution severely impacted both the city's public and private wells. Most wells were less than forty feet deep, and not surprisingly easily corrupted (Koeppel, 2000). A walk through the streets of New York at the time would have not only looked unattractive but was also an invitation for various contagious diseases. The streets were littered with household trash, in many cases simply dumped from residents' windows upon the street below. In addition to trash, the privies of neighborhood residents were frequently simply dumped from windows or surreptitiously carried out to the street at night, and thus the human urine and fecal material was swept to the sides of the street where it mixed with that of the numerous animals that roamed the city. Horses of course traveled through the town regularly, but cattle as well roamed the streets. At various points in the city's history, the Dutch had been compelled to pass laws requiring owners to take better care of the hogs, such as by attaching rings through the nose, who were simply roaming through the streets (Koeppel, 2000). Industrial facilities, in particular tanneries, dumped wastes into streams and city streets as well. Perhaps even more disgusting than the physical ugliness of a typical street during this period was the stench of human and animal wastes, decaying garbage, and industrial chemicals that formed a soup at the edges of every street. And in the center of it all was the public wells from which many New Yorkers were expected to drink.

Not surprisingly, New York welcomed many more epidemics of such diseases as Cholera during the next 150 years. The city was particularly hard hit during the summer months, as the nearby swamps and stagnant pools within the city offered the perfect home to disease carrying mosquitoes. Rat populations were very content living in the shadows of their human overlords, and the summer months brought conditions of warm weather and abundant food during which the rat city could thrive. Rats, of course, carried fleas and the fleas a host of other diseases that were content with humans as well as rats. Storehouses and basements provided excellent cover for the small mammals, and this often kept them in close proximity to the human population.

New York continued to have problems with its water supply throughout the colonial period. By the time of the American Revolution, much of the water in the town was considered fine for laundry and cleaning but not for drinking. The best-known well in the city, known simply as the Tea Water Pump located near today's City Hall, produced drinking quality water that was still best utilized after being boiled for tea (Koeppel, 2000). Beyond the city limits, the Collect Pond was still a source of fresh water, although its abundant supply also attracted numerous industrial facilities, such as tanneries, and in time it too was polluted. A small meadow near present day Maiden Lane similarly was useful for collecting water for household purposes, but again suffered from pollution.

False Starts

New York needed water. Perhaps the best of the early plans for a public water supply came from a most unfortunate character. Christopher Colles was a native of Ireland where he was born into a noble family. Nobility could not save him from a life of mediocrity, however, as Mr. Colles appeared to be one of those people given to unfortunate twists of fate. He came to America in 1772 in order to escape a string of failed enterprises in Ireland and find a start in Philadelphia.

Colles had some familiarity with the underlying engineering of the steam engine, and in 1772 built the second such engine in the soon to be United States. Working on a shoestring budget the boiler of the contraption was too small for constant use, but it did provide a showpiece with which Colles could attempt to lure investors (Koeppel, 2000). He received praise from many quarters, but little actual investment and so he found himself in New York in 1774 promoting a plan for building New York's first water delivery system.

The system itself was to be both simple and sophisticated. The centerpiece of the plan called for the digging of a well in the vicinity of the Collect Pond. The site selected was luckily on the opposite end of the pond from the major industrial facilities and thus considerably less polluted than other sites in the area. A steam engine designed and built by Colles would pump the water to a large reservoir. The reservoir was to be large enough that the pump would only have to operate half the week in order to save operating costs. From the reservoir, gravity would perform the task of distributing the water throughout the city. Colles planned to distribute the water underneath the major city streets—fourteen miles worth—in hollowed pine logs (Koeppel, 2000).

Such a plan was quite novel for the time. There was a rudimentary piped water supply in Boston that was used primarily for fighting fires and laundry. Piped drinking water was also found in Bethlehem, Pennsylvania and Providence, Rhode Island. No other colonial city had piped water service; like New York, they relied on street side well pumps and natural fresh water sources (Koeppel, 2000).

Owing to the fact that the city had, for all intents and purposes, been restricted to only one reliable source of good fresh water (the Tea Water Pump), the city government was impressed with Colles' plans. That summer, the Common Council voted to implement the plan and issued the first of a series of planned promissory notes to finance the plan. Land was procured for the well and the reservoir, and New York's first attempt at a comprehensive plumbed water supply was underway. By the middle of 1775, the well had been dug and tested, the reservoir built, and portions of the steam engine to run the pump had been cast by the New York Air Furnace company. The pipes themselves were being made by a company in the Hudson Valley town of Stillwater, north of Albany and close to the forests of the Adirondack Mountains. For the first time in his life, Christopher Colles was on the verge of a remarkable achievement that would win him the fame and fortune that so eluded him in Ireland.

And then the Americans revolted. New York was occupied by British forces throughout most of the Revolutionary War and the Colles Plan was scrapped. The engine was never used and the reservoir waited in ruin for the water that never came. As for Christopher Colles himself: he was said to have remarked, "Had I been brought up a hatter, people would have come into the world without heads" (Koeppel, 2000, 36). Another victim, so to speak, of the luck of the Irish.

How Not to Build a Water Supply

The Colles plan was to build a truly public water supply, owned and operated by the city for the public good. Water was necessary not only for drinking and household purposes, but also to wash the tepid streets and fight fires. New York has endured several fires that have caused damage over several blocks throughout its history, and each was aided by problems in fighting the fire caused by insufficient supplies of water. A public water supply therefore appeared the most desirable route, and prior to the Colles plan there had been no attempts at doing otherwise.

As the American Revolution came to a close, New York returned to its previous issues of summer fevers and epidemics, filthy streets, and the constant threat of a city-destroying fire. By the later 1790s, the New York Common Council had formed a committee to examine the provision of water in the city, and they sifted through numerous proposals to do just that.

The early republic witnessed the birth of the nation's first two major political parties: the Federalists, or Whigs as they were called by some, and the Democratic-Republicans. The early split revolved around the proper role of government and the extent of the democratic franchise. In general, the Federalists argued for a strong central (Federal) government that would protect the interests of the propertied classes and merchants. Democratic-Republicans, in contrast, supported a more decentralized form of government and wider voting rights for white men, preferring for instance to directly elect federal senators rather than have them appointed by professional politicians at the state level (Phillips, 2002). Not surprisingly, the Federalists did best in areas where great wealth was concentrated such as the big cities (Phillips, 2002). New York, being one of those places, was controlled by Federalists whereas the upstate hinterlands, not yet a highly urbanized region, tended toward the Democratic-Republicans (Koeppel, 2000). The first real attempt at New York's water delivery system demonstrated that politicians of both parties, then as today, were willing to be shortsighted and corrupt.

There is perhaps no more poignant conflict among the leaders of the young republic than that between Democratic-Republican Aaron Burr and Federalist Alexander Hamilton. Burr was a quixotic orphan who as an adult excelled both in politics and business, but somehow left a sour taste on the palettes of his associates (Melton, 2001). In a sense, Burr was the original "slick politician." Hamilton, in contrast, was a staunch defender of the rights of the aristocracy, which were under some attack in the years after the Revolution, and a main author (with James Monroe and John Jay) of *The Federalist Papers* (Hamilton et al, 2003). In 1804, the extent of their rivalry culminated in Burr killing Hamilton in a gun duel (Fleming, 1999). For the New York City water supply, however, they worked together.

In 1799, Burr was one of several New York State Assemblymen representing New York City, a Democrat in a by and large Federalist city. He proposed a bill in the Assembly to water the city, but rather than proposing to do so publicly as the Common Council had intended he proposed the formation of a private corporation to do so. Burr had recruited Hamilton to help convince the city fathers to use a private corporation due to a lack of public funds, suggesting that the city would hold considerable power over the private company. The final product, the Manhattan Company, was very different from what had been described by Hamilton and the Common Council ultimately thought they had supported. Koeppel (2000) found numerous conflicts of interest among the various beneficiaries of the proposed company, including relatives of both Hamilton and Burr. At a time when most private corporations were subject to charters that had finite time limits, the new company would have a perpetual charter. As Koeppel (2000) noted:

> The Company's substantial rights of eminent domain over lands, rivers, and streams were similar to the rights of the state's two private canal companies but, unlike other American water companies, the Manhattan Company did not have to repair streets torn up for pipelaying, could set water rates as it saw fit, and did not have to provide free water to the city to put out fires. . .With these provisions alone, Burr was proposing a precedent-setting company, with broad rights and few obligations. (83)

The truly amazing provision, however, was the right of the company to do whatever it wished with its excess capital. It became the first corporation in New York to have an unlimited charter—all other corporations had charters that limited their business dealings to the purposes for which they were chartered. The Manhattan Company would be capable of entering any business of its choice, and it chose banking. Burr had formed, through a high degree of trickery and corruption, the second bank in New York City. The forerunner to Chase Manhattan Bank, it would compete with Alexander Hamilton's Bank of New York.

New York's experience with the Manhattan Company water system is perhaps best summarized as a slowly evolving unmitigated disaster. Prior to the formation of the corporation, a consensus had begun to take form that the best source of water was had by damming the Bronx River in what was then Westchester County. Water would then have to be brought to the city through the wilds of what is now the South Bronx, over the Harlem River, and down Manhattan Island to the city at its tip. There was some debate as to the specifics, such as whether to use pipes or open canals for transporting the water and the best site for the dam. Nevertheless, a good number of engineers and city residents had rejected not only the Collect Pond as a source of water but the various other sources on the island due to pollution. Even the wording of the Manhattan Company charter, with its allusions to canals and aqueducts, seemed to presume the Bronx as the water source.

It no doubt came as some surprise when the Manhattan Company chose an area near the Collect as the source over the Bronx. The route from the Bronx River was expensive, and the "Manhattan Company had no intention of spending its money on a historic but expensive water supply for New York" (Koeppel, 2000, 86). The company sought the opinions of several engineers who all came to eerily similar conclusions: the Bronx supply was unfeasible, the Collect Pond and the nearby territory in which to dig a well was good water, and there was a need for only 300,000 gallons of water per day. The reports contradicted earlier reports that stressed the necessity of using the Bronx and for a far greater daily supply (Koeppel, 2000).

Work on the water system began during the summer of 1799. The Manhattan Company had settled on a system that was little more than the Colles plan of 1774. (Indeed, Colles was one of the consultants!). They would use a well in the vicinity of the Collect, pump the water to a nearby reservoir, and a distribution system of log pipe. The primary difference was the use of a horse-drawn pump rather than a steam engine of the type originally suggested by Colles in 1774, although in 1802 the Company did convert to steam power. By September, the Manhattan Company was making very good progress on the water system and opened a banking office at what is today 40 Wall Street.

The Manhattan Company expanded water service over the next several years, serving 2000 customers at eight dollars per year by 1802. Water was, however, only one of the company's businesses, and not the most important at that. The Bank of the Manhattan Company became the bank of choice for Democratic-Republicans who were eager to withdraw support of Hamilton's Bank of New York. Aaron Burr's dishonest dealings with Alexander Hamilton likely led to Hamilton's support of Thomas Jefferson for President when he and Burr had tied in 1802, and ultimately the conflict led to the famous duel in 1804 at which Hamilton was slain. The Manhattan Company funded numerous projects throughout the state, including the $150,000 Cayuga Bridge, a mile-and-a-half long wooden bridge spanning the northern end of Cayuga Lake and Montezuma Swamp in western New York (Galusha, 1999). In the city, however, customers complained that "the water it was providing was unfit for consumption and just plain unavailable, its wooden mains clogged by roots or taken out of service for weeks at a time" (Galusha, 1999, 16). In addition, the company rarely fixed the street pavement after laying pipe, leading to conflict with city authorities (Koeppel, 2000). Not surprisingly, Mayor Dewitt Clinton—future builder of the Erie Canal—appointed a committee to negotiate with the Manhattan Company about ceding its water supply privilege to the city in 1804. Clinton was an investor in the Manhattan Company who, shortly after taking office as Mayor, shifted all the city's accounts to the Bank of the Manhattan Company (Burrows & Wallace, 1999). Clinton thus seemed to have a proper perspective on the Manhattan Company: a fine bank, but ill-suited for running the water supply. Unfortunately, nothing came of his efforts to relieve Manhattan of the Manhattan Company.

New York had about 60,000 residents in 1800, but only 2000 customers took what advantage there was of the Manhattan Company supply. The rest continued to use polluted public wells in the streets (soon to be removed to the sidewalks) and, increasingly, private water services that brought water to the city from sources in the country in carts. By 1810, the city's population had grown to nearly 100,000; by 1830, it exceeded 200,000. Unfortunately, the city's water system was far inferior to those in existence or under construction in other major cities, particularly Philadelphia, Baltimore, and Boston (Koeppel, 2000). Pollution of public wells increased with population, along with the overall level of sheer filth in the streets that helped increase wave after wave of disease. The Manhattan Company never supplied enough water to actually adequately serve the entire population. It never provided enough to wash the streets; indeed, who would have paid for it? Water for fighting fires was not required by the charter, and so there was little if any for that purpose. Some of the issues in regard to fire fighting were summarized by Burrows and Wallace (1999):

> (The Manhattan Company's) system was so limited that it reached only a small portion of the city...it had no hydrant, only hard-to-find and hard-to-open fire plugs, forcing firemen to drill holes in the wooden mains to gain access. (362)

Although the charter itself did not allow for a monopoly over water distribution, it did make it difficult for any competitors to service the city—including the city itself. And the situation grew more desperate as the years went by; by the 1820s, the city was squabbling over its water system with one of the most powerful banks in the United States. This was a far cry from what Hamilton had supported in 1799.

In order to counteract the adverse effects of the Manhattan Company supply, the city ordered the construction of cisterns for the collection of rainwater with which to fight fires. Numerous fires, particularly an especially devastating fire in 1828, prompted the city to build its own water system specifically for fighting fires in 1829 (Weidner, 1974; Koeppel, 2000). The public system could only be used for that purpose, however, as the Manhattan Company still had allies on the Common Council. Fighting almost yearly outbreaks of Yellow Fever and later Cholera demanded better sanitation and sewers, both of which required abundant and clean water. The city passed laws requiring property owners to sweep and wash the area around their buildings. The city also hired people to regularly wash city streets with well water. Despite these efforts, the city still suffered devastating epidemics (Duffy, 1968).

As the early 1800s unfolded, some looked to the Collect Pond as both a source of disease and potential new property. Between 1803 and 1819, the Collect was filled in and sold as building lots. By the time of its filling it was less a pond and more of a chemical pit, a convenient place to dispose of industrial chemicals, refuse, and dead animals. (Keep in mind that the Manhattan Company well was nearby). The fill came from numerous sources, both clean and not so clean, including several nearby hills that were leveled. The Collect Pond did not go willingly, however, and the buildings built upon its former site began to sink and sag during the 1820s. The area was subject to putrid smells seeping up from beneath the ground and not surprisingly became an undesirable location in which to live. As such, "Five Points, the nation's first great slum, was born" (Koeppel, 2000, 117).

It took tragedy for the city to finally take action at the source of the problem. In 1832, Cholera visited New York with a vengeance directed at the city's grimy conditions. Devastating as it was throughout North America, New York was especially hard hit. Nearly half of the city's roughly 202,000 residents fled to the countryside—especially the wealthy. Over 3,500 residents died during the summer and fall; 104 during one day in July (Rosenberg, 1962, 28). In response, the Common Council's Fire and Water Committee, responsible for the city's public fire water supply, hired Colonel DeWitt Clinton Junior to explore other options. The Manhattan Company had to go.

Going Croton

In late 1832, the shell-shocked Common Council allotted $1,000 for investigations into how to water the city, hiring Colonel Clinton and forming a special committee headed by former mayor Stephen Allen. Even so, it would not be until 1836 until the city took more concrete action than simply studying the range of options. The report by Clinton and a tour of the Bronx River for city councilors helped to convince them that the Bronx was no longer a suitable option (Koeppel, 2000). The thirty years since the Manhattan Company had turned its back on the Bronx had witnessed not only phenomenal growth in New York itself, but in the surrounding region as well. Southern Westchester County was certainly not immune to such growth, especially in the areas of the major rivers leading to Long Island Sound and the East River. In only another four decades, the first portions of what is today the borough of the Bronx were annexed. The rivers had attracted not only farms and villages, but a variety of mills that required waterpower to operate. On the Common Council tour of the Bronx River area, councilors were informed that the outlet of Rye Pond, the principal source of the river, had been widened in order to increase flow to the urbanizing Bronx Valley. With settlement, industry, and competition for water flow, the Bronx River made the case for the Croton River.

Located thirty miles upstream, the Croton River basin drained a larger area than that of the Bronx. Collecting water from the hills east of the Hudson in New York and Connecticut, the Croton not only featured a more steep shoreline and terrain, but due to such features there was considerably less development along its banks. This, of course, promised a less polluted supply that could be managed more easily by New York interests. The only problem was the price.

If the Common Council was reluctant to pay the high cost of the Croton Water supply in a given year, the mid-1830s had a way of reinforcing the need for it. In 1834, Cholera revisited New York and, once again, devastated the city by sending much of the population upstate and killing several thousand of those who did not leave (Rosenberg, 1962). In December 1835, a fire started in a five-story warehouse and spread over thirteen acres, burning 674 buildings and devastating the entire area south of Wall Street and east of Broad Street. As summarized by Burrows and Wallace (1999):

> Estimates of losses in buildings and merchandise ranged from eighteen to twenty-six million dollars, more than three times the cost of the Erie Canal. Twenty-three of the city's twenty-six fire insurance companies went bankrupt. Four thousand clerks were temporarily thrown out of work, along with thousands of cartmen and porters. (598)

In early 1836, over the fevered objections of the Manhattan Company and property owners in Westchester County and northern Manhattan who would be affected, the Common Council approved the construction of the Croton Reservoir and Aqueduct.

Work on the new water supply progressed between 1837 and 1842. A large dam was constructed at Sing Sing, now Ossining, near the outlet of the Croton River into the Hudson. From Sing Sing, a large iron pipe encrusted in brick conveyed the water from the Croton Reservoir, from the dam to High Bridge over the Harlem River, and from there to a receiving reservoir at Yorkville on northern Manhattan Island. Water was then transported to a distributing reservoir at what is now the corner of Fifth Avenue and 42nd Street on Murray Hill, a two square block masonry structure that is today the site of the New York Public Library. From the distributing reservoir, the water was distributed through iron mains throughout the city.

The building of the water system led to predictably positive results, including less susceptibility to epidemic disease, greater control over fires, and enhanced convenience for city residents and businesses. Of course, the Croton water supply did not alleviate these concerns, but the impact they had on the city was severely curtailed. After the initial building, the new water supply was expanded numerous times through the nineteenth century, growing to include 18 collecting reservoirs capable of supplying the city with 547.5 billion gallons of water per day.

The new water supply was critical to the growth of New York City. As rapid as the growth was during the early nineteenth century, the decades that followed 1840 witnessed phenomenal growth. In response to the famine caused by an infection that targeted potatoes in Ireland, for instance, thousands of peasants from the Irish countryside fled to New York during the 1840s and 1850s. As the century wore on, immigrants from throughout the world clamored for space on Manhattan Island, some looking to find their fortunes, most looking just to survive. Without an adequate water supply, this growth would not have been possible. The obvious necessity for the larger water supply was the need for water for cooking, drinking, and bathing the millions of residents of the city. Also important was the necessity of water for basic industrial functions, from liquefying raw materials in breweries and tanneries to cooling metals in industrial forges. Simply stated, New York needed water for population and economic growth. Less obvious, but nevertheless important, are functions ranging from enhanced fire protection to lessen insurance premiums on both residents and businesses to the perceived psychological comfort of having water available when necessary. In terms of epidemic disease, it is doubtful that the city could have continued its growth if it had fallen significantly behind other New World cities in regard to public health—given the array of differing cities available to a potential immigrant when they left their home country, a city reputed for its disease would not have been high on the list of potential new homes.

The building of the Croton Reservoir and Aqueduct was a good example of utilizing the resources of the hinterland in a variety of ways. The building of the new system did not rely on the resources and skills of New Yorkers alone, but rather on those of the region as a whole. New York City provided the financial resources to attract experienced talent for the design and construction of the Croton System, and this brought people at all levels of the enterprise to work on the system. An examination of the some of the top people in building the reservoir illustrates this point.

The Chief engineer, John Bloomfield Jervis, was born and raised near the present-day city of Rome, New York—the place where the construction of the Erie Canal had first begun. Jervis worked on the Erie Canal, rising from axeman to a superintending engineer for a 52-mile stretch of the canal. He worked on numerous contracts after the canal, all of which connected in one way or another to the developing system of urban political economy developing in the state: the Delaware and Hudson canal, a combination canal and railroad system in New York and Pennsylvania, the Mohawk and Hudson Railroad between Albany and Schenectady, and the Chenango Canal connecting Utica on the Erie Canal to Binghamton on the Susquehanna River (Larkin, 1990). Similarly, Benjamin Wright, Chief Engineer on the Erie Canal and a future New York city water consultant was also from the area near Rome, and Fayette Tower, another engineer, was from the village of Waterville only thirty miles from Rome. Similarly, networks of engineers and others working in similar ventures were found among the graduates of Union College in Schenectady and Columbia College, the forerunner of Columbia University in New York (Koeppel, 2000). At the higher echelons of engineering, the profession was networked across the state and region and, due to this, was ultimately at the disposal of New York when they were needed.

The building of the Croton System utilized the personnel resources of areas outside the city in other ways as well. Many of the laborers on the system were migrants from the rural hinterland upstate and from Connecticut and New

Jersey. In addition, thousands of Irish immigrants labored on the water system during the 1830s, ultimately becoming some of the first Catholics in northern Westchester County (Koeppel, 2000). In time, many chose to settle there.

There was conflict on the project. Although there was no organized labor union movement in New York during the 1830s, there had been a series of organized work stoppages on the waterfront and in some other industries throughout the decade. This, however, slowed by the end of the decade as a recession hit the region and anxieties over job security increased. Such concerns were less crucial for the workers on the publicly funded Croton System, and there were only a few minor strikes and labor problems during construction. The major conflicts during the planning and construction did not revolve around labor, however, but rather around land confiscation.

The state had retained the power of eminent domain that had evolved during feudal times, but now it would be used in a different way. The state granted the city the power of eminent domain for the purpose of constructing the Croton Water System. The legal theory revolved around the notion of the public good: New York City was growing and needed a sound water system, and this objective need on the part of the city was considered to outweigh the property rights of landowners in the vicinity of the new reservoir and along the route of the aqueduct. In practice, however, the imposition of the city's will also inspired mixed reactions on the part of the rural population of northern Westchester County. Of the 813 acres necessary for the project, the city still needed to purchase 454 acres (Koeppel, 2000, 196). "Purchase" was something of a misnomer; city appraisers would judge the value of the property, and the city would pay the owner that amount. The landowner had the right of appeal, and indeed many did, but ultimately the state had the legal power to forcibly take the land provided there was some form of compensation. In the end, the appeals were heard in state court, and thus it was the state that ultimately acted as both arbitrator of conflict and agent for the city. This of course led to some residents, correctly perceiving the ability to save their property as hopeless or simply wishing to profit from the sale, to demand high prices or taking action that would increase the value of the property, such as "dividing their woods and fields into village lots in advance of the appraisers, making acquisition more difficult and expensive" (Koeppel, 2000, 196). In contrast, some chose to fight the forced land takings, arguing that "in reaching the limits of its natural water supply, (New York) had developed all that it should, and other regions of the state, like amply watered Westchester, should be the focus of development" (Koeppel, 2000, 198). In both cases of profiteering and resistance, New York met only its first of numerous similar episodes. Profiteering by and resistance to the city's water plans became regular themes of the reactions exhibited by the residents of the affected places.

In 1842, water from the Croton Water System entered New York City for the first time. Shortly thereafter, the works of the Manhattan Company were drained, eventually dismantled and the real estate sold. For the first time in its history, New York had clean and abundant water worthy of a growing world-class city.

As New York continued to grow faster than even the most liberal estimates, the original Croton water supply grew more and more obsolete. Throughout the duration of the nineteenth century, New York by necessity expanded the system by building new dams upstream, an enlarged Croton Dam (New Croton Dam), and more miles of aqueduct. By the 1880s, the Croton System was in an almost constant state of upgrading as the city required ever-increasing supplies of water. The system grew until 1911, when the last of the reservoirs for the system were finally completed, but by then nearly everyone familiar with the issue recognized the city's need to look even further afield. And as time went on, the conflicts that arose over the city's use of eminent domain to not only force landowners to give up property for the reservoirs themselves, but to remove any building sited near a reservoir in order to protect its water quality, resistance to water projects in northern Westchester and southern Putnam Counties grew. Rural politicians scored points with voters by voicing opposition to city plans, but often had little support from theirs peers in state government. Due to the fact that representation was determined by population, New York City politicians often dominated both houses of the state legislature and had aligned themselves with political interests in the upstate cities who often had similar though smaller issues to consider (Galusha, 1999; Burrows & Wallace, 1999). The Croton System thus expanded until it could expand no longer, and the growing city needed still more.

What to Do?

By the 1880s it was apparent that the seemingly endless supply of the Croton River was not endless after all. Even as the original reservoir was enlarged and the system itself was expanded, city planners and entrepreneurs began to look farther afield for a new source of water. There were several options.

Perhaps the most obvious potential source of water for New York City was the Hudson itself. This was no doubt done upstream in informal ways throughout the early settlement of the island, but it did not have the best quality of water due to high salinity. In 1834, Bradford Seymour proposed building a dam across the Hudson from lower Manhattan to New Jersey, thus keeping the salt water out of the river and creating a useful reservoir for the city (Galusha, 1999, 12). A set of locks would allow navigation along the river. This was also a problem with the plan as the Hudson was, due to the Erie Canal, one of the most heavily traveled rivers in the United States. The city wisely built the Croton System instead, but building the Croton Reservoir was not the end of speculation for using the Hudson River as a source of fresh water. In 1876, Harvey Eastman suggested building a pumping station near Poughkeepsie, sixty miles upstream, which would pump water to augment the Croton water supply (Galusha, 1999, 12). In 1950, Lawrence Beck proposed a dam at Haverstraw, fifteen miles south of Poughkeepsie, which could provide the city with freshwater and double as a causeway over which the New York State Thruway, then in planning, could pass (Galusha, 1999, 12). In each case, the Hudson River as a source of water was frowned upon. Upstream, factories lined the river for miles in Albany and such industrial suburbs as Watervliet, Troy, and Cohoes. Further upstream, factories also crowded the Hudson at Glens Falls and its suburbs. The principal tributary of the Hudson, the Mohawk River, was also heavily urbanized with major Erie Canal cities like Utica, Schenectady, Rome, and Amsterdam. Smaller cities and towns, such as Herkimer, Hudson, and Kingston, lined both rivers and likewise contributed to pollution problems in the Hudson. In all, millions of people lived in the industrial towns and on farms that dumped their wastes into the river heading to New York City. Not surprisingly, few New Yorkers perceived the Hudson as an appealing option for their water supply.

Other sources were also contemplated. In 1830, Francis Phelps proposed a supply from New Jersey's Passaic River. In 1905, Charles Armstrong suggested that New York pipe water from the Great Lakes, perhaps near Oswego, and run an aqueduct along the route of the old Erie Canal, which had recently been abandoned in favor of the new Barge Canal. Various reports during the twentieth century recommended rivers and streams throughout eastern New York and New England, some as far away as the Susquehanna Valley near Oneonta, the Hoosic River near Albany, and the Black River north of Utica. Perhaps the most ambitious plan dated from 1966, which suggested damming Long Island Sound in Queens and building a causeway from Orient Point on eastern Long Island to Connecticut, thus forming Long Island Sound into a large lake. Salt water would have been pumped to sea, hopefully leaving a freshwater supply for New York (Galusha, 1999, 12).

None of these plans were built, in part because of the interstate cooperation that would be required to make the plans work. For instance, the Housatonic River in western New England was suggested several times. The Housatonic was an attractive option due to its proximity to the Croton System; the water could have easily been transported into the existing water system. To effectively build the system and then properly manage it, however, would have required the cooperation of New York, Connecticut, and Massachusetts. Although the city had considerable power in the New York legislature, it did not in the other two states, and this would have made it difficult if not impossible to use state government as a tool for performing the tasks New York needed done. When recommendations for annexing the affected regions in those states to New York met with opposition from the locals, the Housatonic plans were dropped. Plans for a Long Island Sound lake and tapping the Great Lakes would have similarly required such interstate planning, and thus were not seriously considered workable options.

A 1903 report on additional sources of water cited the Fishkill Creek, Wappinger Creek, and Roeliff Jansen Kill in Dutchess County near Poughkeepsie as potential new sources of water. In addition, the report also suggested the Esopus and Rondout Creeks west of the Hudson River in the Catskills, although they were complicated by the river crossing. In addition, development of the Schoharie Creek watershed was recommended only after the development of the Esopus and Rondout creeks. When alarmed Dutchess County residents lobbied and won a legislative injunction against the city developing county creeks, the focus of a new water supply turned to the Catskill Mountains of necessity (Galusha, 1999, 92-3).

Crossing the Hudson

The idea of crossing the Hudson River to the Catskills was first seriously discussed in an 1886 *Scientific American* article. A year later, the private Ramapo Water Company was formed with the express purpose of developing several Catskill Mountains watersheds into water supplies that could be sold to any municipality willing to tap into this supply. Although there were potentially several possible customers, New York was the obvious municipality both in terms of need and profit. In 1898 the Company submitted a proposal to the city that would have cost the city $200 million over forty years that gained some support among the city's Board of Public Improvement, then the entity overseeing the water supply, but it went down to defeat after a public outcry pressured some members to withdraw support. Perhaps it was the $200 million price tag, or perhaps it was the specter of another private water company supplying the largest city in the country, bringing back bad memories of the Manhattan Company. In any case, it was the city and its new Board of Water Supply that would have to build the new Catskill System.

It would be the Esopus creek, west of the small city of Kingston, which would be the first to develop. The Ashokan Reservoir would become the major facility of the new Catskill System. It was built after the practices developed during the building of the Croton System, such as community removal, water treatment, and shoreline protection, had been established. It also established the dynamics that ultimately led to the response of the local community when New York next turned its attention to the Schoharie Valley. The development of the Ashokan Reservoir allowed the city to make its case for the new Catskill System. Perhaps more importantly, its successful completion demonstrated the futility of fighting the city. In both cases, it set the stage for the building of the Schoharie Reservoir and the destruction of Gilboa. Before a discussion of the building of the Catskill System and the Schoharie Reservoir in particular, it is important to understand the development of Gilboa as a community.

6   The Perfect Rural Village

The 1916 Annual Report of the Board of Water Supply announced the selection of Gilboa as the site of the new dam to build the Schoharie Reservoir. It featured a photograph of the village from a hill overlooking the valley. Nestled in the narrow hollow, the bucolic village sprawled along its single street, with only a side road along the creek itself and another crossing to the other side. The points of wooden houses give way to the dense agglomeration of downtown, less than a dozen commercial buildings strong, and a church steeple rising in the center of the photograph. In the background, the rounded hills rise from the valley and overtower the hamlet, farmers' fields giving way to trees and in the distance still more mountains. A perfect postcard to entice the traveler to the Catskills for a season, a weekend, a day. The grayscale photo holds a moment in time when the grass and trees were green and the shallow Schoharie rushed through the ravine on its way to the Mohawk, the Hudson, and the Atlantic. The caption below the picture explains that the church steeple is the site of the dam that will forever destroy this scene.

Trends in the Outside World

In order to understand this region of the Catskills it is first necessary to understand the processes that have marginalized the region and then to understand the ramifications of that marginalization. It is helpful to understand the pattern of growth and decline (both relative and actual) experienced by Schoharie County during the nineteenth century. In 1800, the first federal census showed that Schoharie County had a population of 9,808 people. Ten years later the population had nearly doubled to 18,945 and by 1860 the county's population had peaked at 34,469 residents. Except for some small-scale manufacturing, the county was primarily agricultural and this was ultimately the reason for its peak. Beginning with the 1850 census, the proximity of a county to

Table 6.1: Fastest & Slowest Growing New York Counties, 1850-1910

Fastest Growing	Percent Change	Slowest Growing	Percent Change
Kings	1076.79	Lewis	1.16
Queens	671.16	Wyoming	-.32
Richmond	470.81	Otsego	-2.92
New York	435.84	Livingston	-6.94
Erie	423.78	Madison	-8.78
Westchester	385.82	Greene	-8.79
Schenectady	339.99	Yates	-9.46
Monroe	223.12	Chenango	-11.75
Rockland	176.34	Tompkins	-13.16
Suffolk	160.38	Schoharie	-28.89

SOURCE: New York State Department of Economic Development, 2000

either the Erie Canal corridor or the New York Metropolitan Area became the most reliable predictor of its health. This was true for the next 150 years, including through 1910—the last census year in which Gilboa was not aware of its ultimate fate. As the manufacturing centers of the state grew they also attracted people from around the world. Some of that world from which the immigrants arrived was rural New York State itself, as shown in table 6.1.

Of the ten fastest growing counties during the 1850-1910 time period, seven are today classified by the United States Census Bureau as being part of the New York Metropolitan Area; indeed, four of the ten are boroughs and the Bronx would not be spun off from New York County until 1914. When it was, it already registered over 730 thousand residents in the 1920 census. Erie County is home to Buffalo, the Erie Canal outlet and Great Lakes port that was by 1910 a world class manufacturing center. The other two, Monroe County and Schenectady County, included Rochester and Schenectady respectively. Both cities were the high technology centers of their day, as Rochester was a home to photography and optics and Schenectady was a home to the budding electricity industry. Of the next fifteen fastest growing counties, all but five are today classified as metropolitan, including the cities of Binghamton, Syracuse, and Utica.

In contrast, the ten slowest growing counties all had one interesting variable in common: each county bordered on one of the Erie Canal Counties. In fact, the nine counties that lost population were all immediately south of the Canal and, perhaps more importantly, fell within 60 miles of the nearest major city. It is not necessarily surprising that a rural county might reach a plateau in population. There is a point when the land available for cultivation requires so much time and energy that it is better left to the wild, and when this point is reached those without farms or farm employment must often seek another way of making a living. As those family members who cannot inherit a piece of property for fear of diminishing the farm are forced to leave, the population not surprisingly remains stable as the number of those family members who can remain on the farm remains the same. Each of the 10 slowest growing counties listed above experienced population stability through the 1870 census and then began to register the more steep declines reflected in the 1910 figure. Part of the reason for this is the mechanization of agriculture. As labor saving devices were introduced on the farm a large number of hired hands became increasingly unnecessary. But mechanization is not solely responsible. Earlier in the century, farms were considered to be independent entities geared toward subsistence. In those times, an added number of farmhands, whether family or not, eased the workday. As long as the farm could support the entire household and perhaps produce some for trade, a large number of farm workers was desirable. As New York farms became more centered on trade and the money economy, however, additional farmhands came to be seen as more of a liability against the potential profits to be made. As a result, the desire to produce more agricultural goods for market with the least amount of labor drove the mechanization of agriculture, which ultimately forced many farmers (and particularly farm laborers) away from rural counties and into the cities.

Figure 6.1: Average Population of New York Counties, 1820-1930

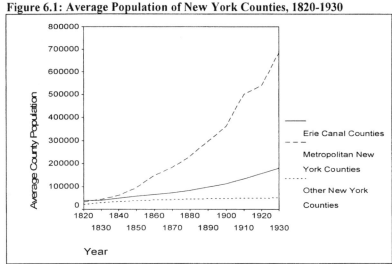

SOURCE: New York State Department of Economic Development, 2000

It is interesting to note, however, that not all New York counties lost population during this time period. Agricultural counties along the southern tier of New York State and in the Catskills grew. For instance, Schoharie County's neighbor to the southwest, Delaware County, grew by over fourteen percent during this same time period despite the fact that there are no cities in the county. Other counties, such as Allegany and Steuben Counties in western New

York and Saint Lawrence and Franklin Counties along the Canadian border also gained population. The decline of population in rural areas was thus not only due to the push factor of land shortage and eventual mechanization, but to the sheer draw of urban life and wage labor itself. Schoharie County youth were exposed not only to rural life and the small market towns found in their own region, but they had access to rapidly growing cities within a day or two of travel and typically had relatives in those very same cities.

Because economies of scale encouraged similar types of businesses and their support services to locate near one another, various cities in the state were known for particular items: Rome was known for copper goods, the Oneida-Sherrill area for silver, Buffalo for steel, and so on. In addition, the growing cities featured the true high technology of the era, whether they be the huge coal steam generators powering Utica's textile mills, the mysteries of photography found in Rochester or the dynamism of electricity found in Schenectady. Albany had the intrigue of the state capital and New York was, of course, the most cosmopolitan city on the planet. Even a small city such as Oneonta could claim in 1910 to have the largest railroad roundhouse in the world. And the children who lived so close to this new world were the ones most drawn to it and away from the rural life of their parents.

In 1850, the advantages conferred upon a county for having access to the growing urban system had a significant advantage in growing the county ($F=3.15$; $p=0.05$). It would grow more important during the next 150 years. As shown in figure 6.1, the average county in the New York Metropolitan area grew to enormous proportions, and even the average Erie Canal county showed continued growth. In contrast, the rest of New York stagnated.

Growth in the future counties of the New York Metropolitan Area was not the steady expansion of a great metropolis as it is sometimes portrayed. Instead, the New York Metropolitan Area was in reality a microcosm of growth throughout the state as a whole, with the ideally positioned urban centers (especially New York itself) growing rapidly and the rural counties primarily stagnating through 1910. This is evident in Table 6.2.

As discussed in chapter 4, the county statistics themselves cover population trends that also reflect preexisting communities. New York City expanded up Manhattan Island and absorbed the villages of Greenwich, Harlem, and Washington Heights, for instance. Similarly, the Kings County village of Bedford predated its suburban and ultimately urban character. As shown above, this is true at the county level as well. For instance, the now-suburban counties of Orange and Dutchess both included growing industrial centers in the form of Middletown, Newburgh, and Poughkeepsie. Similarly, Westchester County included large towns like Tarrytown and White Plains. Each of these counties was, in 1850, relatively independent of the metropolitan area of which they would eventually be part, but due to their position in the growing urban system along the Hudson River and Erie Canal corridor they also experienced growth.

Table 6.2: New York Metropolitan Area Population Change by County, 1820-1910

	1820	1850	% Change 1820-1850	1880	% Change 1850-1880	1910	% Change 1880-1910
Bronx[1]	--	--	--	--	--	--	--
Kings	11187	138882	1141.46	599495	331.66	1634350	172.62
New York[2]	123706	515547	316.75	1206300	133.98	2762520	129.01
Queens[3]	21519	36833	71.17	90574	145.90	367971	306.27
Richmond	6135	15061	145.49	38991	158.89	85969	120.48
Dutchess	46615	58992	26.55	79184	34.23	87661	10.71
Orange	41213	57145	38.66	88220	54.38	116001	31.49
Putnam	11268	14138	25.47	15181	7.38	14665	-3.40
Rockland	8837	16962	91.94	27690	63.25	46873	69.28
Suffolk	24272	36922	52.12	53888	45.95	96138	78.40
Westchester[2]	32638	58263	78.51	108988	87.06	283055	159.71

1. Bronx County not formed until 1914
2. New York County annexed part of Westchester County in 1873 & 1895 which were later included in the Bronx in 1914
3. Nassau County was formed from part of Queens in 1899; the 1910 statistics for Queens therefore reflect both Queens and Nassau County in the interests of consistency.
SOURCE: New York State Department of Economic Development, 2000

Table 6.3: Erie Canal Corridor Most Populous & Least Populous Counties, 1850-1910

	1850			1880			1910	
County	Population	County		Population	County		Population	County
Largest:								
1. Erie	100993	Erie		219884	Erie		528985	Erie
2. Oneida	99566	Albany		154890	Monroe		283212	Monroe
3. Albany	93272	Monroe		144903	Onondaga		200298	Onondaga
4. Monroe	87650	Onondaga		117893	Albany		173666	Albany
5. Onondaga	85890	Oneida		115475	Oneida		154157	Oneida
Smallest:								
10. Niagara	42276	Madison		44112	Herkimer		56356	Herkimer
11. Herkimer	38244	Herkimer		42669	Ontario		52286	Ontario
12. Montgomery	31992	Montgomery		38315	Wayne		50179	Wayne
13. Orleans	28501	Orleans		30128	Madison		39289	Madison
14. Schenectady	20054	Schenectady		23538	Orleans		32000	Orleans

SOURCE: New York State Department of Economic Development, 2000

The growth, however, more closely resembled that found in the Erie Canal corridor (see table 6.3) than what was found closer to the major growth areas of what was then the metropolitan area. Major growth in Westchester, Orange, and later Dutchess County began when the New York suburbs reached those counties due to advances in transportation technology. The two Hudson Valley counties without a major trade or industrial center (Putnam and Rockland) experienced slow growth until the expanding ring of suburbs reached their borders. A similar pattern is noticeable within the counties of the city itself, first in Kings County (Brooklyn and environs) and then in Queens and Richmond County (Staten Island).

By 1850, the five major cities outside of the New York metropolitan area— Buffalo, Rochester, Syracuse, Utica, and Albany—had been established. Although their populations changed in relation to one another through the last half of the nineteenth century, by 1910 the basic proportions of each metropolitan area had been established. The five metropolitan areas are ranked in the same order today as they were in 1910. Once the cities had been established as major centers for commerce, industry and culture they continued to attract both investment and immigrants. This was nowhere more apparent than in Buffalo (Erie County), where access to the Great Lakes market and its pivotal position at the end of the Erie Canal transformed the city into one of the great cities of America by 1910. Albany similarly benefited from the canal as the city and a string of northern suburbs—Menands, Watervliet, Cohoes, and Waterford—lined the canal as it paralleled the Hudson River en route to the Mohawk Valley and the west. Syracuse (Onondaga County) and Rochester (Monroe County) both afforded the canal outlets to Lake Ontario to the north. Utica and its sister city Rome (Oneida County) had intersections with the Chenango Canal and Black River Canal respectively. Even though the importance of the canal waned as increased competition from several rail companies made it most useful for freight, the new transportation corridors by necessity went through the established cities. The metropolitan areas would be the main attractors of investment for the rest of state history.

In contrast, the rural counties of the canal corridor grew more slowly. Orleans County, for instance, spawned several large towns but no cities. This was also true of Wayne County. But access to the urban system was still a benefit, as none of the counties actually lost population during this time period. In fact, access to the system translated into most of the rural counties having small cities, such as Lockport and Niagara Falls in Niagara County, Amsterdam in Montgomery County, and Oneida in Madison County. The access to markets afforded by their placement in the Canal Corridor allowed some cities to industrialize later as new technologies created new economic niches. For instance, Schenectady benefited as a high technology center in the late nineteenth and early twentieth century as Westinghouse and General Electric pioneered electricity technologies. This was also true of Niagara Falls, not strictly speaking a canal city but close enough to benefit from its influence, which featured not only the spectacular waterfalls but the also impressive electrical power generation capacities afforded by the river. Although the smallest canal corridor counties were not necessarily larger than those outside the corridor, the position within the system privileged these counties with opportunities for growth that many other counties did not have.

When examining the counties lying outside of the urban system, two major variables explain much of what is found. Geographic area explains the position of several of the five largest and smallest counties. For instance, at over 2,800 square miles, Saint Lawrence County contains over twice the area as Rhode Island. Similarly, Steuben County also is a large county. As of 1910, however, the most populous counties were all those with access to the urban system. Rensselaer County, always the largest non-canal county, is located directly across the Hudson from Albany and the Erie Canal. Its principal cities, Troy and Rensselaer, both received a considerable amount of trade and investment due to this position. Similarly, Ulster County includes Kingston, a small Hudson Valley city and former state capital. Oswego County contains the city of the same name that grew as a result of the opening of the Oswego Canal that ran from Syracuse to Oswego on Lake Ontario. Oswego County fell out of the top five in 1910. The addition of Chautauqua County in 1910 reflects growth of its principal city, Jamestown, in part as a result of the dominance of railroads that enabled other regions to compete against the canal. The Jamestown Metropolitan Area is today the eighth largest in the state. A noticeable absence is Broome County (Binghamton), today the seventh largest metropolitan area in the state, which experienced its most impressive rates of growth between 1910 and 1930.

The least populous counties all had problems with access to the transportation network. In the cases of Hamilton and Lewis Counties, the minimal transportation network (which included the Black River Canal in Lewis County) was compounded by a climate that dumped exorbitant amounts of snow blown off the waters of Lake Ontario due west. Schuyler and Yates Counties are both among the smallest counties in terms of area in the state.

It was within this context that Schoharie County existed. Being remote, rugged, and relatively close to major cities caused the county to lose population throughout the time period leading to and even after the building of the Schoharie Reservoir. From its peak population of 34,469 residents in 1860, the county slowly lost population in every census until bottoming out at 19,667 in 1930. The area's marginalization was thus not simply a fact but a process as well.

Table 6.4: Most & Least Populous Counties in Remainder of New York State, 1850-1910

| | 1850 | | 1880 | | 1910 |
County	Population	County	Population	County	Population
Largest:					
1. Rensselaer	73363	Rensselaer	115328	Rensselaer	122276
2. St. Lawrence	68617	St. Lawrence	85997	Chautauqua	105126
3. Jefferson	68153	Ulster	85838	Ulster	91769
4. Steuben	63771	Oswego	77911	St. Lawrence	89005
5. Oswego	62198	Steuben	77586	Steuben	83362
Smallest:					
10. Lewis	24564	Cortland	25825	Lewis	24849
11. Yates	20590	Warren	25179	Schoharie	23855
12. Fulton	20171	Yates	21087	Yates	18642
13. Warren	17199	Schuyler	18842	Schuyler	14004
14. Hamilton	2188	Hamilton	3923	Hamilton	4370

SOURCE: New York State Department of Economic Development, 2000

Suffering in the Sisterhood

The forces acting upon the communities in Schoharie County were not unique to Schoharie County. It is therefore helpful to look at other communities that were similar to those found in Schoharie County. There are four Catskill Mountain Counties that do not border on either the Hudson River or the Erie Canal: Schoharie, Otsego, Delaware, and Sullivan. As Sullivan County does not border on Schoharie County, this analysis will focus only on the communities found in the other counties. What becomes apparent is that the trends found at the state level were also found, at a smaller scale, in the three county region.

At first glance, the range of population from the least to most populous townships is rather minimal. Much of the variation can in fact be explained by differences in land area among the towns. For instance, the town of Cherry Valley was divided into two smaller entities in 1854 (Cherry Valley and Roseboom), which reduced the population of both. As the nineteenth century wore on, however, the pattern of urban dominance found at the statewide level became more pronounced in the three-county region as well. Although three of the five largest townships in 1850 were almost exclusively agricultural (Cherry Valley, Middlefield, and Gilboa), by 1880 all five had significant commercial/industrial centers (Cooperstown, Oneonta, Middleburg, Cobleskill, and Schoharie, respectively). Both Cooperstown and Schoharie were county seats. By 1910, some level of industrialization was necessary for a town to rank in the top five, and only the city of Oneonta achieved a five-digit population. In fact, Oneonta, a small railroad center in southern Otsego County, was the only community to have growth rates that even distantly mimicked those found in the Erie Canal corridor.

The smallest townships were all primarily agricultural that in nearly every case witnessed sharp declines in population during the late nineteenth and early twentieth centuries. The largest townships had the advantage that they were capable of attracting investment and population as the urban money-based political economy became dominant. In contrast, the rural townships lost population as farms themselves became oriented toward producing for profit and not for sustaining the household. Access to the urban political economy was not enough: the fastest growing communities in the region all had access to the urban political economy through railroads and had some industry. As the twentieth century wore on, those communities that did not hold onto major industries, such as Hancock and Cooperstown, watched their town populations stagnate or decline. By the end of the twentieth century, *major* outside investment and growth occurred in only three of the region's communities:

Table 6.5: Most & Least Populous Towns in Three County Region, 1850-1910

Town	1850 Population	Town	1880 Population	Town	1910 Population
Largest:					
1. Cherry Valley	4186	1. Otsego	4690	1. Oneonta	10798
2. Otsego	3901	2. Oneonta	4461	2. Hancock	5191
3. Middlefield	3131	3. Middleburg	3376	3. Walton	5088
4. Franklin	3087	4. Cobleskill	3370	4. Otsego	4287
5. Gilboa	3024	5. Schoharie	3350	5. Sidney	4148
6. Tompkins	3022	6. Hancock	3238	6. Middletown	3802
7. Middletown	3005	7. Middletown	2977	7. Cobleskill	3579
8. Middleburg	2967	8. Delhi	2941	8. Colchester	3193
9. Delhi	2909	9. Colchester	2941	9. Delhi	2815
10. Roxbury	2853	10. Franklin	2907	10. Middleburg	2553
Smallest:					
				48. Conesville	963
				49. Masonville	933
50. Pittsfield	1582	50. Wright	1450	50. Exeter	.917
51. Harpersfield	1550	51. Broome	1420	51. Richfield	912
52. Summit	1526	52. Pittsfield	1405	52. Plainfield	885
53. Exeter	1502	53. Bovina	1353	53. Esperance	844
54. Westford	1450	54. Roseboom	1271	54. Westford	803
55. Plainfield	1428	55. Plainfield	1195	55. Bovina	708
56. Blenheim	1423	56. Westford	1191	56. Blenheim	616
57. Conesville	1316	57. Conesville	1127	57. Decatur	476
58. Bovina	1314	58. Blenheim	1022		
59. Decatur	927	59. Decatur	779		

1 Oneonta incorporated as a city in 1908 and thus became a separate legal entity from the town. For consistency, however, this table reflects the combined population of the city and town.
SOURCE: New York State Department of Economic Development, 2000

Oneonta, Sidney, and Cobleskill. All three were located along the Delaware and Hudson Railroad and later Interstate 88[1].

Only Oneonta experienced the type of spectacular growth found in the Erie Canal corridor between 1850 and 1910, and even then grew to only little more than 20 thousand residents by 1970. In Otsego County, Oneonta's fortune helped to stave off a considerable population decline that would have resembled that off neighboring Schoharie County. Indeed, the northern townships of the county mirror the trends found in Schoharie County. Of the fifty-nine townships in the three-county area, only eleven gained population during this time period. The remaining 48 communities lost population—the average township losing over 31 percent of its 1850 population. Only 17 towns would ever see their 1850 populations again. The regional economy thus reflected the wider pattern of the urban political economy favoring larger communities over small, and Gilboa was caught in such a dynamic when New York was looking for a site for a new reservoir. Although there were several small hamlets that had formed in the immediate area, at about 400 residents Gilboa was the largest.

Gilboa's Growth

In 1848, the town of Gilboa was formed out of a large township named Blenheim. The town of Blenheim was founded in 1797 when a large area of the northern Catskills was divided into several large administrative units. The township already had 783 residents when the 1800 federal census was taken, scattered primarily on farms along the banks of the Schoharie Creek. Many of the oldest settlers were Palatine Germans, although the early decades of the 1800s changed the face of the region. The town added about 500 residents every ten years as new settlers moved to the region from New England to farm the feudal estates that extended into the Schoharie Valley. As the first wave of immigrants moved through the region, the area population peaked. After 1850, however, as the canal corridor and the New York Metropolitan area experienced dramatic immigration from other parts of the world, much of the northern Catskills remained a cultural extension of New England. As the cities in the state continued to gain wave after wave of immigration into the early twentieth century, Schoharie County continued to lose population. To be sure, there were

---

1. This is not to say that there was no growth outside of these three towns, but rather that it tended to be very small scale in comparison. Two Delaware County towns, Delhi and Walton, experienced some outside investment. Delhi is home to a small state college, whereas Walton has a small industrial base. The other major community to win outside investment is the Cooperstown area, home to the National Baseball Hall of Fame. In nearly every other community, economic investment has tended to be locally based and in most cases the economies have actually declined considerably since the 1950s.

new families of Italian, Polish, and of other ethnic descent, but their numbers were never high enough to challenge the supremacy of the Yankee cultural milieu.

As noted in chapter 3, the Anti-Rent Wars took place in the region during the 1840s as farmers rebelled against their feudal masters, and the resulting reform of the land tenure laws made it easier for farmers to move off of the farm. It also made it easier for the former tenant farmers to participate in the money economy.

Under feudal relations, a farm household by necessity paid a portion of their earnings, either in agricultural products, labor, money or some combination of all three, to the landlord. Such a system was perhaps never truly desirable from the perspective of the tenant, but it did allow prospective settlers a lower cost option to buying their own land somewhere else. On the Blenheim Patent, as it was called, rent was paid in money. The goal for many settlers in the early nineteenth century was the ability to be relatively autonomous, and the land-lease system by and large allowed for a fairly independent existence based on subsistence farming. It also encouraged large farm households as any excess labor was used to conserve energy and time.

After the reform of the land-lease system, many now-independent farmers strove not for bare subsistence but instead for profit through the money economy. Many farmers raised not only food, but concentrated on the growing of wheat, rye, oats, and potatoes. In later years, hay was grown to feed cattle on large dairy farms that sold milk and other dairy products in urban markets, and numerous small towns had dairy production companies such as cheese factories and creameries. But the big profits came from Hops.

Hops cultivation spread throughout central New York in the 1850s and 1860s, and many Schoharie County farmers, newly liberated from their former feudal landlords, joined the industry. Hops was grown and sold in urban markets to brewers who sold beer to increasing numbers of German and Irish immigrants. In 1886, the region was struck by a malady called the Blue Mold that destroyed much of the crop. By the early twentieth century the center of the Hops industry had moved to more efficient areas of the Pacific northwest, and central New York farmers were forced to move on to other crops. What the reliance on a cash crop introduced to Schoharie County farmers was the business cycle of booms and busts, and the Hops industry was but one of the first industries in the region to go through this cycle.

One way of dealing with the new realities of farming for profit was to lower overhead on the farm. As discussed earlier, part of this involved an increased reliance on mechanical aids on the farm. Mechanization of farming did save time, but it most often allowed the farmer to grow more product with fewer farm workers. What this ultimately allowed, even demanded, was that fewer people live or be dependent upon the farm because every acre devoted to subsistence deprived the farm of some level of profitability. Hence, the exodus of both children and farm employees from rural counties in search of work in the urban centers throughout the state. In fact, the first major restructuring of the American family took place partly as a result of such trends as the extended family was weakened in the countryside and the nuclear family became increasingly dominant in the cities.

The population of the town of Gilboa dropped from 3,024 in 1850 to a pre-reservoir low of 1,448 in 1900, rising to 1,467 by 1910. Much of this decline seems to have occurred in the more marginal land away from the Schoharie Creek, and the population of the village most likely climbed during this period. Part of the impetus was a small cotton mill and the village's status as the trade center for the surrounding area. In 1872, at a time the town had a population of a little over 2,200 residents, the Schoharie County Directory listed 152 different names of heads of households in the Gilboa postal district. Of those, 25 (16 percent) of the names included multiple listings of the same name. By 1899, when the town's population had shrunk to only 1,500 residents, the Schoharie County Directory listed 236 names in the Gilboa postal district, 49 (21 percent) of which were multiple listings. Part of the supposed raise in the population in and around the village is due to changes in the post office district, and thus it is difficult to know the exact increase of the immediate area's population. It does seem likely, however, that Gilboa mirrored trends found in its larger neighbors.

The local economy was still dominated by agriculture. Of the 218 heads of household listed in the 1899 Schoharie County Directory for which an occupation was given, 138 (63.3 percent) were listed as farmers. In addition, several others were listed as having land in cultivation but not as counting their primary occupation as farming. Twenty-nine (13.3 percent) were reported as being involved in the provision of services, including two physicians, a dentist, several teachers and attorneys, as well as more specialized occupations such as dressmakers. Nineteen (8.7 percent) were involved primarily in retail trade and another 27 (12.4 percent) pursued a trade, such as carpentry, painting, and one mechanic. Only five were listed as being involved in manual labor, although this figure would seem low[2].

There was considerable population change between 1872 and 1899, as nearly a third (46) of the names listed in the 1872 Schoharie County Directory do not appear in the 1899 version. Those 46 were replaced by a new 48 names in the 1899 Directory; in both years, the majority were farmers. Although there was such population turnover, it did not translate into a new ethnic influx. Indeed, the turnover only amounts to less than two families per year during the 1872-1899 period. Many of the new names were commonly found in other townships in Schoharie, Delaware, and Greene Counties, and it is possible that the turnover reflects moves of comparatively short distances. The vast majority

---

2. It is likely that many manual laborers were teenagers still living at home and thus are not listed as heads of households.

of names in both years were of English extraction, followed distantly by 1 ....es of German and Dutch descent. There were two O'Briens in 1899, but one cannot tell whether they were of Irish or Scottish descent.

Gilboa at the turn of the century was not a large village[3], but it was the commercial center of its admittedly meager hinterland. As Hendrix & Hendrix (1995) described, Gilboa was fairly self-contained:

> Four general stores sold groceries, dry goods and most of a family's needs. An ice cream parlor, feed store, tinsmith and a blacksmith also served the area's needs. Gilboa had two hotels, three churches and a school with not one but two rooms. The post office dispatched two mails daily to and from New York and *The Gilboa Monitor* came out every Thursday. (175)

There was also a theater in which movies were shown and live entertainment was also occasionally performed. There was also, coincidentally, a water system that delivered water from a reservoir on a nearby hill to houses and hydrants in the village. There was also a small electrical generator by the creek. Stratigos (1998) further explained that the village,

> like many of that time, was a world unto itself. The villagers worked together and they socialized together through church services, picnics, and ice cream socials. Men visited one another in the general stores or the blacksmiths. Women visited in each other's homes. During the long winter months, musicals, dances, and debates were held. Everyone knew their neighbors and with the many marriages that occurred within the community, even closer ties developed. (25)

Although there was surely some interaction with the outside world, it was by and large unnecessary in everyday life. This of course had an impact on the local culture.

Culture Effects

As discussed in chapter one, the culture of a community is ultimately produced through the regular social interaction of its members. Numerous urban sociologists (e.g., Wirth, 1938; Toennies, 2001; Durkheim, 1997) have suggested that interaction with large numbers of individuals produces a high level of cosmopolitanism. In small communities, at least historically, the number of people with whom one can interact is much lower. In addition, the people with whom an individual can interact often share similar norms and values, and

---

3. Technically, under New York State law, Gilboa was not a village but rather a hamlet. A village in New York is an incorporated municipality, whereas a hamlet is administered under the auspices of the township in which it is located.

thus the ritual density of the community is high. The effect of high ritual density on the local community culture is that it will reflect a rather insular perspective that stresses conformity and tradition. As Collins (1975) comments:

> There is little privacy, and the individual is constantly face-to-face with the same people. Cosmopolitanism is low; contacts are uniform and familiar. . .These are the conditions for a strong state of collective conscience. (171)

Gilboa did not have the ritual density of a hunting-and-gathering community, but it was certainly not the ritual density of New York City either. It was a small and isolated rural village, and had a very high ritual density as a result.

Accounts of a tight-knit community centered in the village and extending to include the farmers in the village's hinterland show the effects of high ritual density. There was a negative side as well. For instance, the Schoharie Valley had since the early nineteenth century been home to a small population of African-American farmers. Centered in the valley primarily north of Gilboa, the population survived in a manner very similar to the majority white settlers in the region who arrived with hopes of autonomy through subsistence agriculture. As the century wore on, however, many of the black settlers left the valley in hopes of better opportunities elsewhere. This was, of course, a parallel of trends among the white population. As the black population declined, other blacks left due to their experiences with racism on the part of the white majority and the fact that the support network of other black residents was, after all, declining (Daniels, 2000).

Many Schoharie Valley residents also had a rather curious obsession with Gypsies who were said to travel through the county. As they roamed through the region, many valley residents feigned absence from their homes in order to avoid the reviled class. Newspapers up and down the valley warned permanent residents of their impending approach, including a 1916 (17 Jan.) Article in the Gilboa *Monitor*:

> About two weeks ago several gypsy women visited Cobleskill and while circulating about town stopped at the Proper restaurant. They were given coffee without charge and to repay the kindness they stole $10 from the cash register. Monday they came back and Mr. caused their arrest. They were arraigned and on paying the $10 and costs the charge was withdrawn. While going up the stairs to the justice's office they managed to frisk a $1 bill from J. Madison Pindar of Eminence. They returned the money also when about to be arrested claiming they did not want any more trouble. They were ordered out of town on the first train.

The degree to which the migrant population actually engaged in illegal activity is subject to debate, but the reaction of the locals was a familiar reaction in many times and places: the class itself was stigmatized and feared throughout the county. As summarized by Donald Duell (1986), a folklorist at SUNY Cobleskill who collected stories from the county during the 1980s:

> No other visitor to Schoharie County has caused more vexation or been more intimidating by his presence than the gypsy. No matter the occasion or where the event, Schoharie's citizens have beat a hasty retreat before the ominous threat of these mysterious strangers. Each spring their brightly-colored wagons burst into bloom on main county roads, their foreign gabble and colorful costumes setting them apart from others as they moved slowly from village to village, stopping and camping where they pleased. While guests in the county, citizens felt threatened by capital crime (such as kidnapping), abused of their right to property (by theft), and denied their privacy (by intrusion and brazen disregard of social convention). Gypsies generally made nuisances of themselves, and the fact that most of their attempts to swindle and scheme their way through the summer months did not endear them to Schoharie men and women. Somehow, these colorful strangers either out-witted or ignored all attempts at control. . .This stereotype could be an unfair one, but you will never convince those who volunteered their stories about gypsies that they were being anything but even-handed and balanced in their judgment; there was virtual unanimity of agreement. (3)

This is not to say that their urban cousins reacted much better in the face of racial and ethnic diversity. New Yorkers had been known to riot over ethnic tensions several times during the previous century, but the low ritual density forced many New Yorkers to confront their racial and ethnic prejudices in ways that those in Gilboa and other Schoharie Valley towns simply did not.

Coming Changes

The residents of Gilboa entered the years after 1910 oblivious to their own fate. The city was coming closer, first through the building of the Ashokan Reservoir and then through the visits of city engineers looking for yet more water. The events in Gilboa later in the decade and during the 1920s were hardly isolated events, but rather a continuation of a pattern that had been developing since the building of the original Croton River water supply in the 1830s.

An isolated city must face trajedy to be so vulnerable to John's power.

what if city asked for property but he agreed to develop it himself for city

7 A Tradition of Destruction

There was a particular noble aspect of the original plan for watering New York presented by Christopher Colles in 1774. Though the plan called for the city to purchase private property in the area near the Collect Pond, the property itself was to be granted to the city quite by choice. The owner of the property agreed to sell the city whatever was necessary; although this should have ultimately raised the property value of what he retained, there was a sense of mutual benefit between the city and the seller. There were no communities to be removed, no fellow citizens to condemn to anomie as their hometowns were so condemned. There was only an open meadow and a city's need for water to consider.

The Colles Plan was indeed found during a more innocent time for New York. The city was still, by modern standards, comparatively small and water needs were simpler. A water supply near the town was not only practicable but even desirable. The population in its path was minimal and as such there were always areas of large enough size that could be given over to a new reservoir or well system. Indeed, a major aspect of the problems experienced by the Manhattan Company was that the city continued to outgrow what little supply did exist, and over time it became very obvious that Manhattan Island was not a desirable place from which to bring water. This was ultimately the reason for seeking the waters of the Croton Valley, but looking upstate brought new problems.

Racing the Suburbs

As early as the Colles Plan, New York needed to worry about the encroachment of its own settlement space on its water supply. As discussed in chapter 5, the area around the Collect Pond was rapidly developed after the American Revolution as New York spread up Manhattan Island. Eventually, of course, the pond was filled to become the first of the great American slums, Five Points. It was urban encroachment from the future suburbs of New York, though not suburbs at the time, that likewise made the idea of impounding the waters of the Bronx River undesirable as the river was not only the lifeblood of water mills and other factories but their sewer as well. (The Bronx would later be cleaned as part of the Bronx River Parkway project in the early twentieth century). The decision to impound the Croton River in northern Westchester County was thus a necessary adaptation to a growing, multi-centered metropolitan region.

Prior to the 1840s, northern Westchester County was more urbanized than the southern portion—areas today known as the Bronx, Yonkers, and New Rochelle. Large industrial and port towns like Port Chester, Tarrytown, and White Plains were surrounded by farmland and wooded hillsides, and even places such as Morrisania (now part of the Bronx) were industrial communities set among the rural hinterland of New York City. Nevertheless, the county was primarily rural. Even with such urbanization, building a reservoir near the village of Sing Sing would displace a number of farms but not have the impact on the local area that building on the increasingly urbanized Bronx would have had. Moreover, the Croton flowed through more hilly terrain and the high banks of the river impeded the growth of industry on its shores—a fact that would help preserve the city's water supply against pollution.

Even so, the Croton System could not completely outrun the rapid expansion of an urban state, even in northern Westchester and Putnam Counties. As the construction on the ever-expanding system came to a close early in the twentieth century, the displacement of individual buildings, small communities, and cemeteries was an activity in which the city and its employees increasingly found themselves obligated to participate. As the nineteenth century continued and with it the expansion of the Croton Water Supply, the city of necessity honed its skills at displacing people—dead and alive—from the lands near its precious water. By the time of the building of the Catskill System, of which the Schoharie Reservoir was the second major project, the city's skills were perfected. In order to perform such actions, there were three major discursive frameworks that the city needed to develop in order to counter local opposition: a legal framework, a political framework, and an ideological framework that served as the foundation for both.

The legal framework had been developed not as part of the democratic system or through the new corruption of corporate capitalism, but rather was inherited from the old feudal order. As discussed in chapter 3, political power was justified based on the concept of eminent domain: the idea that God was the ultimate owner of all territory and that He delegates his authority to earthly monarchs, who in turn delegate the authority over portions of His domain to subordinate nobles, ultimately trickling down to the various Lords of the Manor. As all land ultimately belonged to God and his earthly representative as represented by the monarchy and the state, the state ultimately had the power to execute whatever actions were deemed necessary. Ideally, this was to be done in the public interest, but in practice in Europe eminent domain was often utilized as the rationale for taking one noble's land and granting it to another. After the American Revolution, the state retained the powers of eminent domain even as the theory of its origin shifted from the heavens to the earthbound populace. Theoretically, of course, eminent domain could be invoked only by a compelling public need.

Like the king, New York State also had the ability to assign an agent the power of eminent domain. The charter of the Manhattan Company, for instance, included a clause granting the corporation powers of eminent domain (Koeppel, 2000). Similarly, the city held the powers of eminent domain in regard to its water system. The city's will to use this extraordinary power grew over time as its ambitions grew. Early on, eminent domain was a viewed as a desperate last resort to acquire property for which the owner was either unwilling to sell or was asking an exorbitant price. As the nineteenth century wore on, however, eminent domain was used not only as a last resort but also as a thinly veiled threat: sell or we'll force you to sell.

The political framework, as discussed in chapter 3, grew out of a combination of the growing urban system throughout the state as well as the local politics that culminated in the Tammany Hall political machine (Allen, 1993). The urban system provided New York with valuable allies in state government. Political machines in the major cities upstate frequently walked a tightrope between pursuing interests for upstate communities and siding with the New York delegation over concerns that were pivotal to all of the state's cities. In regard to water rights, much of the opposition came from the rural areas of the state, especially those in eastern New York where the home district might be next. In most cases, urban legislators from upstate cities would ultimately side with the city in regard to water rights. This was not necessarily because of networking between the various delegations or because of party allegiances, but rather because of an overlap of interests. Significant restraints on New York City's water rights where there was arguably a great public need could form the precedent to deny similar rights to smaller but nonetheless thirsty upstate cities. Conformity to urban interests was thus a requirement of any urban legislator.

The political machines of the state's cities, in particular the Tammany Hall machine in New York, also enforced an emphasis on urban interests. Although its roots are earlier, the Tammany Hall political machine was a potent force by the 1840s, and among its interests was the inexpensive provision of water. Cheap water was an easy issue because it benefited both business interests and the hundreds of thousands of poor who constituted a major part of the machine's power base. Such an issue provides motivation for expansion of the water supply, and thus also ensured that the bad water days of the Manhattan Company would not be seen again.

Undergirding both the legal framework and the political system that enabled continued expansion was a fundamental ideological truth for both New Yorkers and *Star Trek's* Spock: the needs of the many outweigh the needs of the few.

Such a calculus of public benefit is one that always rewards the city at the expense of anyone living by choice or by fate in a smaller community. It argues that the aggregate of many people is of higher value than the aggregate of a smaller number of people. In so doing, it undermines the notion of "all men being equal" by placing a higher value of the lives of those who live in urban areas than those who do not live in urban areas. In practice, it was this idea that functioned as the primary ideological support for the demolition of nearly forty small towns over the course of 150 years. The prevalence of this ethical guideline was so supreme that even many of the townspeople of Gilboa perceived the demolition of their community to be a just cause (see chapter 5). Even today, many people who live near the various city reservoirs defend the city's right to water even as they complain bitterly about the city's methods. One resident commented:

> Sure they can be pricks to people around here. You can't build on the lakes, it's pretty strict for building anything even close to a creek that might flow eventually into the city supply. And since 9-11, ya might get shot if you look too suspicious near one of them. But what can you do? The city needs water, and that's more important than a couple of farmers and hunters.[1]

By the late nineteenth century, such an ideological bulwark formed the basis of the city's arguments for the expanded water system, and thus for the destruction of the many communities that stood in the way. Indeed, many people considered the city's prosperity as necessary to that of the rest of the state.

A Most Unsavory Tradition

From the early work of condemning farms for the original Croton Reservoir to the completion of the Cannonsville Reservoir in 1967, the various city agencies in charge of building the city water supply would eventually destroy all or part of 37 separate communities in the name of supplying the city with water. Curiously, none of the destroyed communities are in what is today the city of New York despite the fact that it was, after all, the city supply and there was some need for infrastructure in the city. In order to save city residents (and their landlords) the inconvenience and expense of displacing urban residents, the largest reservoirs and other infrastructure was built far north of the city and its budding suburbs in the lands left for farmers, small town shopkeepers, and other supposedly less important people.

---

1. It should be noted that there have been no such instances since 9/11, and that this statement is an exaggeration.

The original Croton Reservoir displaced dozens of farmers and other landowners (Koeppel, 2000). As the city grew, however, it needed more water and the city was able to convince the state legislature to pass several laws that allowed the city to manage several lakes in Westchester and Putnam Counties. In anticipation of the expansion of the system beginning with the Boyd's Corner Reservoir in 1866, the city began to dredge the outlets of Lakes Gleneida, Kirk, and several others in order to allow more of their water to flow downstream to the Croton Reservoir (Galusha, 1999). The city was at this time under the control of the infamous Boss Tweed of the Tammany Hall political machine, and Tweed knew that a threat to the water supply was a threat to his power (Galusha, 1999). In 1869, even as the Boyd's Corner Reservoir was under construction, the city's once abundant water supply was subject to a severe draught that created water shortages in the growing metropolis. In 1870, the city began buying water rights upstream and draining the lakes for the city's supply. In 1871, the city won even greater powers to drain upstream waters from the state legislature, although they were repealed the following year. The city also began to implement a policy that forced property owners to remove buildings from the shorelines of the lakes, including numerous tourist hotels, in order to protect the quality of the water heading downstream (Galusha, 1999). In time, the lakes were essentially reservoirs. The control over the lakes was recognized as a temporary measure and that the future depended upon an expansion of the system as a whole.

The control over the lakes and the new Boyd's Corner Reservoir introduced a new era of city domination of the hinterland in pursuit of water. The original Croton Reservoir did displace some residents, but the actions on the part of the city during the 1860s and after marked a decisive escalation. The Boyd's Corner Reservoir was named after the tiny hamlet of Boyd's Corners, whose eleven families were forced to move as the city destroyed their homes for water. Between this action and the control of the lakes in Putnam County, local residents began a series of actions meant to resist further city control of the hinterland. They managed to win an 1877 state law that limited the city's taking of water from Lakes Mahopac and Gleneida between March and September—a concession for resort owners who served primarily tourists from greater New York. There were also several lawsuits against the city and countless newspaper editorials accusing the city of an almost dictatorial power and the will to use it (Galusha, 1999). The Boyd's Corner Reservoir was completed and put into service in 1873, but the city's control over the various natural lakes continued. In fact, it continues today. The following year, the city started construction on the Middle Branch Reservoir, which like the original Croton Reservoir displaced only a small number of people.

The pattern of the 1860s and 1870s merely amplified over the coming decades. There was media condemnation in local newspapers, some lawsuits, and some griping about the city's power and its use of that power. There were some concessions, normally at the behest of the state government, but in the end the city got what it wanted. As the city entered its phase of its greatest water supply expansion during the 1890s and the first decade of the twentieth century, this would become a familiar pattern to all involved.

Ten years after the Middle Branch Reservoir was begun, construction began on the East Branch Reservoir. The reservoir was built near the small village of Brewster, a community home to four city reservoirs. It was part of a project called "Double Reservoir 1" due to it being part of a system with the Bog Brook Reservoir begun a year later and connected via a ten-foot diameter tunnel. The Bog Brook Reservoir was relatively isolated and thus required the removal of few people, but the East Branch Reservoir forced the demolition of the hamlet of Southeast Corner. Harper's Magazine commented wryly at the time, "The million people in the city need a reserve of drinking water, and twenty-one families must move out of their quiet homes and see their hearths sink deep under water" (Quoted in Galusha, 1999, 56). During a time when it was relatively common for rural families to have four or more children, one may conservatively estimate that those twenty-one families translated into a loss of at least one hundred people from the area, and it was likely more. Not only did the township of Southeast where the Double Reservoirs were located lose population (Shupe et al, 1987), but the Tilly Foster Iron mine flooded and subsequently closed in part because of the new reservoirs. Similarly, the Borden Condensary, which produced evaporated milk, was forced to close as the number of farmers supplying the plant dropped considerably. The local economy was severely disrupted (Galusha, 1999).

New York continued to expand its water supply in the Croton watershed. In 1890, the Titicus Reservoir was begun. The township of North Salem lost its namesake village and a smaller hamlet called Salem Center. Again, it can be estimated that over a hundred people were forced to move out of the soon-to-be-submerged valley. Again, a milk condensary serving local farmers and employing some locals in the nearby village of Purdys was forced to close due to the lack of farmers. Some Purdys residents might have correctly considered the closing of the American Condensed Milk Company as a dire omen for the village, as it too was demolished only ten years later to make way for the Muscoot Reservoir.

The 1890s also witnessed the rebuilding of the original: the Croton Reservoir. The New Croton Reservoir was built between 1892 and 1905. It completely engulfed the original Croton Reservoir, dam and all. It also flooded all or part of the villages of Katonah, Golden's Bridge, Purdy's Station, and Croton Falls. The new reservoir offers a stark contrast of the philosophy that accompanied the building of the water system. Whereas the original reservoir displaced relatively few people, the New Croton Reservoir required the removal of over two thousand people and another 1,500 graves. Part of the reason for this is that the population had grown since the 1830s, and one may argue that the original reservoir was built when such disregard for the quality of human life was still rampant but there were fewer lives to ravage. This is, to some degree, true. But it is also true that there had been an escalation of such displacement, from perhaps less than a hundred early in the city's drive for water to the thousands that characterized later development. It indicates an increasing ability on the part of city engineers, lawyers, public officials, and even the public at large, to look at a river valley and see only the water and not those who lived by its shores. It required that those parties place their own interests above those who already lived in the valleys.

The Muscoot Reservoir began in 1901, and was one of the last built in the Croton Watershed. Besides the seemingly cursed village of Purdys, what remained of Golden's Bridge and Croton Falls was lost to the Muscoot. When it was finished in 1905, the Cross River Reservoir was begun, flooding the communities of Cross River and Hoyt's Mills. Along with the Croton Falls Main Reservoir and the accompanying Diverting Reservoir, the Croton System was finished. Thousands of people had been forced to move from their homes, to relocate their businesses, to move elsewhere to find new farms. And the city continued to grow, and so the politicians and the engineers and the populace still feared a return to the dry years before the Croton System.

A Greater New York

In 1898, the New York State Legislature passed a law legally consolidating the greater New York City area into the city of New York. Parts of southern Westchester County, now called the Bronx, Kings County, which included Brooklyn, part of Queens County excluding what is now Nassau County, and all of Richmond County (Staten Island) were legally joined to Manhattan. There were to be many rewards for such consolidation, according to the boosters of the plan, the common provision of water to all the boroughs being one of them. Curiously, it was not necessarily on the top of the list.

As the nineteenth century entered its later years, the Democratic political machine known as Tammany Hall became extremely powerful. The machine followed a pattern that was found in other political machines of the time in that it organized around individual blocks in immigrant neighborhoods. Individual block captains were responsible for organizing the blocks to be loyal to the machine in the voting booth. This was typically accomplished through a loose system of political patronage, social service provision, and at times outright bribery (Allen, 1993; Plunkitt, 1995).

The block captain could use his connections at City Hall to obtain jobs for people living in the neighborhood, and this was a lifeline to the desperate immigrants and their children in need of work. City jobs included the police and fire departments, public works, and a range of other public benefits that not coincidentally expanded during this time.

Block captains would also provide an informal set of social services to neighborhood residents. Often, this was simply acting concerned about the fates of their constituents by attending weddings, funerals, and other family functions. Such functions in inner city "urban villages" were often community events as well, and the presence of such an important figure bestowed a level of prestige on the host family. In addition, the block captain could give loans and cash grants to families in need or seeking to begin a business (Allen, 1993; Plunkitt, 1995).

When all else failed, there was outright bribery and fraud. Scandals frequently erupted over such practices. By a combination of these practices, the political machine was able to control much of the vote at the local level. But Tammany Hall was considered to be a Manhattan phenomenon, and the expansion of the city limits to include Brooklyn—then the fourth largest city in the United States itself—as well as rural areas in Queens and Staten Island was considered one way to mitigate the influence of Tammany Hall.

Nevertheless, the consolidation of city government set new challenges before city leaders. The water system was chief among them. The Croton water supply was built not for the entire region, but for what was then New York City alone. As this included Manhattan Island and the annexed portions of southwestern Westchester County, large swaths of the Bronx[2] and the other boroughs were not connected to the system at all. Brooklyn's water supply was a makeshift system drawing from aquifers near the city and further out on Long Island. Queens for the most part consisted of an urbanized western portion bordering the East River and Manhattan and a semi-rural eastern district that included some large towns, such as Flushing and Jamaica, and a series of rural villages. For the most part, each town fended for itself. Staten Island was much the same.

As the twentieth century began, it was clear that even the new and enlarged Croton System reservoirs were not enough to quench the thirst of the new and enlarged city. There was again some talk of crossing into Connecticut or Massachusetts for additional water. Either state had the advantage of not requiring an aqueduct to cross the Hudson, a technological challenge even today. Most city leaders recognized, however, that the state legislatures in either state could not be as easily swayed as that in New York. New York City had no representatives in either state for obvious reasons, so those states would by nature be predisposed to hold their constituents' needs over that of the metropolis. Moreover, Massachusetts was dominated by Boston politicians, one of New York's prime competitors in the northeast and surely subject to some desire to hinder the city's ability to compete. The reaches of neighboring

---

2. The Bronx was not an independent borough until 1914.

Dutchess County, due north of the Croton System, was off limits due to 1904 legislation that prohibited the city from building a water supply on its waters. And so, without particularly good options on the east side of the Hudson, the city looked west to the Catskills. There was nowhere else to turn.

To the Catskills

As discussed in chapter five, the first attempt at gaining water from the Catskill Mountains first came from a private company called the Ramapo Water Company. Several factors led to its demise, and by the 1890s it was up to the city to build a water supply from the Catskills if one was to be made at all.

In March of 1900, John Ripley Freeman submitted the first of several reports that explored, among other things, the development of watersheds west of the Hudson. Freeman had in the past consulted on both the Panama Canal and China's Grand Canal, as well as the water supplies for San Francisco and Mexico City (Galusha, 1999). It was certainly not the first time that New York sought "world class" opinion, but it nevertheless indicates a change since the original Croton Reservoir was built. Then, the engineering talent came primarily from other northeastern projects, such as the Erie Canal, the Chenango Canal, and the Delaware & Hudson Canal & Railroad, as was the case with John B. Jervis. Freeman had worked the world over, and it was a man of his stature that appealed to New York's elite. An engineer of similar stature during the 1830s could be had only from Europe, but New Yorkers were at that time content with the self-taught Jervis. Three generations later, a competent though experienced engineer was no longer enough—New York demanded a world class engineer for a world class city, and only someone like the Massachusetts Institute of Technology-trained Freeman would do.

Freeman proposed developing the Ten Mile River valley in Dutchess County. This recommendation so alarmed the rural population and, more importantly, the Poughkeepsie elite, that in 1904 residents successfully lobbied the state legislature to pass the Smith Dutchess County Act that prohibited New York City from acquiring water rights in the county. As mentioned, that forced the city to look either east into Connecticut and Massachusetts or west across the Hudson. Freeman had also suggested the Housatonic River system in Connecticut and Massachusetts as, like the Dutchess County water, it could be more easily accessed than the Catskill waters. In order to counter any lack of cooperation on the part of out-of-state politicians, he also suggested a boundary change to place the proposed water system entirely in New York State. Ironically, this would have restored a considerable part of the original Dutch claim to New York. Such a recommendation likely did not play well in New England statehouses or town halls, and the plans were not pursued due to the political realities that made the very idea unfeasible. He also recommended further exploration of the Esopus and Schoharie Creek watersheds in the Catskills, and these were the only truly viable options.

In 1903, Freeman was one of three supervisors of another study that, among other recommendations in the 900-plus page report, suggested filtering Hudson River water, developing the Esopus Creek west of Kingston, and later developing sites on Catskill Creek near the village of Catskill and the Schoharie Creek Valley. Most New Yorkers never considered the polluted Hudson River water appealing despite the proposed filtering or the fact that the city of Poughkeepsie was doing it, and so the Catskill Mountain sources were chosen almost by default.

In 1904 and 1905, three key pieces of legislation were passed that would allow the city to further investigate and develop the so-called Catskill System by creating the Board of Water Supply. Each of the three members was selected by the mayor from lists provided by the Chamber of Commerce, the Board of Fire Underwriters, and the Manufacturers Association of Brooklyn. The state also gave the city the right to take property only ten days after it was appraised and half the money owed was paid to the (former) owner. In order to pass such an act, the state also allowed communities along the water lines to tap into the water supplies themselves, only modestly increasing demand but successfully muting some opposition and dividing the rest.

In order to make the reservoirs in the Catskills useful, the city needed to build an aqueduct to carry the water. The Catskill Aqueduct, as it came to be known, represented a series of technological problems and subsequent innovations. The major problems were related to the landscape of the Catskills themselves, formed as they were by a variety of differing soil and rock types. Of even greater import, however, was the fact that the aqueduct needed to cross the Hudson River. As noted in chapter one, the Hudson is in reality more of a tidal estuary than a river, and even in Kingston, 90 miles upstream, the river still rises and falls with the tides.

Work on the aqueduct began in 1907 but the aqueduct was not filled until 1914. During that seven years, workers used a variety of methods to build the aqueduct. The major project was, of course, crossing the Hudson. There were several possible ways of conveying water across the river. One possibility was to simply lay pipe across the bottom, but this was considered to be costly and not sufficiently stable over the long term. Another idea was to build "shield tunnels" about one hundred feet below the river bottom. Shield tunnels involve the digging of the tunnel and the reinforcement with steel or concrete. The main disadvantage is that a variety of geologic conditions would have to be overcome at the river bottom, including silt, clay, and rock. A third option was to build a bridge over the Hudson. This option, as today, would present engineering obstacles and high construction costs, plus exposure to the elements. It was the fourth option that seemed to have the most benefit in terms of cost and long term stability: a tunnel dug through solid rock well beneath the surface of the river.

Once chosen, the project proved easier said than done as it took four years to find an area of the river that had accessible solid rock from one shore to the next. The result was a tunnel that sank 1400 feet to over 1000 feet below sea level and then rose up again to almost 400 feet above sea level to continue its journey to the city.

At the same time, the Board of Water Supply built the Ashokan Reservoir. As the new reservoir would cover 12 square miles, it was another mammoth project. The Olive Bridge Dam would be almost a mile long, twenty stories high, and span the entire width of the Esopus Creek Valley. Behind it, the waters of the Esopus would fill the new basin and leave even more room for additional projects in the new Catskill System—such as the Schoharie Reservoir. From the dam, the water would be transported via the Catskill Aqueduct. When the aqueduct was first filled with water in 1915, New York City not only had another state of the art water project to its name and millions of more gallons of water, but the beginnings of a new system that could be expanded in the future.

The contractors for the dam built labor camps for the hundreds of by and large immigrant laborers, transforming the local economy and culture of the Esopus Valley. Many of the laborers were newly arrived from eastern Europe, Scandinavia, and Germany. There were also large numbers of Italians and southern Blacks. For the most part, the camps were segregated by ethnicity and race in a manner similar to the urban villages that were found in ethnic neighborhoods in the city itself. There were several camps in the region, the largest being a temporary town built near Brown's Station, which included streetlights, paved roads, police and fire departments, and a hospital. It housed nearly 4,000 laborers and, in some cases, their families in dormitories and cottages for married workers (Steuding, 1989).

As with the other reservoirs, the cost of progress was primarily financial for the people of New York but devastating for those who stood in their way. The area to be inundated with Esopus Creek water, and eventually Schoharie Creek water as well, first needed to be "grubbed;" that is, cleared of all trace of vegetation, animal life, or human habitation. As Galusha (1999) summarized:

> nearly 2,000 people lived in eight villages and outlying farms. The city would claim 504 dwellings, perhaps 1,500 barns and outbuildings, 10 churches, 10 schools, seven sawmills, nine blacksmith shops, and several stores, mills, and other establishments. More than 2,600 bodies in 40 cemeteries had to be exhumed and reinterred elsewhere. The coming of the reservoir also required the relocation of 13 miles of the Ulster & Delaware Railroad tracks serving six stations in the valley. Miles of telephone and electric lines were also moved. (128)

Four of the above-mentioned villages were rebuilt in new locations. In some cases, former residents could buy back their former homes from the city after their property was condemned so that their houses could be moved.

Not surprisingly, there was a wide gulf between the value of property as perceived by local residents and what city appraisers considered to be fair. In 1913, over $600 thousand in claims were brought against the city for condemned property, yet only $123 thousand was awarded (BWS, 1914). There were several reasons for the discrepancies. First, Esopus Valley property owners tended to perceive their homes, farms, and other properties in terms of use value, including their former utility and sentimental value. Many of the dispossessed had been raised in the area, and not surprisingly they placed a higher value on the region than did the appraisers hired by the city. It was this combination of sentimentality and wishful thinking that lead many local residents to demand higher prices than the prevailing exchange values would necessarily suggest. This was aided by the fact that, as in every other water project, many owners of condemned properties took whatever advance notice they had been given to treat their buildings to a new coat of paint and any other aesthetic improvement that might raise the property values (see Koeppel, 2000). By the building of the Ashokan Reservoir, New York had attempted to deal with the situation with the legislation of 1904 and 1905 but many city appraisers and officials alike were skeptical of Esopus Valley residents' claims of higher property values than the New Yorkers had determined. The resultant miscommunication and mistrust likely lead to many local residents in fact being underpaid for their properties.

In Line of Sight

By the time that the Ashokan Reservoir was completed the Board of Water Supply had already started plans for a second reservoir to send water rushing to the Ashokan. It was widely understood that the Schoharie Valley was next in line, although the exact placement of the dam was still in some doubt. Nevertheless, there were two patterns that had been established that carried through to the Schoharie Reservoir project.

The first major pattern was a cultural discourse that held the lives of New Yorkers to be more important than those of rural families. This discourse couched such sentiments in popularly acceptable sentiments such as, "working for the greater good," but the result was still the forced removal of one population from their homes by another more powerful force. The process had been sanitized through a morality that claimed universality and particular honor for perceived rural virtues of simplicity and community, but ultimately was rooted in urban universities and parish houses. The belief was legitimized by utilizing the apparatus of the state to perform the chores of the city, obscuring the power mechanisms dominated by urban interests generally and New York City interests in particular. And in many cases, it was received wisdom for many, if not most, rural residents as well who through its acceptance undermined their neighbors' communities.

The forced dislocation of rural residents was acknowledged as an "acceptable cost" of building the water system. It is tempting to lump this pattern with the first, but the two are distinct. The first addresses the cultural foundation for displacing residents, but still it calls for some restraint. The psychological ability to act with the moral certainty and lack of concern displayed by city engineers and politicians comes not only from a cultural justification but from experience as well. The Ashokan Reservoir was not the first city project to so intrude into individuals' lives, but rather the extension of many similar efforts to displace people and replace them with water. After displacing two thousand people in the Esopus Valley, the demolition of the small village of Gilboa was, for many in the city, of minor significance. Previous support for a great evil makes the lesser evil seem more palatable.

8　　　　　　　　　　　　　Dam

Any particular event is the result of an infinity of possible scenarios having been selected, for whatever reason, seemingly leading to that moment. The unfolding events lead to one another so perfectly that it is tempting to suggest, in retrospect, that there *must* have been some cosmic plan to bring them about. For if any of the events both important and trivial had not occurred and in the manner in which they did, the Schoharie Reservoir might not have been built. The concept of eminent domain came to us from feudalism. Governmental decisions to allow New York to travel over one hundred miles to find water descended from a system of urban political, economic, and cultural dominance. The size of the great cities at the tip of Manhattan and throughout the state was determined by the movements of millions of migrants who chose their new communities based on their own unique situations within the global contexts from which they came. Even the environment itself, without millions of years of tectonic movement, glaciations, and erosion, could have denied Gilboa and New York the pain and promise of the Schoharie Reservoir. And as the Ashokan Reservoir project proceeded quickly to create the first installment of a new water supply system for the growing city, all these forces and more came together in a way that sealed the fate of the small village of Gilboa.

The Protestant Ethic and the Spirit of Gilboa

In a series of classic experiments during the 1960s, Stanley Milgram (1969) tested the willingness of ordinary citizens to electrocute their fellow citizens at the simple request of an authority figure. They were not in actuality electrocuting anyone, but the subjects of the experiments were asked to "correct" people answering incorrectly in a mock psychology experiment by administering increasing levels of electrical shock, often with labels on the machine indicating "fatal" and even in the face of (fake) agonizing cries from the accomplice playing the hapless person answering the questions wrong. In the end, about two-thirds of the subjects were willing to administer the full range of electric shocks, a behavior that had the experiment been real would have resulted in the rather grisly death of those receiving the shocks. Such shrinking in the face of an authority figure may to some be appalling, but it would appear to be a part of human nature.

· Such shrinking was of course found in ample proportions throughout the Schoharie Reservoir project. Most evident was that of the engineers, public officials, and laborers who in the end produced the conditions under which the community would be destroyed. Strengthened by a cultural discourse that held the interests of the city supreme and the destruction of Gilboa a necessity, these actors for the city had plenty of cognitive reinforcement to aid them in believing their job was a moral and respectable one. As considerable attention was paid to this cultural discourse in the previous chapter, it is at this time more interesting to examine the cultural underpinnings of the reactions to be found in Gilboa during the period.

As discussed in chapter 6, Gilboa's population expanded the most prior to 1850 and steadily declined after that year. As with much of rural New York, this demographic trend translated into a population that was by and large rooted in Calvinist Dutch and Lutheran German, and to a far greater degree, Puritan New England immigration. The decline in population during the last half of the nineteenth century occurred during a time when the major cities of the state were all witnessing immigration from diverse ethnic and religious backgrounds and thus had those initial Puritan cultural traits challenged and assimilated with other traditions. As most rural communities were losing population, however, this pattern of cultural challenge was not found in places such as Gilboa. While there is evidence in Gilboa and other Schoharie towns that there was some new immigration, the numbers were extraordinarily low—on the order of individuals and families rather than the entire neighborhoods found in the cities. Whereas urban areas fostered "urban villages" where ethnic identities could be fostered and slowly shared with those of other ethnic groups, immigrants to rural communities seem to have had less of a cultural impact on the dominant culture of the community. The result was, by the turn of the twentieth century, distinct rural-urban differences over a variety of issues, such as alcohol prohibition, religion and science, and socialism, which was ultimately rooted in the fact that urban culture had been forced to accept diversity whereas rural culture had been capable of (relative) cultural continuity during the same time period.

It is thus not surprising that Gilboa still did, and to a large degree still does, engender a local culture closely resembling that of their New England progenitors. Not surprisingly, both of the churches found in Gilboa were protestant, and specifically Calvinist in their orientation. One was Methodist and the other Dutch Reformed; a Baptist Church was in nearby Flat Creek. What the churches of Gilboa had in common with each other and other Protestant churches of the time was the basic theological tenets of Calvinist sects: a conviction that humans exist for the glory of God, that God's knowledge of the future allows Him to predestine believers to Heaven, and that God calls people to their religious and secular roles in life (Johnstone, 2001). Weber (1992) argued that such theological undercurrents inspired believers to work very hard. Hard work allowed people to glorify God and fulfill their calling. In fact, the ability to do one's job consistently well was taken as a sign of God's grace and, therefore, an indication that the individual was one of the saved. Weber called this ascetic Protestantism and posited that it was a primary force behind the beginning of modern Capitalism.

Ascetic Protestantism thus stressed the importance of industry, chastity, and sobriety in everyday life. Various cultural expressions, songs, and writings of the time testify to the importance of such values. Often, the values were blended together. Consider the expression, "idleness is the devil's workshop." The expression immediately conjures the importance of work and activity, of continually working to glorify God and to perform one's calling. It also, more subtlely, directs believers away from temptations of drug use (particularly Alcohol) and sex by prescribing work. Religiosity was an important component of everyday life in the Schoharie Valley; newspapers would regularly run the columns of local and syndicated ministers exhorting readers to follow the straight and narrow. At times, the local newspaper would mention the affiliation of various politicians as a way of indicating the official's respectability. Journalistic accounts of the time, nearly every local history, and interviews with elderly residents from the throughout the region express the view that most people attended church regularly. It was simply expected.

Religiosity was reinforced throughout the community. In a village of only 400 residents, where perhaps another two to three hundred residents lived in the surrounding hinterland, a sizable proportion of one's regular social contacts not only attended church regularly, but a given individual's particular church. That religion was important is an understatement: it was an essential part of the community. What is unclear, however, is the extent to which individual community members internalized religion as spiritual experience as opposed to social ritual and obligation. It is likely that individuals passed through phases of spirituality just as today, but the culture was also infused with the obligations and expectations of religion that it simply, for the majority of modern Americans, no longer found at such levels. What is certain is that, as the regular day-to-day social interaction reinforced such theological tenets, the local culture that had evolved over the generations internalized in even the most agnostic individual the simple morality of the protestant ethic: industry, chastity, and sobriety.

As noted earlier, the cultural ideal of industry encouraged local residents to keep busy. Work was viewed as a calling for the glory of God, and as such it was incumbent upon local residents to accept the lot they were given. If one's destiny was to be a farmer, or a merchant, or a minister, or a teacher, no matter the calling one had an obligation to accept God's mission and work hard to perform their role well and without complaint. Not surprisingly, at a secular level many local residents believed that fate in other realms of life was God's will and thus to accept that fate. This would be apparent in the reaction to the building of the Gilboa Dam.

Chastity in its most obvious form relates to sexual experience, most especially for females. In its broader ramifications, however, it refers to a broader obligation to be honorable and pursue simple pleasures. In this way, the value of chastity was one that demanded the individual to be good parents, obedient children, and honorable neighbors. More than a sexual obligation, it was an obligation to be examples of Christian morality.

Sobriety was an important virtue, but also the one that many local residents appear to have had the most trouble upholding. As early as 1882, William Roscoe in his History of Schoharie County inadvertently commented on this fact:

> The temperance question has engaged the attention of the people for many years and created a distinctive change in the customs and habits of the people, in influencing the mass to refrain from using intoxicating liquors, to which they became habitually accustomed in the early part of the century.

In any case, the hotels of Gilboa stayed in business, and hotels in small towns during this time period typically stayed afloat by serving alcohol in restaurants and saloons downstairs. The temperance movement, however, had an effect of reinforcing community feeling as well. In nearby Hartwick, sixty miles away in Otsego County, members of the Hartwick Womens' Temperance Union utilized the movement as an opportunity to socialize with like-minded people, working on community events, holding meetings, and participating in "bees" designed to make items (food, clothes, blankets, etc.) for sale as fundraisers (Thomas, 1998). It was likely a similar story in Gilboa.

Needless to say, there were certainly those who resisted such a strict culture. Some simply refused to participate. Others, as shown in chapter six, simply left for less green pastures in the cities. Countless others simply went through the motions and played the role of respectable citizen while harboring more carnal desires. But the regular social interaction functioned as a ritual of reinforcement of those same values, and many residents and former residents simply found it difficult if not impossible to believe differently. The values were largely unquestioned even if the beliefs that buttressed them were.

Such was ascetic Protestantism. It was the prevailing cultural discourse, rooted in religious theology and reinforced in rituals of both the secular and the profane, played out in secular interactions. To the most religious, they were simply "living their faith," as one modern Calvinist minister put it. To the less religious, it was the path to respectability that echoed a religious upbringing but carried over into secular life. It produced a local cultural discourse that stressed the supremacy of God's plan for the world and the individual's responsibility to respect that plan. To question one's circumstances was to question God's judgment. The individualism so well fostered by ascetic Protestantism encouraged the individual to accept their own lot while working to help others. Combined with the prevailing dominant cultural discourse that placed the interests of cities above those of residents of rural areas, the good people of Gilboa would respond in accordance with how they believed.

Problems Upstream

As the Ashokan Reservoir was being completed, city engineers roamed the countryside to the north of the Esopus looking for a new dam site. The Schoharie Valley had for years been mentioned as a place for a reservoir, and the logical place appeared to be near the small village of Prattsville.

Prattsville was no larger than Gilboa. It stretched along a single road on one side of the creek. A bridge connected the village to the other side of the creek about midway through the community, and there were some houses on the other side. At the east end of town were the Pratt Rocks, a series of stone carvings made in the nineteenth century paying homage to the town's leading citizen of the time. They are today sometimes called "New York's Mount Rushmore." A little downstream was the Devasego Falls, claimed by both Prattsville and Gilboa, eventually flooded by the reservoir. As late as 1914, the city considered Prattsville the logical place to build the Schoharie Reservoir.

As had happened with the plans to build the Ashokan Reservoir, local residents were angry about the decision to build the reservoir. There were lawsuits and angry residents at city-run meetings. The Gilboa *Monitor* reported reactions to the news that were similar to the response of other communities near proposed dam sites. There were pronouncements against the immorality of the city engineers for proposing the devastation of the lands so near the village. There were cries that the city should be forced to live within its means. In Gilboa and other downstream communities, farmers and mill owners complained that the reduced flow of the creek would hurt their operations. But in the end, none of these protests mattered to the Board of Water Supply. What did matter was that city engineers had determined that nearly double the water capacity existed by building the dam just five miles downstream. In downtown Gilboa.

For Prattsville, the selection of Gilboa as the site of the dam spared the community of much of its own suffering. They would lose a waterfall, and the creek would flow higher at the west end of town, but the village was left intact. In fact, Prattsville, among other upstream villages, would gain a new sewer system courtesy of the city of New York in order to spare the new reservoir to come of the problems associated with raw sewage flowing into the stream. For Gilboa, the challenge had begun.

The City Cometh

It was Thursday, April 25, 1912. The Gilboa *Monitor* went on sale in local shops, the front page devoted to disaster. The H.M.S. Titanic had struck an iceberg and sunk in the North Atlantic as the band played *Nearer, My God, to Thee* carrying nearly 1,600 people to their deaths. The story would haunt the American psyche for generations, and it sold papers on that spring day with the details of the crash, interviews with the survivors, and stories of heroism:

> "Mrs. Astor was sent away in the tenth boat," said John Kuhle of Nebraska. "Just as she was about to be placed within the boat, Colonel Astor embraced her." (GM, 25 April 1912, 1)

It was a horrific disaster, but one that ultimately had no victims in this remote Catskill town. *Monitor* readers indulged in a vicarious tragedy that was a world away. In the meantime, their neighbors in the Esopus Valley to the south were being displaced for the Ashokan Reservoir and the good people of Prattsville were facing a similar fate in the so-called Schoharie Development. Perhaps it was the sudden onset of human tragedy that drew writers and readers alike to the Titanic, but most tragedies are simply not Titanic in scope but tragedies just the same.

On June 20, the *Monitor* reported the results of a meeting of the New York City Board of Water Supply and the State Conservation Department. Following the meeting it was announced "that a decision has been made to construct the next reservoir in Schoharie County. . .the dam to be erected at Prattsville" (GM, 20 Jun. 1914, 1). The newspaper was quick to point out that:

> Prattsville is in Greene, not in Schoharie County, and the borings made for bedrock were made near the "Big Rock" a mile or so away from that village, but the dam will be in Schoharie Creek. (1)

It was a tinge of cynicism well earned by the state and city planners who apparently cared little about such details as the county in which their development would take place. They were aiming their statements primarily at the audience in the great city and few of them would know the difference. It is worth noting that it was a simple mistake as well, an easy confusion of the creek's name for the county name. That the newspaper would take offense is also understandable: other news of the day reported that the national presidential election would cost up to $10 million—an alienating figure to the residents of a poor farming village that obviously excluded all but the wealthiest from entering national politics. Another article bemoaned the cost of the military, arguing, "we should make more homes and not so many fighting machines" (GM, 20 Jun. 1912, 1). And directly beneath, the core of Gilboan culture—an article on an approaching conference of Sunday school teachers. Virtue was experienced at the local level in everyday interactions with neighbors and Sunday services in the protestant churches. And thus the derision toward state and national politicians.

The meeting itself was not a public affair, but rather one attended by several lawyers representing property owners, several attorneys representing townships to be affected by either landtaking or reduced downstream flow, and another attorney representing the Middleburg Light, Heat, and Power Company. The lawyers were necessary due to the fact that the precise writing found in legal documents more or less required the presence of a trained practitioner to interpret them—it was not for the commoner. They discussed matters with representatives of the Board of Water Supply and the whole meeting was hosted by the State of New York. The state had been crucial in legitimizing the appropriation of territory by the city for decades in other projects, so its presence was expected. The added legitimacy convinced some that the city's dealings were valid, although many were convinced that the state was not an unbiased participant. As one former resident commented in 2002:

> My mother used to talk about it. People would get all riled up, and it'd go to court or some meeting, and—surprise, surprise—they'd find for the city. A Lot of people would be pissed, but they'd say they tried.

In either case, the presence of the state in the process of appropriation for the city effectively split the opposition. The use of state mechanisms, such as the courts and the various state agencies, gave the appearance that the city was being restrained. The *Monitor* also noted that "so far as can be learned there was no appearance for the property owners of Gilboa village which will be damaged to a great extent by taking of the Schoharie and diverting it to the Esopus" (GM, 20 Jun. 1912, 1). The concerns were the reduced flow of the creek to power mills and irrigate fields. The concerns would soon escalate.

As 1913 came and went, Gilboans were preoccupied over many of the same concerns. Numerous articles attacked the Tammany Hall politicians who ruled New York City and corrupted the state government as well. At times the articles discussed the proposed upstream dam, but most often the articles simply seemed to gripe about a range of issues in state and federal government. There were positive stories as well, including numerous stories about the expanding network of improved state highways that made automobile travel—and commerce—possible. A new state campaign aimed to convince farmers to grow more Alfalfa—it was good for pigs (GM, 28 Aug. 1913). And every week one or more articles instructed residents to live the good Christian life and announced activities at various churches in and around the village. At one point the courts ruled that New York City could not take the Schoharie Creek water as "the plans proposed are not justified by public necessity" (GM, 8 May 1913, 1). The ruling was later overturned by a more city-friendly higher court. In short, there was a heavy dose of condescension of urban society during 1913, and 1914 was much the same. Articles concentrated on state and national issues and local stories were often instructional (particularly in agriculture and religion) or gossipy in orientation.

It is rather perplexing how the people of Gilboa were informed by their newspaper of the city's intent to flood the village. On December 20, 1915, the *Monitor's* headline declared, "City Gets Half of Water it Pays For." The Ashokan Reservoir delivered 250 million gallons of water per day to the Catskill Aqueduct, which was designed to handle twice that amount. The city's original plan, then over a decade old, was to develop not one reservoir but three, and as such the underutilization was by design. The headline was thus somewhat alarmist, but it concealed a greater issue. The article explained that the site of the third reservoir on the Rondout Creek had undesirable soil and bedrock conditions for the dam. The city decided to forego the Rondout Reservoir in lieu of an enlarged Schoharie Reservoir. In order to increase the watershed to divert another 250 million gallons per day the site of the dam would be moved to Gilboa. This fact was buried in the fifth paragraph. The reason was that the newspaper relied on a number of articles reprinted verbatim from other newspapers, and this particular article originally appeared in the New York *Sun*. Although it would appear strange that the article was not paraphrased into one more appropriate to the local audience, it is even more strange that it was the only mention of the plans in the issue. One week later, a legal notice appeared which announced that the maps and plans of the proposed dam site could be viewed. In New York City. Below the notice, Luman Hildreth offered for sale four of his wood stoves in a classified advertisement.

The plans called for a reservoir five miles long. The dam would rise 160 feet above the creek on a line that ran through one of the village's two churches. In order to build the reservoir, seven new roads, simply named "road one," "road two," etc., would be constructed at higher ground to get crews and traffic to and around the reservoir. The village would, of course, be destroyed in the process of building the dam, with any remaining buildings and vegetation to be burned at a later date (BWS, 1916, 1917, 1918). The entire village would be engulfed under more than 150 feet of water.

The remarkable aspect of the response to the plans to demolish Gilboa in order to build the Schoharie Reservoir is not the level of opposition but rather from where it came. On January 27, 1916 the *Monitor* reported that opposition was building to the project in an article entitled "Oppose Schoharie Water plan." On closer examination, however, the article notes that the opposition came not from residents of Gilboa but rather from two city groups: the United Real Estate Owners Association and the West End Taxpayers Association, who declared that the Ashokan system was adequate. The president of the United Real Estate Taxpayers Association opined:

It would be reckless folly to expend $22,000,000 before we know whether the system will be sufficient. Engineers inform me that Catskill Water cannot be pumped into Brooklyn or Queens without danger. (GM, 27 Jan. 1916, 1)

The water was eventually brought to Brooklyn and Queens, and Staten Island too. Nevertheless, the opposition found in the city cared little for the well being of Gilboa but rather about their own taxes.

Opposition in Gilboa itself tended to be informal and muted, as one former resident related about the experience of a close relative:

My grandmother would talk about old Gilboa and what people said. People would apparently gripe about the city and ministers would tell people to persevere. They'd complain a lot but, you know, there was nothing they could do.

One can picture the scene repeated daily for the last years of village life. A cynical comment at the grocery, a snide remark after church. Schoolchildren telling stories, tall tales, of evil city engineers. Frustrated homeowners, sorrow filled farmers. But one cannot find evidence of Gilboa's bitterness in the public record. Throughout 1916, there was nary a word about any level of local opposition though the events relating to the dam were watched closely. Occasional stories of the challenges by the city taxpayers associations, but no riots, no rallies, no apparent oppositional groups. The *Monitor* carried no editorials decrying the loss of the community despite the obvious willingness to disparage the urban dominated political system. No guest editorials. The 1917 Board of Water Supply Annual Report had no mention of opposition or vandalism during 1916. It was over a year, on March 29, 1917, when the *Monitor* finally published a soulful passage about the destruction of the town. Local resident Harry Jackson had written his poem, "The Probable Passing of Gilboa:"

According to all reports
The old town must soon go,
And where old familiar sites now stand
Will rippling waters flow.
Compulsory eviction will be the order of the day,
But ample compensation will ease the trip away;
All to quench the thirst of the growing mass
Over a hundred miles away.

Let kerchiefs fly as we wave good-bye
To the town with the Biblical name,
1st Samuel 31-8 tells us that was where
Saul and his three sons were slain.
It's seven roads of access
Will serve as exits, then

We can look right straight at the cause
'Tis the Old Schoharie flow

So let us all keep cheerful
And love one another more;
Absence makes the heart grow fonder
May we meet on the other shore,
Where living waters flow forever—
No more parting, no more pain,
Where no earthly thing can sever
Families re-united again. (GM, 29 Mar. 1917, 1)

The passing of the town was considered by many of the local residents a *fait accompli*. There was sadness, there was anger, but there was no consensus as to what to do. For some, the inevitable destruction of the town was an opportunity, albeit one borne of coercion, to seek fortunes in distant places. For others, there were other nearby communities within a short distance of the new reservoir. For still others, there were hopes of a new Gilboa planned from the beginning. A 1916 letter to the editor—the only one of the year—captured the mood:

> Mr. Editor—
> As the dam seems to be an assured fact, it is timely to consider the proposition for the new settlement for those who may wish to remain in this vicinity. Some may think it is too soon at this time to think of the possibility of there having to be a new Gilboa, I think it is none too soon to give some things proper and careful thought. For instance we will take our water system, the lighting plant, the cemetery and all public necessities should be owned by the new village and not by individuals and operated by and for the people. More anon. Yours for a bigger and better new Gilboa.
> Fred Siebel (GM, 10 Feb. 1916, 1)

War loomed. The December 20, 1917 *Monitor* headlines an appeal for Gilboa residents to join the Red Cross "to provide for the men who are at the front and who are putting their lives in peril for our country" (GM, 20 Dec. 1917). The appeal went on to argue that "perhaps that dollar means a bit of sacrifice on your part but WAR MEANS SACRIFICE" (1; emphasis in original). In the next column, the Christmas sermon discussed God's mercy. Non-local issues abounded throughout the year. Women were afforded the right to vote, the newspaper commenting that "women suffrage was carried in New York by pro-Germans, pacifists, and Socialists" (27 Dec. 1917,1). In Gilboa, 1917 again passed without protest or vandalism as well.

In May of 1918, owners of lots in Gilboa Rural Cemetery were advised to meet and find a new location (GM, 16 May 1918). Soon the occupants of the cemetery itself would be moved. In June, it was the living that was told to move "not immediately, perhaps, but sooner or later, and on 80 days notice...We therefore suggest that NOW is the time to decide where you are going to locate"

(GM, 27 Jun. 1918, 1). The advertisement, which like so many others appeared to be a news article, went on to suggest "the beautiful and fertile valley of the Susquehanna in the vicinity of Afton, N. Y." over sixty miles away (1). Other advertisements enticed residents to Middleburgh, Bloomville, and Oneonta (GM, 20 Jun., 1918).

On October 10, 1918, the final issue of the Gilboa *Monitor* was published. The editors wrote simply that:

> The time has come when we must say good-bye to the readers of the Monitor. . . The future of Gilboa is such that all, sooner or later, must bid adieu to one another and seek homes that only the Good Lord knows where. (GM, 10 Oct. 1918, 1)

They sold their readership to the Middleburgh *News* and moved to Oneonta, a small but growing city on the tracks of the Delaware and Hudson Railroad. They finished with an expression of the spirit of Gilboa, advising their readers that, "the latchkey will always be found hanging out and it will afford us genuine pleasure to have our friends from this way visit us...Don't wait for business to call you there" (1). It is unlikely that a similar offer has ever been made by the editors of the New York *Times*.

Like the years before, 1918 passed without incident. There may have been oppositional opinions, but there were few if any oppositional behaviors.

Fait Accompli

For a writer, the story of a community opposing its oppression in the face of injustice makes for great reading. For the social scientist, however, the far more likely but far less inspirational scenario of community resignation to defeat is arguably a more useful case. Contemporary urban theory suggests that in the face of such an external threat the community should unite across class boundaries to oppose the common foe (Castells, 1977). But many studies have found a different scenario of near apathy (Nash, 1989; Rabrenovic, 1996; Tauxe, 1993). Resource Mobilization theory suggests that collective behavior such as an oppositional movement develops if there are sufficient resources to sustain it (McCarthy & Zald, 1977), and it is true that a village of only 400 residents hardly had the resources to mobilize against the most powerful city in America. Nevertheless, the response of Gilboa deserves—demands—analysis.

Gilboa had resources. The village was still, as of 1918, a relatively autonomous community. Agriculture had been oriented to sale for a generation or more, but the potential for supporting itself was still present. The village had a water system and electricity, both produced by private entrepreneurs. Although the village's connections to the outside world were not as developed as that of a small town today, it was certainly not a subsistence economy either.

Nevertheless, this level of self-sufficiency was not complete—the villagers had come to appreciate some manufactured goods from other communities—and the raw economic power found in other communities was far greater. Whereas a century or more earlier the key components of a modern village included developed agriculture and industrial autonomy, the nineteenth century had transformed American society such that the ability to produce and attract capital was increasingly vital. Based as it was on the money system, the reality of a community's full development and potential for self-sufficiency was worth little in the "new" economy. It was no longer acceptable to pay a qualified lawyer from another town in chickens or beef; money was a necessity.

The money necessary to compete against the interests of other communities could not be had through agriculture, but rather it depended upon the circuits of trade that distorted values and thus created profit. Just as the Dutch had done nearly three centuries earlier, New York City businesses traded money for raw materials, transformed them, and in many cases sold the finished product back to the suppliers of the raw materials. To use a hypothetical example: a farmer might sell a bushel of wheat to an urban producer for one dollar. The producer would transform the wheat into twenty loaves of bread, building the costs of the transformation into the bread. The additional cost arguably came from the expended labor, but if additional labor was required then the price necessarily needed to cover their costs as well. Even though the added value of the bread came from the expenditure of labor power, the employer paid a set wage to the employees and appropriated a portion of the added (surplus) value. Marx (1990) believed that the cost of labor was constrained by the fact that the employer needed to pay the laborer enough to stay alive, but as noted in chapter one the bottom limit of the wage structure could be manipulated by lowering the costs of the raw material bought from the farmer. As such, the original bushel of wheat transformed into twenty loaves of bread is valued at five cents a loaf, but in fact the price charged might be ten cents per loaf. The additional nickel in this instance is the result of the expended labor, but each laborer might only make two cents per loaf with the additional three cents appropriated by the owner. The profit (three cents) comes from both the appropriation of the surplus value of the worker and the distortion created by trading between the rural producer and the urban producer. In order for the owner to increase the profit, the price of the bread could be raised, but this could result in a competitive disadvantage if other producers fail to follow suit. Additional profit could also be gained by lowering the cost of labor by cutting wages, although this was sometimes difficult, especially as labor unions gained power during the early twentieth century. Profit could also be increased by lowering the costs of raw materials, which allowed for both a lower wage for urban workers and for greater distortion between the use value and the exchange value of the rural product (e.g., wheat). In short, Gilboa, as with any rural village, was in the wrong place in the capitalist economy to attract capital.

Not surprisingly, the ability of New York City to pay fair market value for hundreds of properties split the community. For some, the village was worth saving regardless of money. For others, particularly those who might have flirted with the idea of leaving, the land purchases by the city provided a unique opportunity. The region had been losing population for decades, and there was a low population to whom to sell properties. Particularly desirable properties might sell easily, but what of those a bit more marginal? Further, people witnessed what soon-to-be-former residents were being paid; for those who perhaps did not learn through word-of-mouth, the newspaper published their names and awards (GM, 3 Oct. 1918, 1). This split between those who cherished the community and others who looked upon the land sales as a new lease on life in a community of only 400 people would have made any agitation rather small. Without the comfort of a mass of the malcontented, such mobilization simply did not occur. As Harry Jackson commented in his aforementioned poem, "ample compensation will ease the trip away" (GM, 29 Mar. 1917, 1). It certainly did.

Even without the reservoir issue, local residents spewed venom toward New York City with its corruption, immigrants, and perceived immoral living. Accepting the city's money was easy compared to accepting its power. Had the city attempted to do such a thing by itself, the land acquisitions would have been seen for what they in fact were: the confiscation of the territory by a more powerful community. The state was, in theory at least, a product of all communities and thus had legitimacy in Gilboa. This idea was continually reinforced in the local discourse and in the newspaper. The political involvement of the state further split the community as some believed the state officials to be tools of the city, whereas others believed the mechanisms of the state to be valid. In either case, disappointments were addressed in respectable outlets operated by the state, generally the courts.

For example, when the Proper Commission, which was charged with awarding property owners compensation for their condemned property, issued its awards, one of the two attorneys retained by the area property owners opined that:

> The principal factor in the condemnation proceedings was the city of New York and that in making awards to people whose property was condemned for the use of that city the commissioners were of the impression they were bestowing benefactions instead of awarding what the constitution and the laws defined as a just compensation for property taken for public use. (GM, 6 Jun. 1918, 1)

Not surprisingly, a majority of the affected property owners appealed the commission's decision. For its part, the city believed itself to be paying a considerable price, even more than the properties were worth. When the commission formed to hear the appeals upheld the awards of the original commission, the *Monitor* simply commented that they were "as a whole unsatisfactory to the claimants" (GM, 3 Oct. 1918, 1). The case would continue for years, but the goal was restitution, not salvation.

It is unlikely that the political reality facing the village was not apparent. The previous decade had witnessed the similar debates involved in building the Ashokan Reservoir less than twenty (rugged) miles away. There were five times as many people displaced for the reservoir as for the Schoharie Reservoir, that fact making it apparent to many if not most that the city and state were going to build the reservoir, period.

These factors all interacted with the cultural tradition of ascetic Protestantism. Many residents perceived this episode as a test from God, a life event to be endured. The response of a good Christian person was to try to identify God's intentions, to endure the suffering and trust in God's will that His plan be fulfilled. And each person met that plan as an individual to make things right for themselves: A December 1917 article called "Economics in the Bible" encapsulated the cultural mood when it advised good Christians to:

> Be selfish nobly. "Love thy neighbor as thyself." When Christ said that, he set it down as an everlasting truth that man must love himself in order to achieve anything at all in this world, and that the attempt to love another as he does himself is to struggle toward an ideal. . .To be selfish in a fine way is to carry out one's highest destiny. That is real philosophy. It is also real common sense. Why is a man put into the world if it is not to make the best of himself? (27 Dec. 1917,1)

To fight was to work within the system for justice, and if that justice did not appear then to trust that God knows what is ultimately for the best. To cause a ruckus, to rally, riot, or destroy—these things are against the will of God. "Give unto Caesar," they would say, "and give unto God that which is his." New York was indeed a new Rome.

9

Burn, Gilboa, Burn

The construction would begin in 1919. As 1918 progressed, realtors from communities far and near advertised for the business of the soon-to-be-homeless. The hill which contained a church and a handful of houses would need to be de-populated before any construction could begin, and the rest of the village would need to follow suit soon thereafter. The end had begun.

Depopulation

As 1919 began, subtle changes in village life became more apparent. Some families had moved, but most were preparing for the event. Some were traveling great distances to find new homes, many were simply touring the region searching for a new community that could meet that combination of comfort and opportunity for which the refugees were looking. The newspaper had been discontinued and its former subscribers were receiving the Middleburgh *News* instead. The paper concentrated, for obvious reasons, on events that occurred in that downstream community and not in Gilboa. As spring came, city engineers and representatives from Hugh Nawn Contracting Company of Roxbury, Massachusetts were staying at the Gilboa House and surveying the countryside, pointing fingers at condemned buildings and marking trees. The villagers had known for over three years that Gilboa was condemned, but it was only now that that fact impressed itself on them. From late 1918 through early 1919 the coming destruction was transforming itself from a curious news story reporting on some future episode to an inevitable fact.

Every week, the *News* carried advertisements for realtors trying to sell the refugees property in their own communities, companies willing to buy furniture and other household wares, and publicizing the advantages of the automobile.

Local and immigrant laborers worked in the cemeteries exhuming bodies and transporting them to higher ground. Where possible, the city would advertise to local residents their intentions to move the bodies and request that family members claim their departed. The vast majority of rural remains were claimed, and those that were not were moved to a new cemetery on higher ground. The newspaper diligently reported such movements, such as a January report that Eugene Mackey was taking bodies from the old cemetery and reinterring them in the cemetery at nearby Grand Gorge (MN, 23 Jan. 1919). The process took several years of almost continual digging.

The Middleburgh *News* reported in a similar style as the Gilboa *Monitor*. Most of the news covered discussed state and national events, such as the end of World War I in 1918. There were the weekly articles detailing new agricultural techniques or economic conditions, the messages of area pastors for their communities, and small sections devoted to surrounding communities that functioned as gossip columns. There was the occasional substantial article discussing local events, but those events were in Middleburgh or, perhaps, its neighbors five miles away in Schoharie. Gilboa was most often relegated to its gossip column and the occasional article updating the public on the progress being made on the new dam or the Shandaken Tunnel being constructed to carry the water to the Ashokan Reservoir. The mundaneity of the stories, such as the decision in Schoharie of the Women's Christian Temperance Union to not seek prohibition of tobacco on the heals of their success with regard to alcohol (alcohol prohibition had recently gone into effect) but rather to educate people instead, functioned to focus attention on issues other than the reservoir in other area towns. In Gilboa, life simply was not normal. People and institutions were leaving, and there was a ripple effect. The closing of the dairy creamery, for instance, resulted in area farmers not in the way of the new reservoir selling cows for lack of a place to process their milk.

From time to time, there were articles reflecting the mood of the village as people faced the community's demise:

> There is a note of sadness in the business transactions occurring at Gilboa almost every day. The separation and scattering of the big family of village residents, people who for long years have lived together, means a whole lot, for sentiment and friendship are more than commonplace terms, better appreciated and understood when boyhood and girlhood homes and scenes of a life time are taken from you, and when your neighbor of to-day becomes your far away friend of tomorrow. (MN, 17 July, 1919)

As 1919 continued, this feeling became more pronounced as people were leaving town. In January of 1919, R.O. Lewis purchased a home in Unadilla and town supervisor Southard bought a farm in Otsego. They soon left the village.

In February, workmen for the city were busy tearing down the former Hall's Store. In March, George Mattice and his family moved to seek their new fortunes in Bridgeport, Connecticut. Mary Dickinson bought a house in Wisconsin after having moved the previous fall. In April, the Ellerson house was being torn down.

As houses were vacated, remaining area residents would sometimes stay in vacated homes until they were either moved or demolished. For instance, a May

News story reported that Newell Miller had moved to West Conesville and his former premises were to be inhabited by Floyd Roe (MN, 29 May 1919).

The changes took their toll on area residents. In June, Ray Lewis suffered a nervous breakdown (MN, 19 Jun. 1919). He was later reported to be doing better, but the cause was attributed to the obvious stress of the times. A former resident unrelated to Lewis mentioned in 2003:

> My father never forgave the government over that one. The dam ruined alot of lives —lots of people were just devastated, you know, emotionally. People always talk about the loss of the town, but think of the people who lived there.

The impact on individual lives was incalculable.

Summer was a particularly busy time for moving. In July alone, the month in which work on the dam itself began, Luman Hildreth (who had previously sold his stoves) moved to Potter Hollow, Frank Mattice moved to Catskill and the Wyckoffs, whose family owned several shops in the village, went to Conesville. Relatives of theirs, Mr. and Mrs. Clinton Wyckoff, moved to Roxbury (New York). Sidney Rivenburgh moved to West Conesville but bought a house in Prattsville for his mother. Raymond Cronk bought a house in North Kortright, Dr. Persons bought one in Slingerlands, and Laura Tonsley's parents moved to Catskill. August witnessed even more intense activity as villagers bought homes elsewhere and left their hometown behind. In some cases, they could purchase a lot and move their old house there after buying it back from the city. In other cases, they could buy a neighbor's house. Still others bought or built new homes.

By autumn of 1919, the majority of Gilboa residents had moved on. There were 38 families who were listed as having moved in the Middleburgh *News* between January and October 1919. Some had by this time already left, as was the case of the former editors of the Gilboa *Monitor* who went to Oneonta in October and thus were not listed. Some others, in particular young men who could find employment at the jobsite, stayed in town and also were unlisted. The *News* commented wryly, "Several of our townsmen are working for the construction company" (MN, 21 Aug. 1819, 1). Of those that were listed, sixteen (42.1 percent) moved to communities within a ten-mile radius of Gilboa. Of the remaining 58 percent, 2 families had moved out of state—one to Wisconsin and one to Connecticut. Seven families (18.4 percent) had moved to one of the small cities in the region, specifically Catskill, Kingston, or Oneonta. None had moved to one of the state's metropolitan centers. The remaining 13 families (34.2 percent) were scattered among ten different rural towns over ten miles from Gilboa. In all, former Gilboa residents moved to at least twenty different communities, and half of those new communities received only one Gilboa family. In some cases, individual family members were separated from one another. Although Supervisor Southard moved to Otsego, Ellery Southard moved to Schoharie—over 45 miles from Otsego. Similarly, the Wyckoff family was spread out in nearby Conesville, somewhat more distant Roxbury, and in Oneonta 45 miles away from Gilboa. Although the data as presented in the Middleburgh *News* is not perfect, it is a good indicator of the fates shared by the former residents.

Building the Dam

If the years leading up to the dam were sad for Gilboa, they were remarkably uneventful for most New Yorkers. All attention was diverted to the Great War then being fought and won in Europe, Gilboa being mentioned only occasionally in New York newspapers. In contrast, the annual reports of the Board of Water Supply detailed the city's dealings in Gilboa. In 1917, for instance, the BWS claimed that:

> buildings within the Schoharie taking were measured and their volumes computed. Searches for deeds were made at various county seats. Supplementary sheets for taking and residue parcels were prepared, necessitated by the subdivision of several of the parcels, the data warranting such changes having developed since the original maps were completed. (BWS, 1918, 41)

And thus was the coming destruction of the village reported to city leaders—if they read the report.

As 1918 set in, the city continued to remove corpses from the seven cemeteries in the future reservoir. There were 1,328 graves in the area, and 643 were moved by the end of the year. The largest number was from the two large cemeteries in and near the village—Gilboa Old Cemetery and the newer one built by the Gilboa Cemetery Association. The non-dead were paid 12.5 cents per square foot for what was meant to be their own final resting places. The owners were required to travel to Stamford, ten miles away, to prove the ownership of their plots in order to receive payment.

In 1919, as Gilboa residents were reading the newspaper of a community twenty miles away and preparing to leave town forever, the city worked on the new highways on the eastern side of the reservoir. The routes were cleared and some excavation work had begun on several roads. Road eight, today the main highway into the reservoir area from New York route 30, was begun.

The Shandaken Tunnel, running at one point over 2,200 feet below the peak of Shandaken Mountain, had been started in 1917. At over 18 miles, it was then the longest tunnel in the world for any purpose. It would connect the Schoharie to the Ashokan Reservoir as water flowed through the tunnel to Esopus Creek and eventually into the Ashokan. As the Gilboa Dam got underway, crews were already at work sinking eight shafts in remote locations in order to construct the tunnel.

On June 20, 1919 the contract for the dam itself was officially awarded to the Hugh Nawn Contracting Company of Roxbury, Massachusetts. By the end of July, the final destruction of the Church Hill area at the north end of town had begun:

> It is with sadness we note that work has begun on Church hill by cutting down shade trees. Some of the trees in the yard of the Reformed Church have been cut down and the schoolhouse grounds are being cleared up and some of the pleasant homes have had the shade trees cut away. (MN, 31 July 1919, 3)

Although the trees were an obvious sore point, it soon included more:

> Streets are being made unattractive by the cutting down of shade trees and buildings are being demolished. The Reformed Church, an old landmark and a sacred place to many, is now being razed. The city of New York presented to the society the memorial windows, the seats and furnishings, and the society has graciously given the property to other societies of like domination. . .The seats and windows will go to South Gilboa church, the carpets to the Blenheim church and the organ will become the property of the Grand Gorge church. (MN, 14 Aug. 1919, 1).

The city never reported such specifics but rather reported them as such in the BWS annual report:

> The sites of the main structures at the Gilboa dam were cleared and earth excavation for the dam and spillway channel was started on September 24, at which time excavation was begun at Station 13 with one of the steam shovels released from work on the highways. . .Rock excavation was begun at Station 14+10, starting at the level of the present road and working back into the hill. The holes were drilled about six feet deep and loaded with two or three sticks of 40 percent dynamite. A Thew revolving shovel was used to load the muck into wagons which transported it to the crusher on Church Hill. (BWS, 1921, 68)

Property owners in nearby communities benefited. In Grand Gorge, the site of the nearest station of the Delaware & Ulster Railroad, the Board of Water Supply established a field office. In Prattsville, the southerly terminus of the new reservoir that narrowly escaped being the site of the dam itself, another field office was established. In Stamford, at over 2,000 residents the largest community for twenty-five miles in any direction, the main Board of Water Supply offices for the project were established. There was a field office in Gilboa, as well, which concentrated specifically on the dam itself. The owners of the properties were afforded generous rent for these offices.

As construction began, a flood of laborers came into the area to augment the rather small pool of labor found locally. As Beatrice H. Mattice wrote:

> Many workers of all nationalities moved in to work on the dam. A construction camp was set up to house the workers and a police force organized to try to keep

order. Local men were also hired and paid wages unheard of in these parts. (Quoted in Stratigos, 1998)

From the perspective of New York City, the wages were decent in order to attract the largely immigrant labor force, mainly Italian and Irish but also many ethnic Poles and southern African-Americans, into the mountains. The contractor building roads paid workers four dollars per day (MN, 10 July 1919). Skilled laborers on the dam itself fared even better:

> Wanted Immediately: 20 form carpenters for Gilboa Dam. Wages 70 Cents per hour; eight hours and overtime. (SMR, 12 may 1925, 4)

The Board of Water Supply apparently would have preferred a better pool of laborers, however. Nearly every annual report lamented about the workforce, finally concluding near the end of the project in 1925:

> The labor conditions were similar to those of the previous year; the supply of labor, while generally ample, was of poor quality and the turnover was large. The average number of men employed during 1925 was 425, with a maximum of 760 and a minimum of 79. (BWS, 1926, 59)

The fluctuations were generally due to the fluctuations in the seasons and which phases of the project were being conducted.

In addition, thousands of workers needed housing at the various job sites in the region. Landlords in Prattsville, Grand Gorge, North Blenheim, and Stamford were able to charge rents in excess of what could have been charged without the surge in demand created by the influx of so many workers. In Gilboa itself, many of the properties formerly owned by village residents were rented by the city to various workers at the job site. Even so, the number of workers engaged in the building of the dam was far in excess of the total number of residents who once lived there, and the contractor had to build temporary housing for many of its workers:

> The construction company that has the contract for building the dam is busily engaged in constructing a camp for their employees. The camp is made up of units, a unit consisting of four buildings arranged in the form of a square, and a building in the center. The four outside buildings will be used to lodge the workmen; each building to accommodate twenty workmen and the center building to be used for baths, washing, etc. . . .There will be a big commissary building to be used for a store, barber shop, etc. (MN, 21 Aug. 1919,1)

A week later, the *News* made it clear that it was not only the laborers who were looking for a place to live:

The city police that are here are very busy looking for homes for their families. It is said all the houses are taken with the exception of the postmaster's house which will not be taken. The merchants' homes will not be disturbed for awhile. (MN, 28 Aug. 1919, 1)

Several merchants were permitted to stay in the village and continue their businesses as construction continued. It was, in a real sense, a final opportunity to earn money before finally leaving town. For the laborers, the cost of housing ate up some of the good wages that were being paid: housing could range up to $1.25 per day.

By the end of 1921, Church Hill was a muddy mess of construction with steel towers rising overhead, a stone crusher on site, and the constant clatter of trucks, mule-drawn wagons, and foreign languages spoken to one another. The invasion of the community, those who remained at least, was total. Their Dutch Reformed Church had been demolished, its articles given away, and its site defiled as a construction site. The school next door had been demolished as well, and for several years school was conducted in the Baptist Church outside of the village. The Methodist Church, still standing but on higher ground with fewer parishners, was kind enough to share its building with the numerous Catholics who had no place to worship. The Catholics said mass in the morning and the Methodists held services in the afternoon. The valley itself was becoming more narrow as the earthen portion of the dam closed in on the shores of the creek. The masonry section of the dam, today the most pronounced feature at the site, was rising above a small outlet through which the creek water was allowed to run.

The amount of materials used was phenomenal. By the time the dam was completed in 1926, 449 thousand cubic yards of earth had been excavated, 482 thousand cubic yards of masonry had been placed on a dam structure that contained over a half million barrels of cement. The embankment that composed a large proportion of the dam itself contained an additional 733 thousand cubic yards of earth. In addition, 119 thousand cubic yards of earth had been excavated for eight new highways to and around the reservoir. Constructed of nearly three thousand barrels of cement, over four thousand cubic yards of masonry, 10 thousand cubic yards of crushed stone and almost ten thousand feet of paving, the highways were, for the time, among the most advanced anywhere in the state. Similar highways had been constructed in the state's urban areas, but it was rare to find such roads in the mountains (BWS, 1927).

In 1923, the city began the serious job of grubbing the dam. Grubbing involves the clearing of vegetation, buildings, and any other potential debris from the basin of the reservoir. Without grubbing, the vegetal matter of the reservoir, such as dead trees, shrubs, grass, etc., decomposes in the water. Although small plants decompose quickly, large trees can become waterlogged and thus may acts as pollutants in the water supply for years afterward. The entire basin was thus cleared of all plant and animal life.

By the end of the summer in 1925, the dam was nearly complete. The roaring twenties roared in New York, a continuous party for those of proper social status. In Gilboa, the final destruction of the town was finally near.

Fire

It was October 18, 1925. At around 10:15 that night, a construction foreman named simply "Wolf" was walking through the business district of the doomed village. While walking through the empty street, the sounds of laborers gambling and drinking in the background and the silhouette of the looming dam in front of him, Wolf noticed something peculiar. It might have been the smell of smoke, wafting through the street from a ways away. Fire was used to clear brush, but not at 10:15 on a Saturday night. By the store of H. S. Slover in the Lawyers Building, the flicker of flames through the windows was accompanied by the crackling of the burning wood frame structure. Concerned, he summoned George Angermuller of the Board of Water Supply police, who was at that time walking his beat in the village until midnight. The two conversed and walked, maybe ran, toward the doomed building. They approached the door and entered. The whirr of a swelling fire as flames leapt up the walls and climbed to the ceiling convinced the duo of a fatal truth: the store was lost, and the heart of the village itself was in jeopardy.

The two men found Hugh Nawn, the owner of the contracting firm, who sounded the company fire siren. About three hundred villagers, not of the old village but of the one assembled to build the dam, were called upon to help fight the fire. They brought out the company's own fire fighting equipment, assembled brigades of buckets to bring water from the nearby creek to the besieged building. Like any other urbanized area, however, downtown Gilboa was a densely settled area. Many of the buildings stood within six feet of each other, some were touching their neighbors. Not surprisingly, the fire hurdled the narrow crevices in the building line, spreading at first to the buildings on one side of the street and then to the other. The Prattsville Fire Department was called, and they arrived within twenty minutes. The Stamford Fire Department was called, traveling a greater distance they nevertheless arrived within forty minutes—traveling the twelve miles over poor roads in darkness in only twenty minutes. The Stamford Fire Chief assumed control, bringing their pumper and attempting to save the condemned community. As eighteen buildings, two and three stories tall, sent spits of fire into the dark sky it was obvious that the village needed to be evacuated. As the Stamford *Mirror-Recorder* reported:

As soon as the fire had gained headway so that it was quite certain that the village would be destroyed, many of the tenants were ordered to vacate, as owing to the wind it was difficult to fight. Through the courtesy of Moore Brothers, the Hugh Nawn Contracting Company, and Wyckoff Brothers, much of the personal articles of the victims were saved, as they put their entire force of trucks running to the scene of the fire, carting to safety the belongings of the tenants and commercial people, and everybody was busy in saving what they could. (SMR, 21 Oct. 1925,1)

The roar of the trucks and the glow of 18 buildings afire and fire fighters and frantic tenants and drunken laborers scarfing their gambling winnings and the roar of an unrelenting wind as the heat of the blaze turned one side of a man's body warm while the other remained cool in the October air. Amid the chaos:

It was found necessary to dynamite one of the buildings at the upper end of the village on the south side of the street, occupied by Sergeant O'Sullivan of the B.W.S. police and known as the Hattie Gaylord residence, to prevent the fire from spreading and this was done under the supervision of the Hugh Nawn Company. (1)

The fire raged. The Middleburgh *News* noted:

The fire was spectacular in appearance and lighted up the heavens so that the light could be seen far and wide. Telephones helped to spread the word and soon autos from far and near headed that way. It is estimated that fully 5,000 assembled to watch the doomed village go up in smoke. (MN, 22 Oct. 1925, 1)

As a most welcome dawn arrived, the heart of the village was smoldering in ruins. The wood frame buildings had by and large collapsed, their charred remains smoking on either side of the blackened and muddy street. Twelve buildings on the south side of Main Street had been destroyed despite the creek directly behind. Six, including the three story Gilboa House hotel, in the shadow of the hillside and the embankment of the growing dam, were gone. A construction tower was also in ashes. Three hundred residents had been displaced from the boarding rooms they had been renting in the village center, their belongings thrown onto the backs of trucks or heaped in piles away from the ruins. The city claimed $150 thousand in damages. Gilboa was no more.

There remained only a mystery. There was speculation about the cause of the fire, but no real facts. The Cobleskill *Index* reported:

The fire is believed to have originated in the back room of the Slover store and is thought to have been started from a rubbish fire left burning on the bank of the Schoharie Creek near the rear of the store. (CI, 22 Oct. 1925, 1)

This opinion of an essentially accidental, even innocent, origin for the blaze was not unanimous. The Stamford *Mirror-Recorder* noted:

Another story was that a hilarious party was held that evening and that jollification of the evening might have resulted in the fire. It is also said that the residents of Gilboa were unwilling to have motion picture concerns thrive on pictures made of the village, when the time came for destruction of their old home, for sentimental reasons. Consequently, no definite cause of the fire has been learned and it is believed that there will be no investigation of the origin of it. (SMR, 21 Oct. 1925, 1)

There was, indeed, no investigation of the fire's origins.

There were thus three theories as to the fire's origin. As for the theory that the fire began as a result of a brush fire left smoldering behind Slover's Store, it was the most widely reported at the time. What is unclear is why there would have been a need for a brush fire. It was likely started to burn some garbage from the store, a common practice at the time. The fact that the fire was behind the store implies a personal, as opposed to social, use for the fire. Reports of the time suggested that the fire was left smoldering, implying that the fire starter stayed with the fire until it was thought safe. As the night was windy, it is likely that he preferred to be indoors and thus was not as inclined to watch the fire as he would have been during the summer. That same wind would have been capable of growing the fire given the right angle, and even helping it spread. One major question remains, however: why was the fire so close to the building and not closer to the creek? The likely answer again seems to be that it was a cold and windy night, and the starter preferred not to travel too far from the warmth of indoors.

The second theory suggests that the fire was somehow started during a night of partying among the workers. The worker housing was full of hundreds of young men who were somewhat inclined to drink alcohol (then illegal), gamble (also illegal) and generally participate in other such behaviors. Although it is possible that there were some laborers near the original brush fire, it seems unlikely that it would have been over by 10:15. It is more likely that partying young men were scapegoated as a group due to the conflict between the local culture, especially among older residents, and the more freewheeling young urban (and often immigrant) men.

The third theory was that the local residents had started the fire themselves. A 1998 local history quoted the following:

An unidentified writer for the Albany Evening News wrote in July 1925, "The dramatic story of a river turned back from its course and tunneled beneath a mountain and of a prosperous village buried 150 beneath an artificial lake unfolds toward its pathetic end here today. Last groups of Gilboa's 200 citizens are watching their hometown fall slowly in ruin, so that New York City's water supply can have a new reservoir. Before the town was to be flooded, it was supposed to be burned to the ground. There were a few movie companies competing for rights to film the final fire, before they were able to, however, the villagers torched the town to save what was left of their village's dignity." (Stratigos, 1998, 73).

The story actually dates from that date in 1926 in the Albany *Evening News and Albany Evening Journal* and already provided a new narrative for the last days of Gilboa. Newspaper accounts at the time (in October 1925) reported the story of the movie rights differently. The Cobleskill *Index*, for instance: ". . .it had been rumored the city of New York had sold the right to burn to a moving picture company" (CI, 22 Oct. 1925, 1). The Middleburgh *News* had the exact same quote (MN, 22 Oct. 1925). A week later, the Cobleskill *Index* reported:

> Rumors are rife to the cause, but these are only conjectures, it is said. . .One report has it that the fire was caused by a hilarious party, while another rumor persists that the fire might have been designed to prevent moving pictures being taken when the doomed buildings were razed. (CI, 29 Oct. 1925, 1)

Given that 38 families left Gilboa in 1919 alone, the number of local residents remaining was surely very low. The final vacating date was November 1, and in anticipation some of the local merchants, "had allowed their insurance to lapse because of depleted stocks" (1). Given foreknowledge of a great fire, why would a merchant allow insurance to lapse and forego the payment of the insurer?

Although the timing was right for a political statement, the people left in the area had at that point benefited financially from the project. There had been better timing for a political statement, such as the time of the original takings of the property six years earlier, or the beginning of construction, or even when city engineers first arrived. There was no mass resistance to any of the events up to this time, although there was clearly some bitterness. If some local residents purposely started the fire, it was a very small group of conspirators. Perhaps the rumors that the city was planning to contract with a movie company to film the final burning of the town was too much for this small group, and that explained the timing. Curiously, the Board of Water Supply never mentioned the possibility of filming the burning of Gilboa, and it is likely that if this was in fact the case then the arsonists torched the community for nothing. In fact, the Board of Water Supply never conducted a full investigation and barely acknowledged the incident at all in the annual report for that year:

> Areas of the Village of Gilboa and vicinity lying outside of the limits of the contractor's operations under contracts 203 and 205 were cleared by the labor forces of the Board of Water Supply. A fire, of accidental origin, on October 17, destroyed the buildings on nineteen real estate parcels in the heart of the village, and the remaining buildings in the village, with the exception of those on Parcel 180, were burned on November 23; the buildings on the latter parcel and on Parcel 4 were burned December 4 and those on Parcel 190 on December 10. (BWS, 1926, 76)

It was bureaucratic treatment of the end of Gilboa. Perhaps that was why the Board of Water Supply failed to investigate further. Certainly that was how the City of New York found it possible to condemn the community in the first place.

The cause of the Gilboa fire can never be known, but it appears most likely that it was an accident. Like a *Red Badge of Courage* (Crane, 1997), however, the fire created a sense of resistance for a population that had been embittered by their treatment but had done little outside of the courts to fight for their homes. Area residents had arisen to defend their homes only three generations earlier during the Anti-Rent Wars, and the fire made it appear that the their efforts had not been in vain. As discussed in chapter 11, it is this appearance of resistance to which many villagers attach themselves today.

A New Gilboa

As the letter of Fred Siebel (GM, 10 Feb. 1916, 1) showed, there were those who were committed to the idea of a new Gilboa. For many, this was a community in which they had been raised, in which they themselves had fallen in love, gotten married, bore and raised children of their own. For them, the heartbreak of Gilboa's passing was the panic of losing the only home they had ever known, and many were not surprisingly reluctant to let the community go the way of the town. "Yours for a bigger and better new Gilboa," Siebel concluded, "More anon." There were no more letters from Siebel or anyone else, and it is debatable how much planning ever went into the new Gilboa. With the emigration of residents at the end of the decade, there were considerably less community members to mobilize as the roaring twenties began.

Nevertheless, the parishioners of the Methodist Church had planned to salvage as much as possible from their former building and construct a new one on higher ground. Alas, the church was lost during the fire but the new building was built across the creek and up the hill above the new water line. New York City built new Gilboa a school, but it was across the reservoir from the new post office and the church. Carved into the side of the mountain, the location was never one in which there was a high likelihood of new settlement.

Perhaps the most successful attempt at a new Gilboa was located a few miles from the new reservoir. Small business owner Imer Wyckoff began Imerville, a small development consisting of a "Socony garage, the general store of Leland Lewis, the East Side Lunchroom which also housed the post office" (Galusha,1999, 165). By then, however, many of the townspeople had scattered to other towns and begun new lives. Even members of Imer's own family had moved away. In 1928, an oil lamp exploded and the resulting fire destroyed the fledgling settlement.

A new Gilboa never materialized. The settlement's key institutions were too spread out, the church and Imerville being on one side of the reservoir and the school being on the other. The population had moved to new homes, and for many the trauma of a second move to a new Gilboa was not an attractive option. As the roaring twenties turned into the Great Depression, Gilboa had been reduced to a township with no village, a community with no center, and a distant memory for an entire generation.

On July 24, 1926, the reservoir bottom had been grubbed and the sluice gates on the dam were closed. Over the next several months, in the midst of a draught, the Schoharie Reservoir was filled and the village flooded. On the night of November 24, Florence Brandow witnessed the first water roll into the intake of the Shandaken Tunnel:

> A group of us went down that night. They had a big searchlight they fixed with car batteries so we could see when it first went over. There was loud hollering: "there is goes. It did it!" (Quoted in Galusha, 1999, 165)

The Schoharie Reservoir was born.

As for New York City, the dam was filled, new trees were planted on the hillsides, and Gilboa was nothing more than another supply of water. By the end of the 1920s, the Board of Water Supply was investigating the feasibility of yet another entire water supply: the Delaware System.

10 Power to the People

The completion of the reservoir would seem to be the end of the story. It was a compelling tale of injustice and of redemption through fire. By 1930, most of the claims had been paid and the trees had been planted, transforming the once agricultural hillsides into a dense forest. But just as it was important to examine the social dynamics that brought these two communities—New York and Gilboa—into such sharp conflict with one another, it is also necessary to examine the dynamics as they have developed since the completion of Gilboa Dam. The dam signified not the end but rather the beginning of a new relationship with New York through one of its most important organs: the Department of Water Supply, Gas and Electricity that became responsible for the reservoir upon its completion. It was a relationship with challenges and one that was further tested when New York State again chose the Gilboa area for a unique power station. As New York turned its attention to the Delaware River system to the west, the people in and around Gilboa learned what ordinary life in the watershed of the reservoir would demand.

The new Delaware system was first subject to a bitter federal court battle in which the states of Pennsylvania and New Jersey, whose shared border is formed by the Delaware, argued that New York City's plans for the Delaware River in the western Catskills would impinge on their own water rights. New York City won the day and went on to build the Cannonsville, Pepactin, Rondout, and Neversink reservoirs after World War II. And as in Gilboa, thousands more residents were displaced from their homes in communities like Union Grove, Arena, and Cannonsville.

The 1954 Supreme Court decision that allowed the Board of Water Supply to build on the Delaware also required the city to install mechanisms that would help maintain the flow of water to the south. The reservoirs of the Delaware would thus have valves designed to release water downstream. The Pepactin, Neversink, and Rondout reservoirs were connected to the city by way of the Delaware Aqueduct. The Cannonsville Reservoir, the farthest west on the western branch of the river, was also connected but its primary purpose became not the supply of water to the metropolis but rather for controlling the flow of the Delaware River. The last of the major reservoirs, Cannonsville chewed up half of the land in the Delaware County township of Tompkins, resulting in a loss of over 700 residents. Due to its use primarily as a flood control dam, many area residents believed (and many continue to believe) that the reservoir was unnecessary (Galusha, 1999).

Urban Views

There would be many opportunities and many reasons for conflict and ill will between the city and local residents after completion of the dam. Lingering resentment toward the city for the village's destruction was evident even in 2003, but the major sources of contempt revolved around two of the city's concerns: 1) the cost associated with maintaining and running the system, and 2) the sanitary conditions of the water supply. These two major interests have guided New York's dealings with the people of the Catskills, not only in Gilboa but throughout the Schoharie, Esopus, and Delaware watersheds. In many instances throughout the years, New York City acted from their own interests and by doing so tread on the sympathies of many, though not all, of the people in those areas.

To a large extent, the obvious supply of water for New York City is the Hudson River. Forcefully flowing from the shadows of Mount Marcy, the highest peak in the state, the Hudson broadens and meanders through the mountains into an ancient fault line at a series of rapids at the Glens Falls metropolitan area. The river thus travels south through industrialized towns like Hudson Falls, Mechanicsville, and Waterford. At Cohoes, the Mohawk River, derisively called the Muddy Mohawk due to its own pollution problems, merges with the Hudson and continues through Troy, Albany, Kingston, and Poughkeepsie. As late as 2000, conflicts raged over pollution in the river despite remarkable progress in addressing it since the 1960s. In short, any supply from the Hudson River needs a heavy dose of water treatment and filtration. Not surprisingly, this was not considered to be a viable option. As early as 1914, even such bastions of progressive media as *The Nation* had rejected the Hudson in lieu of the Catskill Mountain streams:

> those (sources) on the westerly side (of the Hudson are) the only practicable sources of additional supply, except for the Hudson River itself; but inasmuch as the latter water would require filtration from the outset of its use as well as the construction of costly storage reservoirs in the Adirondacks, the Catskill Mountain streams were selected for the necessary additional water supply of New York city. The wisdom of this selection is enhanced by the fact that the waters of the Esopus, Schoharie, and Rondout Creeks are almost ideal for a public supply in consequence of their softness and purity and their comparative freedom from pollution due to drainage of populous areas. (*The Nation*, 5 Nov. 1914, 557)

The goal of not adding filtration to New York's water system has been a driving force in its policy toward its neighbors in the system's watersheds to this day. Even before the dam had been completed,

> surveys and studies were continued on the sewerage systems proposed for the Villages of Tannersville, Hunter, Windham, Prattsville, and Grand Gorge in order to protect from pollution the City's sources of water supply in the Schoharie watershed. (BWS, 1926, 79)

The Board of Water Supply targeted the larger settlements, each of under a thousand residents, for sewer systems. Tannersville, for instance, was a small village on Gooseberry Creek. As one of the larger tributaries to the Schoharie, the city proposed to build for the village a sewer system that would cleanse water before it was released into the creek. Had the water not been treated, it would pollute the reservoir and potentially the entire system. The city provided the funds and the engineers, while the village and adjacent town of Hunter were required to negotiate the sale of the required properties and the right-of-way that were required for its construction. For the most part, local officials were willing to help the city in this matter as their communities were benefiting from the new sewer systems. This same process was repeated in the other four communities as well.

In 1953, in accordance with the New York State Sanitary Code, the city adopted a series of regulations governing activities in the watershed areas. For instance, farm runoff was not supposed to reach a stream that fed into the watershed. Certain types of buildings, agricultural, industrial, even residential, could not be located too close to a feeder stream. There could be no swimming or wading in city-owned reservoirs and even some streams. In short, a large portion of the watershed was unavailable for use by local residents. From the point of view of New York City, the regulations made considerable sense: with nearly 8 million people, the sanitary condition of the water supply was of utmost importance. As one former city employee commented in 2002:

> Yeah it was a pain in the ass for local residents. They couldn't, they still can't, go swimming in the reservoirs. Ya got this beautiful lake here and you can't swim in it, sometimes you can't even walk around it. But ya gotta think: it's inconveniencing a few people up here, but their happiness isn't as important as the 7 million people downstate. I know a lot of people would be pissed to hear me say it, but it's true.

But for many local residents it was a simple matter of being told what to do by a government they had no say in electing. As one lifelong resident of a community near the Pepactin Reservoir commented in 2002:

> It's not taxation without representation exactly, but it's somethin' just as bad. The city comes in here, steals the land, and then tells us we can't use the lakes they created. You go up to Downsville, and there's this beautiful lake that you can't even

really walk around. Ya gotta ask the city for permission to do anything like build a building, and look, I didn't vote for Giuliani—I think he's a creep. But the city has these rules, and we gotta live by them even though we have no say in them.

Such sentiments were not new at the time of these interviews but rather had been growing for generations, as the initial announcement of the regulations in 1953 "aroused considerable consternation among householders" (Quoted in Galusha, 1999, 255). As a Gilboa area resident stated in 2003:

> It's not just that they killed the town. They regulated the hell out of this place, and you can't even enjoy the reservoir. I've been to places like Boston and they turn their reservoirs into parks, you know, like the Chestnut Hill Reservoir. My father used to say that if you get caught over there they might shoot you. I don't know if that's true, but a lot of people here were told by their parents to stay away and, let's face it, you can't expect that kind of abuse from the city to not get people here riled up.

A fact of life, but one that elicited numerous expressions of ill will toward the metropolis and its people when watershed residents were asked about the reservoirs[1].

Over the years, New York had become rather lax about the enforcement of such regulations. As one resident pointed out:

> They came down hard at first, but by the time I was in my twenties, that's the sixties there, the inspectors weren't around all that much and as long as you didn't build a shithouse next to the creek nobody'd say anything. People around here talk like the city was this tyrant, but it was more a matter of how the laws were enforced. You weren't supposed to swim, but the kids did it and the locals knew and the city didn't make a real hard effort to find them.

As the oil shocks of the 1970s helped create the worst fiscal crisis in New York City history the enforcement personnel in the watershed was spread thin. As one resident, a teenager during the 1970s and early 1980s, related:

> You'd go to a farm, and I don't think anyone paid attention to where the runoff went. I got caught a couple of times down on shore just hanging out with some friends and the guy didn't seem to care. "Just don't piss in it," he'd say. You know, the water laws were kind of like the drinking laws: you knew you were doing something wrong, that you might get caught, but everybody does it so you don't really care. They're only gonna prosecute if you spike the water with acid (LSD) or something. Actually, the CIA did that and they didn't get jailed.

---

1. It should be noted that regulations vary by reservoir. Some do allow walking near the shore and boat permits are available for people to go fishing. Nevertheless, the reactions are rooted in the perceptions of the regulations, and it seems likely that there is some exaggeration and hyperbole in some of these statements.

And another resident:

> There are these waves. You got the sixties, and everybody in New York is shittin'
> bricks that someone's gonna dump LSD in the drinking water. And then you'd see a
> cop here and there, but let's face it—there are thousands of miles of streams here.
> Then you get the seventies, and there's, like, nobody up here. Ya get the 80s, and
> nothing happened in the 80s because they were still recovering from the 70s. Now,
> you got enforcement here again, but ten years from now. . .I don't know.

There was a change in the 1980s.

In 1986, the United States Environmental Protection Agency issued a series
of new regulations passed as amendments to the Clean Water Act. As a result,
the city's Department of Environmental Protection issued a new set of
regulations for the watershed in September of 1990. Knowing that the
regulations were on their way, rumors again abounded throughout the
watershed, and many people were positive that the city meant to take through
eminent domain even more property and heavily restrict development near
streams. As one Catskill watershed realtor commented in 2002:

> You have to understand that nobody comes up here looking for a little cabin next to
> a cliff, that there's usually some water involved. With these regulations the city's
> got it so we can't build any kind of major industry because of the runoff, and they
> really don't want us to farm because of the runoff, so that city guy looking for a
> hunting cabin is pretty much all we got left. You bar building too close to streams
> and we're all gonna have to move. . .that's probably what they want.

Among the regulations was a rule prohibiting all farm activities, particularly
animal grazing and the use of fertilizers (including manure) within 100 feet of
any watercourse eventually leading to the reservoirs, the storage of highway
road salts by municipalities in sealed buildings, and prior approval for sewage
disposal systems as well as an outright ban on those situated near a stream
feeding into the reservoirs.

Throughout the watershed, there was anger and resistance to the new
regulations. Senator Charles Cook held hearing in Albany on the fate of the
Catskills and encouraged residents, including the powerful Catskill Mountain
Builders and Contractors Association, to fight. In March 1991, the Coalition of
Watershed Towns, composed of 35 municipalities, was formed specifically to
retain legal and scientific assistance in fighting the city. For many residents of
the region, the city's demands for a pure water supply seemed out of kilter with
the treatment of various rivers in urban areas, one Delhi area resident
commenting in 2003, "apparently you can dump poison in an urban river but a
cow can't shit in the creek." Other residents, however, had a different take:

> Urbanization's a problem here. Ya got city people building cabins and vacation homes up in the woods that they may only use twice a year, but it looks like shit and dumps pollution in the water. We should control growth.

Many others correctly perceived the issue as being primarily about finances:

> Look, New York City doesn't care what happens up here. Half the city wants a summer home up here anyway, and they probably don't want this place to develop because that would ruin their views. It's better to keep the rest of us poor so they can have their woods and ski slopes. But more important than that is money—they don't want to build a filtration plant, and that means we can't use the streams. They'll shoot a kid for playing in the creek if it'll save 'em a buck. And they've always been like that.

Indeed.

Financial concerns had plagued the New York City water system from the beginning. The Dutch were unwilling to pay for numerous public projects for fear of the ever-important profit margin for the West India Company. The British procrastinated. The Americans privatized the water system with results that stain the history of both the city and Chase Manhattan, the modern incarnation of the Manhattan Company. It was finances that convinced the city of the need to build a larger Schoharie Reservoir at Gilboa due to unfavorable conditions on the Rondout, thus condemning the village. It was specifically financial concerns that barred the city from taking and filtering water from the Hudson. And as the Gilboa Dam was completed, the wrangling over finances became more severe.

There were claims against the city for losses far from Gilboa itself. For instance, the Cohoes Power and Light Corporation, based in an industrial suburb of Albany at the confluence of the Hudson and Mohawk Rivers, sued the city for $1.5 million. The company claimed that the Gilboa Dam reduced the flow of water on the Schoharie Creek, which as a major tributary of the Mohawk River affected that river and thus the power generation capabilities of the company. A state commission later estimated that the flow of the river was perhaps six percent less than before the construction of the dam, and added that "experience in other counties has shown pretty clearly that New York City has richly paid and frequently overpaid, for every bit of damage, direct or indirect, resulting from its work" (Quoted in Galusha, 1999, 235). Awards in Gilboa were typically far lower than the claims. As Galusha (1999) noted:

> Property damage awards ranged from $10 to more than $12,000. The First Dutch (Reformed) Church got half of what it wanted—$6,200. The Gilboa School District was awarded $1,900, the Gilboa Hose Company $1,850. A sampling of business damages awarded by the Schoharie Commissioners included $6,000 to Joseph Zeh for reduction in the value of his real estate in Fulton and Blenheim downstream; $2,500 to Josiah Mann for disruptions of his Gilboa dental practice; $10,000 to

Wallace Stryker for the decrease in his Gilboa dairy business and $3,000 to Rose
Telephone Company for a decrease in its business. (235)

In most cases, the original claim was much higher than the award. For New
York, of course, the awards were often considered to be excessive. Indeed, the
city did have to contend with some level of profiteering as residents would often
treat their homes and businesses to a new coat of paint, flowers, or new
outbuildings in order to increase the value. In one case, a beekeeper who lived
on Shandaken Mountain claimed that blasting for the tunnel below resulted in
the loss of several hives, forcing the city's attorney "to study literature on bee
culture in order to question eight apiarists who were witnesses in the case"
(236). In some cases in Gilboa as well as in the Ashokan Reservoir watershed,
the legal battles continued for decades. This, of course, shaded perceptions of
the city in the eyes of local residents. Similar battles began and continued as the
Delaware system was constructed at mid-century, the Commission of Appraisal
not finishing its work until October of 1993!

Gilboa was also at the center of a dispute over taxes. Throughout the
nineteenth century, the city paid taxes on its properties in various watershed
communities based on the value of the property when it was "unimproved." In
1905, Westchester County won in court the right to tax the city on the
improvements made on the property, such as dams and aqueducts, which had
previously been exempted. The case, when upheld by the state Appellate
Division, was a windfall for local communities in which the facilities were
located. New York City was, of course, distressed by the turn of events and
again attempted to use the state legislature as a tool for subduing what it
considered to be "exorbitant valuations" on its water system. In both 1913 and
1927 the city attempted to have a law passed that would exempt its water system
from taxation, but both times it was blocked by upstate legislators. The state had
effectively blocked an overextension of city power. During this time, however,
Gilboa Dam was designed and built.

Empowered by the battles in Westchester County, the town of Gilboa raised
the assessment of city properties each year between 1925 and 1927 to account
for new levels of property "improvement." The Board of Water Supply
characteristically reported in 1926:

> The assessments of the City property in the Towns of Conesville, Prattsville,
> Roxbury, Lexington, Shandaken and Wawarsing were held to last years values. The
> assessors of the Town of Gilboa, in which the partly completed Gilboa dam is
> located, increased the city's assessment by adding $3,666,000.00 to the 1924
> assessment of $117,279.00. . .the increased assessment was protested on Grievance
> Day (BWS, 1926, 15)

By 1927, the assessment had been raised to $5,101,000 for which the town
expected to be paid taxes of over $96,000; the city refused to pay, as it had done

in response to the $55,000 tax bill in 1925 and the $80,000 bill for 1926. Instead, the city appealed the assessments in state court. The city's position was clear and unchanged as stated in the 1927 Annual Report:

> Where the City of New York formerly paid about one-sixth of the taxes of the Town of Gilboa and less than one percent of Schoharie County's taxes, it would be compelled to pay about five-sixths of the town's expenses and 21 percent of those of the county if the assessment is upheld. The City refused to pay the taxes, whereupon the County Treasurer advertised its lands and the Gilboa Dam for sale, but a court order was obtained which served to stay the sale pending the determination of the proceedings before the referee. (BWS, 1927, 14)

Later that year, a court-appointed referee agreed that the city had been over-assessed by over half but that the city should nevertheless be taxed on its improvements. Other watershed towns followed suit, and the Ashokan Reservoir had been successfully placed on the auction block in 1931. As the Delaware System was constructed, similar battles continued and by:

> 1997, the City of New York paid a total of $54,999,757 in taxes to municipalities in nine counties. It's buildings, dams, and 84,769 acres of watershed lands were assessed for $333,219,036. (Galusha, 1999, 243)

The additional cost of a new filtration plant at an estimated cost of over $8 billion in 1990 was thus not one the city wished to expend.

Mobilization against new restrictions in the watershed continued throughout the early 1990s as New York City negotiated with the Environmental Protection Agency for a plan that could save the city the expense of building a filtration plant. Throughout 1992 and 1993, protests flared at city-run hearings. As Galusha (1999) related:

> One of them, in Walton in September 1993, drew 700 people and elicited six hours of mostly negative comments and testimony. Protestors carried signs reading, "Free the Watershed" and "Remember Arena," a reference to one of the many communities submerged beneath city reservoirs. (257)

People were angry not only at the city but any group perceived as siding with urban interests. Various taxpayer groups, opposed to a the expense of a filtration system, and environmental groups who found the environment friendly proposals gratifying regardless of their intentions were held in particular ire. As one Stamford resident commented in 2003:

> Ya had these fucking environmentalists, they act like they care about the
> environment, but they're just trying to make the city's actions seem somehow less
> reprehensible. . .You know, these liberals, they care about you if you're black and
> oppressed, or if you're an owl, but us fuckin' rednecks are just trash and we deserve

to get rolled over. So they side with the city and call it environmentalism. You think these people care about these things away from their friends. . .You think they have any black friends that aren't rich too?

Late in 1991, a coalition of area farmers agreed with the city to create a system of "Whole Farm Planning" meant to protect the watershed and the farms themselves. This was partly due to the opinion of the city that farming and open space was preferable to new urbanized development, and as such the city was willing to relax some of its regulations in regard to agriculture. The program consisted of a ten step planning process:

1. Inventory of farm's current land, livestock, equipment, and management
2. Setting of long-term management goals and objectives
3. Inventory of pollution problems
4. Prioritization of problems
5. Development and evaluation of conservation and management alternatives
6. Setting of goals for BMP implementation
7. Development of implementation plan
8. Implementation
9. Annual progress review
10. Evaluation and update of plan

A similar agreement for communities might have been reached in 1994 had it not been discovered that the city had agreed to more land acquisition as part of a deal with the Environmental Protection Agency that it acquire more land in order to not build a new filtration system.

It took another two years of negotiations, but in 1996 a deal had finally been reached. The city, the state, even many local residents considered it a step in the right direction. An Environmental Protection Agency press release summarized:

The City will finalize its regulations for watershed land uses, acquire sensitive lands to protect key reservoirs and waterways, conduct more extensive water quality testing in the watershed, and support upstate/downstate partnership programs (including major investments in wastewater treatment facility upgrades, a fund for compatible economic development in the watershed, and a regional watershed partnership council). New York State will adopt the City's watershed regulations and land acquisition permits consistent with implementation of the overall agreement and establish a new Watershed Inspector General's Office to ensure that the City's regulations are implemented to protect public health. EPA will continue to oversee New York City's filtration waiver and the City and State's action to implement the agreement. Finally, watershed residents can develop property to the extent the regulations allow, or sell it to the City if they choose. In addition, upstate community representatives will participate in the regional watershed partnership council, which will include representatives of the State, City, and downstate consumers. (EPA, Dec. 1996)

It was a historic agreement. When asked if it would work, a Schoharie County resident simply commented, "we'll see."

An Unusual Power

Amid the decades of debate and mistrust throughout the watershed, Gilboa experienced yet another incursion into its community. By 1968 the town of Gilboa was sparsely settled and many of the residents who had lived through the destruction of the village were dead. There were some, of course, but there were a far greater number of children and grandchildren who had only heard stories about the village, looked at old photographs and wondered about the lives lost in that little town. And now there was a new threat.

The Power Authority of the State of New York (PASNY) had plans for an intriguing electrical power plant. Electricity is subject to wide swings in demand. At certain times of the day, on weekends, and at night, demand is relatively low. During the workday, however, electricity demand increases sharply. During these "peak" demand times, energy consumption is high and electricity prices are as well. The proposed power plant would take advantage of these swings in electricity demand by "storing" power during periods of low usage and producing electricity during peak periods. As explained on the power-plant's website:

> Each of the reservoirs—one atop Brown Mountain, the other at its foot—holds five billion gallons of water. When we're generating power, the water cascades down a concrete shaft that's five times taller than Niagara Falls. When we're storing water—usually at night or over the weekend—we reverse the process and pump the water back up the shaft for storage. The system allows us, literally, to "go with the flow"—to take advantage of the daily highs and lows in statewide electricity demand. In other words, we can generate power when we need it—generally in the late afternoon or early evening—and store the water that fuels the power when we don't need it. The electricity Blenheim-Gilboa uses to return water to its upper reservoir is inexpensive surplus power made available during low-demand periods. The cost of this power is cheaper than the electricity our project replaces the following day during peak-demand periods. (PASNY, 2003)

But it needed to be built first.

PASNY was apparently somewhat oblivious to the concerns of some in the local community, the Chair at the time justifying the project in the following terms:

> The need for electricity is doubling every ten years, that what happened in the city of New York is that they just plain do not have enough generating capacity. (Quoted in Alleyne, 1980)

The event to which he referred was a major blackout, but the expectation that the residents of Gilboa would have strong sympathies with the metropolis was rather misguided. Local residents were concerned with the potential loss of farmland and tax revenue for the townships and the school districts involved. There were also concerns that stream flow, already weakened by the original Gilboa dam, would decrease even more. By the 1970s, this had an impact primarily on irrigation and recreational uses of the creek. But perhaps the most sore point was the "continued exploitation of Schoharie County for New York City residents" (5).

In a prequel to the mobilizations of the 1990s, the Valley Emergency Citizens' Association (VECA) was formed. They agitated and argued that the agricultural character of the region should be preserved and that New York City should be more self-sufficient. PASNY countered that:

> They need the power plant that we hope to build here in New York City. . .I am aware of the emotion of some of the individuals in this area that has been expressed of their feelings that Schoharie County resources are being tapped for the sole benefit of New York City. . .remember people lying in hospitals. . .people who are abandoned in elevators or subways. . .In the city of New York. . .they just plain do not have enough generating capacity. (Quoted in Alleyne, 1980, 5)

In response, a Gilboa area resident commented upon hearing that quote in 2003:

> Think about the fact that we don't have a town, that the city had broken promises to us before, and they (the people at the time) had every reason to expect that they were getting' screwed again. What about the thousands of lives that New York City has ruined up here? Are these people worth anything?

Another area resident who lived in the area at the time commented:

> I said it then, I still think it today. New York's got too many people. You can't live within your means, it's like anything else, you gotta be cut off. The city didn't have enough water, they needed to be cut off and the people needed to move somewhere else. . .I'm sure those Gilboa merchants back then would have welcomed some new customers back then. It's like those cities out west, Las Vegas and L.A., they ain't got the water then they shouldn't be allowed to grow. As far as the new dams go, if New York couldn't generate enough power on its own then maybe they ought to move up here.

In New York City, one might surmise that there were very few people who shared such an opinion.

The Blenheim-Gilboa Power Project, consisting of two actual projects, was completed over the objections of VECA. A local resident commented in 2003:

> People bitched about Blenheim-Gilboa, and they bitched about the new regulations a few years ago (during the 1990s), but there was only a small number of them. Most

people either didn't care or just didn't care enough to bitch about it. I think that's why the city was able to build the dam to begin with. It's not that people didn't care, but people have got their own lives, and not enough of them had the time or energy to bitch and become one of "those people". . .You take the opposition to the (Blenheim-Gilboa) power project or the new regs, and you got people from all over the Catskills. If it takes that huge area to build that kind of opposition, why would you think a little place like Gilboa had a chance?

Why indeed.

11

Making Trouble

She stopped me at a store in a village near Gilboa, commenting about my class discussion earlier at the high school and asking about the book. She commented about the tragedy suffered by the village, but showed pride, even delight, in the community's final act of defiance. She was certainly confident in her assertions:

> They didn't want the city to come in and make money off burnin' the village down. They were gonna burn it down and have a Hollywood movie picture made of it. So they (the villagers) got pissed and burned it down themselves. They weren't gonna get rolled over.

As discussed in chapter 9, of course, is the fact that a definitive cause of the fire was never truly discovered or, for that matter, sought. What was reasonably certain, however, is that the story of the townspeople rising up against their oppressors was grounded in a particular mythology that has developed since the building of the dam..

The Power of Myth

Some in the local area have never heard the story or responded with a dull, "oh yeah, I think someone told me that once." Others, however, can hardly contain their glee at the mythological episode, as this adult woman commented:

> They started this fire, burning down their own town. I mean, the city was gonna do it anyway, and they didn't want the city to make any money off it. So they got together—can you see it? Hundreds of people setting fire to the place. Sticking it to New York City for killing their town.

A high school student similarly commented:

> I don't know if it's true or not. I mean, I don't study history or nothing, but the city freakin' deserved it. They deserve it now, but I guess the town's gone now. I mean,

the city came in and flooded the place so they could have water. Why didn't they go somewhere else? Why didn't they pick on another town? They thought they could just kill anyplace they want. I hope they (the villagers) did burn the place down—I think they should've burned Manhattan.

Even three generations later, there is some latent resentment of the city due to the destruction of the village and to subsequent injustices as well.

Resentment is not universal, however. For some, the dam and other past injustices are historical relics that should be treated as such:

Some people just seem to hate. They hate the city for building the dam, for making you get a permit to do anything. I think some of them just hate the city on principle. But you know, you gotta let it go. The dam's here, and it's got a beautiful lake behind it. The town was nice too, but now we have the lake.

For others, the dam was a necessary evil, as one student commented:

Yeah, the dam sucks. We used to have a town, and now we don't have it anymore. But the city needs the water. I mean, you can't have the city without water. If they hadn't built the dam here, maybe the city would've stopped growing and then where'd we be.

For many in the community, the dam is simply a fact of life.

The mythology of the dam, however, is informed by a combination of resentment for the fate of Gilboa and of awe for the engineering marvel in their midst. In a classroom in 2003, the following exchange occurred:

Student 1: There's cracks in the dam again.
Student 2: Yeah, one of these days it's just gonna bust, and that new building the city's building just below it will be destroyed.
Student 1: They have to fix the cracks every few years because they buried the town in it.

The linkage of cracks in the dam to the destruction of the town through some supernatural force is consistent with other local myths. For instance, several students in one class insisted upon the existence of ghosts in the school because the building was built on an old cemetery. It is claimed that the old headstones were moved but the bodies left behind, and as a result the school is haunted *ala* the film *Poltergeist*. However, Board of Water Supply Reports, early topographic maps, and photography do not show a cemetery in the vicinity of the current school, thus undermining the notion that the school is haunted by spirits angry at being displaced from their former final resting places. Indeed, the city would not have moved a cemetery in the vicinity as it was well above the water line of the reservoir. Other myths include a multitude of ghosts apparently ringing the reservoir, one spirit who likes to cross the road and disappear when an approaching car hits the breaks, and an unfortunate man and his donkey who fell into the concrete in the middle of the masonry portion of the dam. He and his donkey are reputedly still buried in the concrete. There is no mention of such an incident in city records. Of course, in each case, similar myths exist across the country. A ghost avenging a dishonored burial ground is a common theme in American folklore, as are ghosts who cross in front of cars and then disappear. Numerous building projects are claimed to have the remains of unfortunate victims buried in their concrete, from reputed mobsters in Albany's Empire State Plaza to labor leader Jimmy Hoffa embedded in New Jersey's Meadowlands Sports Complex. Like grey-green aliens and the occasional headless horseman, such tales are embedded in American culture.

One curious source of myth or, at the least, historical distortion, is the size of the former village and its disinherited future. Asking current area residents, both in the community at large and in the local school, provides a variety of answers:

- At least as big as Oneonta at the time: Oneonta, a small city of about 13,000 in the city and surrounding suburbs in 1920.

- It was bigger than Cobleskill: Cobleskill, the largest locality in Schoharie County, had about 3,800 residents in 1920.

- The biggest town in Schoharie County: That was Cobleskill, although Gilboa was the largest community in southern Schoharie County.

- 5,000 people: No estimate of the village's population at the time of the community's condemnation exceeds 400 residents, and the township as a whole included only 1541 residents in 1920. The drop in population for the town between 1920 and 1930 of 563 residents to 978 seemingly confirms these estimates when the effect of condemnation on surrounding farms and ordinary population decline is considered.

- About the size of Middleburgh: Middleburgh's population in 1920 was 2,109 in the township, a substantial number of which lived in the village.

Nearly everybody asked seriously overestimated the village's population at the time of the condemnations.

There are three major functions associated with the overestimation of the community's size. The first is that the dominant American culture stresses the importance of larger communities over small, and that by overestimating Gilboa's population the village appears more impressive. As one area resident commented in 2003:

I like to go into Albany. It's, like, civilization. . .It's got lights, and real roads, and you don't have to drive 20 minutes to buy a soda. This place—Gilboa, Prattsville, Grand Gorge—it's not real. They're too small to really be anything.

To varying degrees, this was a common sentiment, especially among younger residents.

The second function is that overestimating the village's population, and thus perceived importance, heightens both the sense of drama around the event and the collective guilt due New York City. As an older man opined:

> Ya gotta think that New York City really killed the place. They came in and displaced thousands of people from their homes, and that's a sin that the whole city shares. Every millionaire down there, every poor (black resident), everybody—they owe us. They're drinking water they got by ruining thousands of lives, and that's just here. Think about how many lives were destroyed so they could have water.

Another woman commented, "We're one of those stories about people losing everything when the government comes to town."

The third major function is that overestimating the village's population at the time aids in displacing responsibility for the state of the region today. As one resident stated:

> Think about what the place coulda been. It was as big as Cobleskill and still growing when the city destroyed it. We could've had factories and stores, and people today wouldn't have to drive to Oneonta (45 miles) or Albany (60 miles) for work. There'd be a lot more money here. We wouldn't be so poor.

Another resident commented:

> This place was booming. We'd have a lot more here today if they hadn't built the dam—maybe you could get a job around here. But the city killed all that. Now everybody drives somewhere else—and, I mean, really long distances sometimes—just to find a job. One person works all the way in Utica! That's over an hour and a half. But if you don't, you live in poverty. . .see a lot of that around here, too.

Rather than seeing the dearth of opportunity in the area as a function of combined and uneven development, area residents have a ready scapegoat in New York City and the myth of Gilboa's past size. As one woman summarized nicely:

> A lot of people blame the city for the poverty around here. Other people blame them (the poor) for not trying to get real jobs. I don't think it's either. . .If you want a good job around here you're gonna have to drive to it, and not everybody can do that. They've got kids, or the car's falling apart, or they're just too old. But it's not the city's fault either: we're just too far from anywhere you can get a good job, and I don't think saving the village would've made us any closer.

And then she asked me, "Do you think Gilboa would have been what people say it would be?"

Table 11.1: Population Trends in Gilboa Area Townships, 1860-2000

Town	1860	1880	1900	1920	1940	1960	1980	2000
Gilboa	**2541**	**2040**	**1448**	**1541**	**1061**	**782**	**1078**	**1215**
Blenheim	1367	1191	768	516	415	345	292	330
Conesville	1478	1127	793	652	673	593	681	726
Fulton	2944	2683	1998	1227	1010	1008	1394	1495
Jefferson	1716	1636	1409	1065	845	800	1108	1285
Roxbury	2558	2344	2134	2258	2277	2238	2291	2509
Stamford	1661	1638	1997	2104	1993	2103	2038	1943

SOURCE: U. S. Census of Population, 2000; Shupe et al., 1987

What If?

Many area residents have commented about the missed opportunities that resulted from the building of the Schoharie Reservoir. The truth has been nicely summarized by several residents as, "nobody can know." Had the dam not been built at Gilboa, any number of possibilities could have dramatically altered the community's course over the ensuing decades. Such transformative events have repeatedly happened in many other communities. For instance, the current city of Oneonta was a small village prior to the arrival of the railroad in the 1870s. Similarly, Philadelphia was a spot on the Delaware River, without any obvious reason to become a great city, before a developer named William Penn designed a city plan in the seventeenth century. San Francisco was transformed from a frontier outpost to an important city as a result of the Gold Rush. Although such comparisons of Gilboa to Oneonta, Philadelphia, or San Francisco appear unrealistic, each of these very different places has experienced some moment of transformation that resulted in growth and tremendous social change. Certainly, the possibility of a similar transformative event—a new railroad, the advent of some new product, perhaps—could have transformed Gilboa from the village it was into a somewhat larger small town. But beyond a seemingly random event bringing prosperity to the town, there is a path that Gilboa is more likely to have taken. It is the path shared by its neighbors and structured by its geographic and social position vis-à-vis New York City. It is a path of probability, not of spectacular good fortune. Despite the fact that the community's fate was ultimately molded by spectacular (but not random) bad fortune, probability remains the best measure of what would likely have happened had the dam not been built. It is helpful to examine Gilboa in the context of surrounding townships, as shown in table 11.1.

As shown in table 11.1, by 1920 the population of the town of Gilboa had already been declining steadily since the mid-nineteenth century. Part of the reason for this decline is that after 1850 rural families began have fewer children, but this only explains part of the decline. Rural to urban migration, even from farms to small villages, was already having an impact as well. Of the above townships, the most drastic declines occurred in the townships without significant villages and their attendant economies of retail and small-scale urban production (e.g., blacksmiths). Blenheim, for instance, lost 62.3 percent of its population between 1860 and 1920, a trend that continued until the late twentieth century. Similarly, Fulton lost 58.3 percent of its population during the same time period and continued to lose residents until the 1980s. In contrast, Stamford showed growth of 27.7 percent between 1860 and 1920 owing to a dynamic urban center, and the township has shown relative population stability since 1920.

Gilboa, in comparison, lost 39.4 percent of its population between 1860 and 1920, reflecting the lower birthrate and some limited opportunities in the village, but not to the same degree as nearby Stamford and certainly not in comparison to the cities. Given that the overall pattern for rural townships in the area has historically been population decline, and that larger communities even as early as 1920 had an advantage in attracting population and economic opportunities to bring more people, it is unlikely that Gilboa would have grown much had the dam not been built. There may have been some increased concentration of population and economic activity in the village over the next generation, perhaps bringing the village's population up to five to six hundred, but perhaps not. What is certain is that without a major (and positive) transformative event Gilboa would most likely today resemble its upstream neighbor Prattsville (which narrowly escaped the dam itself), which itself has substantially less than one thousand residents.

Perceiving the Dam

Three generations after the building of the reservoir, students at Gilboa-Conesville Central School continue to have mixed, even contradictory, feelings about the dam, as shown by a survey conducted in 2003. There are advantages to surveying high school juniors and seniors. The school is an ideal place to find a cross-section of area residents. The students themselves are a reflection of the opinions expressed (if any) in their home environments and in the educational system. In addition, the school is directly across the road from the reservoir, making it impossible to miss. Thus, area students are confronted with the reality of the dam almost every day. There are some disadvantages as well. Aged only in the late teens, some students know relatively little about the reservoir, and some simply do not take it seriously. Nevertheless, the opinions of area teens are telling of wider attitudes found throughout the area. The results of four questions asking specifically about the reservoir are shown in table 11.2.

Table 11.2: Opinions of the Dam among 11th & 12th Graders at the High School, 2003

Statement	N	Agree (%)	Disagree (%)
Gilboa Dam was a good idea	38	21 (55.3)	17 (44.7)
Gilboa Dam helped the local area	38	14 (35.9)	24 (63.2)
Gilboa Dam should not have been built	38	18 (47.4)	20 (52.6)
Gilboa residents should have resisted more	37	26 (70.3)	11 (29.7)

Survey conducted during Social Studies classes April 29,2003 for all juniors and seniors in attendance that day; the students were presented the findings one week later and asked to comment.

Three generations after the City of New York arrived in the Schoharie Valley, condemned all the property from downtown Gilboa south over five miles, destroyed buildings, starting with churches and the local school, and flooded the site under 150 feet of water, 55 percent of the students surveyed considered it a "good idea." In focus groups during which the survey results were revealed, students explained why:

- Well, I mean, it was good for later generations. We've got a beautiful lake here now, and they didn't have that in old Gilboa.

- It preserved the landscape. The village might have grown, but with the reservoir it's keeping it from getting all built up here.

- I think it's good for us. I mean, it's not good for the people who lived here then, but now its okay.

What the comments reveal is a desire for epistemological stability. Today's youth have grown up in the environment as it is now, and under the circumstance it is not surprising that over half of them would indicate a preference for the Gilboa that they themselves know rather than the one that was destroyed. Nevertheless, almost half of those surveyed disagreed with the statement, preferring the unknown to what they did know. This, too, was marked by a desire for epistemological stability as many of these students referenced the myth of a big Gilboa in focus groups:

- Yes, I disagree…Look at what they (New York City) destroyed. They forced a lot of people, thousands of people, to lose their homes. That's wrong.

- I don't think that people in Gilboa should've suffered so New York could have water. We'd all be better off if the city hadn't come.

In a sense, the statistics thus hide a similar desire on the part of the individual students. Not surprisingly, a similar proportion believed that the dam should never have been built when compared to those who agreed that it should have been.

In contrast, almost two-thirds (63%) of students believed that the dam did not help the local area. While this appears to contradict the previous question, focus groups revealed the motivations behind their answers. One student, who agreed that the dam was a good idea but disagreed that it had helped the local area, commented:

> It was a good idea for the city. They needed the water, and they needed to get it from somewhere. They got it from here. . .Do I think they should've gotten it elsewhere? Yeah; but I live here. If they got by burning down Tannersville, maybe, I probably wouldn't care but there'd be kids there who do.

The student had internalized an ethical standard that serves urban interests: urban interests are more important because they affect more people. Another student echoed this sentiment:

> New York's much more important than Gilboa. They needed the water and we had to move. It's as simple as that.

Nevertheless, most students believed differently:

> New York thinks they can just come in here and run our lives because we're not New Yorkers. They destroyed the town, and now we don't have a town anymore. And they're still doing it. . .They shut down a car wash because of septic problems . . . Why don't they pay to fix the problems? Because they don't have to—we don't matter.

And another:

> They're (New York City) stupid. Ya got the lake and ya can't swim in it or take out a boat or nothin' without a permit, and ya need a permit to do just about anything. You know up in Prattsville, the bridge, if you swim on one side of it you're fine but on the other you can get a ticket. That's right—you can get a ticket for swimming. But only on one side of the bridge...I mean, you can swim upstream of it (the reservoir), the water all flows into it anyway.

Local residents, despite their opinions of the reservoir itself, are quite aware of who benefits.

Mixed reactions toward New York City are accompanied by the desire that Gilboa residents of the time had shown stronger resistance than they had. Seventy percent of the students surveyed agreed that residents "should have resisted more," and classroom discussion reflected this opinion. One student summed up the feelings of her classmates quite well:

It's just that nobody wants to be a loser. The city came in and ruined the place they (the residents) didn't do anything about it. I know there were lawsuits and some people say that they burned the town down, but they didn't do anything when they could have made a difference. What's the point of burning your town down after it's already condemned? Why didn't they do something sooner?

They are good questions, in particular since the population of the region has revolted against outside oppression in the past: during the Anti-Rent Wars of the 1840s, against the Blenheim-Gilboa Power Project, and during the Watershed Movement during the 1990s.

Resistance

What leads a population to either compliance or revolt? Or, more specifically, why is it that residents of southern Schoharie County would revolt during some time periods and not in others? An analysis of events in the Schoharie Valley might be illuminating.

There were four periods that stand out as periods when some form of rebellion was possible: the Anti-Rent Wars of the 1840s; the building of the Schoharie Reservoir between 1916 and 1925; the building of the Blenheim-Gilboa Power Project during the late 1960s and 1970s; and the resistance to new environmental regulations during the 1990s.

As discussed in chapter 3, the Anti-Rent Wars were a regional conflict in which the tenants of the large estates revolted against the rents of the landed gentry. By refusing to pay their quitrents, the tenant farmers of the region not only defied the landlords but the power of the state as well. Several factors allowed this to happen. Politically, the 1840s marked the dawn of the urban system. This had two major effects. As the cities along the Erie Canal corridor grew, New York political elites could increasingly side with their compatriots in central and western New York. This, over time, shifted political power away from the landed elites of the Hudson Valley. Moreover, the engine of growth in the western cities as well as in New York was fueled by the Industrial Revolution, and as such the claims of the Patroons seemed outmoded in comparison.

Economically, the tenants had an obvious incentive to incitement. Living on leased lands, in many cases for two or more generations, the rhetoric of Jacksonian democracy during the 1830s contradicted the reality experienced by tenant farmers who neither owned their lands nor could easily control their own destinies. For many farmers who had over decades built from scratch entire communities, the lure of rebellion and being able to remain in their hometowns outweighed the incentives to move west in search of new lands to buy but with the responsibility to begin a community all over again. Perhaps for an earlier generation, but no longer. But such contradictions between the ideology of the new country and the economic realities were hardly limited to the tenant estates of the 1840s, and as such the economic incentive alone was not enough to lead to the Anti-Rent Wars.

The generations following the American Revolution were characterized by attempts to define its significance. By the 1830s, there had developed an ideology that equated freedom and opportunity as access to property (Zinn, 2003). Once the privilege of the upper class, the ownership of property came to symbolize independence and self-sufficiency, thus driving American policy toward the native population and inspiring the ideals of "manifest destiny." In essence, the landed gentry were themselves becoming increasingly defined as relics of the European past, the estates themselves as "un-American." The Anti-Rent Wars were therefore not perceived as rebellion against wealth but rather were characterized as fulfillment of the American Revolution. In fact, the basic legal framework of land ownership as summarized by eminent domain—that property is passed down from God through the state to landed gentry and finally to tenants—has not changed significantly. Arguably, only the landed gentry has been dissolved—"landowners" even today must pay their taxes (quit-rents?) or risk losing their property. And as experienced firsthand by Gilboa residents, the state can take property without such cause through the powers of eminent domain.

The environment played a crucial role in the Anti-Rent War as well. The southern Schoharie Valley had no telegraph, telephone, or cellular service during the 1840s as these technologies had not yet been invented. As the local residents had essentially adopted defensive positions in their own communities, they had the "home advantage:" an intimate knowledge of the terrain, the road and trail system, and sympathetic residents. In contrast, the county sheriffs and state posse that were dispatched often had little or no knowledge of the terrain and the sentiments of particular local residents. Lacking a modern communications infrastructure gave the advantage to the local residents while hampering the efforts of the sheriffs responsible for keeping the peace. Such an advantage allowed the local residents enough time that eventually the political system caught up to their demands and reformed the land ownership laws.

The two modern periods of activism—the building of the Blenheim-Gilboa Power facility and the resistance of the 1990s—are similar to one another but very different from the Anti-Rent Wars. The major distinction was that in neither case did local opposition lead to significant episodes of violence.

Politically, both the fight against the Blenheim-Gilboa power project and the resistance to more stringent environmental controls in the watershed resulted in the same basic tactics. Community interest groups were formed to organize resistance through education and legal action. Particularly during the 1990s, area legislators, public officials, and other elites participated in the opposition to the more stringent regulations.

The major difference between the two time periods is substantially related to the economics of the two issues. The Blenheim-Gilboa power project was built in response to the 1968 New York City blackouts. Electricity is like water to a modern city: the city cannot operate without it, meaning that electricity must be gained at all costs. Not surprisingly, the protests against the Blenheim-Gilboa project by and large fell on deaf ears. The city *needed* electricity, and as nice as it would be to have the support of the local population it was only the power of the state that was necessary. Gaining electricity was, for New York, worth the ire of a few thousand people upstate. As so often occurs, economy and polity were intrinsically linked. In contrast, the more stringent environmental regulations were ultimately the realm of the federal government, with which New York City has less persuasion. More importantly, however, is that the economic and environmental interests were not as diametrically opposed as the rhetoric sometimes suggested. New York City would benefit considerably by not building the multi-billion dollar filtration plant, providing a real incentive to bargain with local residents. For their part, local residents needed assistance with implementing the plan as it was clear that some form of restrictions would go into effect. In the end, of course, watershed communities would benefit from the regulations themselves by ensuring a cleaner environment. This is a decidedly different economic incentive for both sides than that found with the power project and hence a very different political outcome.

In cultural terms, both movements rapidly assumed the language of individualism and fear of government power characterized by the ascetic Protestant local culture. But something had changed: the use of violent or even non-violent resistance had come to be defined as disreputable. The following comment by an area resident illustrates this shift:

> Well, the anti-rent wars did not occur in Gilboa, of course. There was some activity in Blenheim Hill and of course a lot of violence in Delaware County, but not here. We didn't have those troubles here.

Of course, aspects of the Battle of Blenheim Hill did involve Gilboa (see chapter 3; see also Christman, 1945; Mayham, 1906). And in the case of both Blenheim Hill and the Delaware County actions, they were in many cases within twenty miles of Gilboa in every direction. In fact, Gilboa was quite in the center of such resistance, but such sentiments today are relatively common. Ultimately, many of the local elites in the Anti-rent Wars, such as clergy, physicians, and lawyers, were fairly independent of the wider state political economy. In contrast, local elites in the 1970s and 1990s typically had strong connections with wider institutions. Even without them, however, the interrelatedness of the local economy with wider systemic concerns hampered the willingness of local leaders to oppose the system itself. Overall, there was an acceptance of the system.

Ultimately, the environment of Gilboa has changed dramatically. By the late twentieth century, forms of electronic communication such as the telephone, fax machine, and later email have allowed for people in distant locales to organize. This was an advantage over those involved in the Anti-Rent wars that had more difficulty. In addition, however, whereas the rebels of the Anti-Rent wars had the advantage of fighting in their own territory, rapid transportation, excellent maps, and spectacular weapons technology make the violence of that era nearly impossible today. As a local man remarked, "if we did today what they did, they'd fuckin' nuke us." Overly dramatic, yes, but not entirely wrong.

The building of the dam itself inspired comparatively little resistance despite the gravity of the situation. There was some legal action, prefiguring the actions later in the twentieth century, but there seems to have been little else. To the degree to which it existed, a striking aspect of the Gilboa Dam project is the degree to which it represents an intermediate form of resistance. The conditions of late modernity that characterize the two later periods of resistance had not yet been achieved, but the rather more primitive conditions of the 1840s had been far surpassed.

As discussed in chapters 7 and 8, the dam was built during a period when the classic urban system was dominant. This meant that Gilboa had few supporters in government as even the most powerful upstate interests identified with New York City's need for new supplies of water. As the project only truly impacted the area immediately surrounding Gilboa, there was little help from those in other communities. In effect, Gilboa was isolated in its fight against urban interests—a sharp contrast to the regional actions of the other three time periods. Within the area itself, the Board of Water Supply was able to divide potential opposition through generous land purchases, employing local labor, and reference to the experience of other places, such as the fruitless resistance of those in the nearby Ashokan Reservoir project.

Similar to the Blenheim-Gilboa power project, New York City needed water and its interests were thus diametrically opposed to Gilboa. This contrasts to the Anti-Rent Wars when there was little compelling interests for the rising urban Capitalist elite either way. There was therefore comparatively little room for negotiation. From an economic perspective, Gilboa residents should have more actively resisted given that their collective economic lives were to be objectively destroyed—although it is doubtful that they could have won. Ultimately, however, New York City had the power (with aid from the state) and the financial resources to divide any opposition. Schoharie Reservoir is thus more similar to Blenheim-Gilboa—there was no room for negotiation as there was with the resistance to the environmental regulations in the 1990s.

The lack of widespread resistance to Schoharie Reservoir is perhaps more readily explained in cultural terms. Ascetic Protestantism had by the early twentieth century transformed itself in perceiving the dam as "God's will" rather than a mere human activity. The appropriate reaction was thus acceptance of His will and to perceive the dam as a signal that He wishes you to restructure your life. Translated into a secular worldview, it would have been inappropriate to "make trouble," as more than one area resident referred to a more spirited resistance. Or as one resident commented, "shit happens. . .you just have to accept it and move on."

Culture had another source of influence. The Ashokan Reservoir was in the late stages of completion as Gilboa learned its fate, and there had been a tradition of failed resistance against other city projects. This knowledge became a part of the local culture—a sort of collective learned helplessness—and many, if not most, of the local residents correctly perceived the fight to save the village as unwinnable. A string of successes on the part of the powerful spawns yet more success, much to the chagrin of those in opposition. Regionally, this knowledge led many to consider the dam as "Gilboa's problem," partly because the dam was in fact Gilboa's problem and partly because successful resistance there would have forced the Board of Water Supply to find another dam site in another area town. As with Maslow's (1968) hierarchy of needs, it appears that successful resistance requires a basic level of personal security.

Gilboa also faced aspects of the environment that placed it at a disadvantage. Geologically, downtown Gilboa, specifically Church hill, was a great place for a dam. Resistance was further hindered in that the technology available in terms of mapping and equipment meant that incursions into the area were easier than during the Anti-rent wars, but the communication technology required for a successful modern resistance had not yet fully compensated.

Defining Success

Defining the success or failure of a resistance movement is far too broad for the context of this work, but some attempt should be made in regard to the movements at hand. Success, of course, is a fluid concept that is ultimately defined by the members of the community. During the Anti-Rent Wars, for instance, success was defined in terms that the local tenant farmers would be given the opportunity to buy the land on which they were living. For residents of Gilboa, the obvious success would have meant saving the village from destruction. During the Blenheim-Gilboa power project, the goal was again to save the condemned lands from the dam—although there was not specifically a village to save. During the 1990s, success for most was the development of a plan that would not put an undue burden on residents for the sake of saving New York City the cost of a filtration plant. By these criteria, the Anti-Rent Wars were an obvious success, and the Watershed Agreement was a less obvious success. In neither success was there unanimous acceptance but rather a desire to minimize further costs associated with conflict. In contrast, the attempts to save Gilboa from the building of the Schoharie Reservoir were an obvious failure, as were attempts to stop the Blenheim-Gilboa power project.

The Anti-Rent Wars present a curious fact: the most radical change was brought about through the use of force. At first glance, it appears that violent resistance was successful. On closer examination, however, it was not the violence per se. Violent resistance (and oppression) is an outgrowth of the decline in some segments of the population of the hegemonic order. This is true for both sides of the conflict as the resistance resorts to violence when it appears that there is little to lose as well as an acknowledgement on the part of the oppressor that they cannot convince the oppressed of their legitimacy. For the tenant farmers of New York, the conditions for violence were suitable for a precipitating event—the death of Stephen van Rensselaer. Combined with the fact that the older landed elite was losing power to the merchant and budding capitalist classes, it is not surprising that the tenants were able to find supporters in high places. Ironically, the success of the Anti-Rent Wars set the stage for the later failures by enabling the farmers to own their land and thus perceive a stake in the maintenance of the system overall. It is thus the last major instance of violence, although not of coercion. The other success—the watershed pact during the 1990s—was due in large part because of federal orders for the city to build a filtration plant if a mutually agreeable solution could not be found. This was not coercion from below as with the violence of the Anti-Rent Wars, but rather coercion from above in the form of the federal government. In both cases, however, coercion arising from conditions allowed Gilboans to resist elite prerogatives as part of a large and powerful group rather than as a solitary community. In contrast, the one time Gilboa attempted solitary resistance was during the Gilboa Dam period with very poor results. Mobilization of local residents was extremely difficult with the net effect that there was little tangible resistance at all to the community's destruction. Such networked resistance, however, is not a guarantee of success: there was some (limited) networking during the resistance to the Blenheim-Gilboa project, and it was nevertheless a failure. The large networks of resistance have two functions: 1) the networks across geographical space make the complaints appear regional (instead of local) and thus more deserving of attention; and 2) a larger pool of participants makes it more likely that high status individuals who command respect from elites are involved.

Political power and economic dominance build on one another dialectically. In the present cases, it was the economic interests of New York City that prevailed. In both cases where the interests of the city and those of local residents were diametrically opposed the locals could not resist effectively. The obvious example is the Schoharie Reservoir itself. New York City needs water for its population and industry, and as such there is no room for negotiation. No change of party and indeed no change in urban elite could have changed the needs of the city and therefore the reservoir was built. This condition is similar to the case of the Blenheim-Gilboa power project: New York City needs electricity—an objective need in a any modern society—and there was little room for negotiation. In such instances, one witnesses the brutal exercise of raw power. In contrast, the centrality of the federal government in the negotiations of the 1990s not only gave local residents bargaining power but in a sense created a common political and economic foe. The local residents and the city elites both identified the federal government as a threat to their economic interests. In the case of the local population, the imposed restrictions on property appeared designed to forever inhibit economic development in the region. In the case of the city, the threat of the costs associated with a filtration plant was also potentially damaging. Thus there was a synergy in the economic interests of the two regions and an impetus for negotiations. In addition, the region of the reservoirs is increasingly a vacationland for metropolitan area residents—much as the lands of Westchester and Putnam Counties were before being swallowed by the expanding rings of suburbs. The proposed restrictions would have affected not only local residents but downstate developers and owners of vacation homes. The Anti-Rent Wars, in contrast, were also successful because of bargaining power on the part of local residents, but in this case came from disruptions to the status quo. A similar movement today could achieve similar results with a concerted campaign of non-violent resistance.

An Ongoing Relationship

Gilboa today looks with pride over its reservoir. It is an irreversible fact of life that both builds pride and masks chagrin. On a sunny day when the water is quite low, residents will sometimes collect at the shore and look at the foundations of their community sunk beneath the waves. For them, New York is not only a distant city in the southeast corner of the state but is a daily presence in their lives.

12

Pastoral Ideals, Rural Realities

The spillway of the brownstone dam flows down from Church Hill, a small parking area with a sign at the east end of the dam in the middle of the woods dedicated to the village sacrificed for New York's seemingly endless growth. Today, New York City remains one of the largest cities in the world with a population of over 8 million residents amid a total metropolitan population of nearly three times that. The sprawl of the city stretches 40 miles, and often more, in any direction, nearly to Ulster County and the reservoirs built to service the city. It would take a subtle change—a high-speed bullet train perhaps—to further bring the suburbs to the countryside. New York has appeared past its peak several times in its history, the most recent time during the 1970s, and it has recovered each time. The metropolitan area today is larger and more powerful than at perhaps any time in its history.

Schoharie Creek is a different place than it was during its settlement. Its water is taken for the Blenheim-Gilboa Power Project, Schoharie Reservoir, and even to make snow for the Hunter Mountain Ski Resort in Tannersville. Unlike its parent river, the Mohawk, which was dammed and converted into the Barge Canal early in the twentieth century, the Schoharie runs free for most of its length. But it is not like its Adirondack Mountain cousins, either, flowing free from beginning to end. A local college student commented in 2003, "The creek's funny; it's in the middle of nowhere, pretty much, but it's got the power project and the reservoir." The Schoharie Valley continues to do what it has done for generations: it works for New York City.

World Trade Center

The October 22, 2001 issue of *Business Week* magazine summarized what was lost in the terrorist attacks against New York's World Trade Center on the previous September 11:

(The attack). . .was the single worst blow New York has ever sustained. In an Oct. 4 report, New York City Comptroller Alan G. Hevesi estimated that the attack caused

$34 billion in property damage. The amount of Class A office space destroyed—about 13 million square feet—was equal to the entire office-space inventory of Atlanta or Miami. The loss of life not only sapped the city's spirit but also destroyed about $11 billion in "human capital," the productive power of those killed (BW, 22 Oct. 2001).

Such figures set New York apart not only from the cities of upstate but from other cities of national importance, as with Atlanta and Miami mentioned above. By the end of the twentieth century, New York had not only joined but in fact dominated the ranks of global cities. It's economy was being transformed from one based on manufacturing to one based heavily on information technologies and services—one of only a handful of national and international cities that could do so (Fainstein, 1993). As Sassen (1994) summarized:

> Today there is a general trend toward high concentration of finance and certain producer services in downtowns of major international financial centers around the world. From Toronto and Sydney to Frankfurt and Zurich, we are seeing growing specialization in financial districts everywhere. . .In the United States, New York leads in banking, securities, manufacturing administration, accounting, and advertising. (61-62)

In essence, New York does what it was founded to do: trade.

The position of New York grew from its original economy based on Wampum and furs. By the turn of the twentieth century, New York worked politically with other upstate cities to ensure its ability to use the state for its own interests, such as the building of the Schoharie Reservoir. Economically, however, the city has always looked upon some or all of the state as its hinterland—its property, even. During the Colonial period, upstate functioned as a producer of furs and other products for trade. As the city grew, it utilized upstate for food production as well. When the Erie Canal opened, the growing cities were themselves part of an "urban hinterland" producing goods for trade through the great city of New York. With each period, the geographic area functioning as New York's hinterland grew, from the immediate area around the city, especially on Manhattan, during the colonial period, to the lower Hudson Valley for food by the mid-nineteenth century. By the end of the nineteenth century, New York depended upon goods made upstate—textiles from Utica, copper and brass from Rome, steel from Buffalo, for example—to bolster its position as a trade center. By the early twentieth century products from as far away as the Great Lakes were funneled through the port of New York and the city's merchants exacted their share of the profits. The trade carried out in New York was never simply about facilitating the movement of goods and services, but rather about the accumulation of capital. The profits were driven into financial markets through banking, insurance, the stock and bond markets, and real estate.

New York's rise to dominance relied on its source of wealth. Ultimately, the value of the products manufactured and traded in the city came from the labor expended on the transformation of the raw material into a finished product. Such is the relationship between rural and urban production: the value of a rural product comes from its transformation into a useable product, i.e. food or iron ore. The value that further is added through urban production is the value of the labor expended to make a useful product, such as a shovel or a basket. But the value added in New York City often came from trade—not a profit based on expended labor but rather on the powered relationship between the producer and the merchant. New York was at the critical junction of land routes throughout the northeastern United States and ocean-going sea traffic. Producers needed the city—or another like it, such as Boston or Philadelphia—in order to bring their products to market. This gave New York merchants a degree of power in the social-financial interaction that enabled them to charge a price in accord with this power. Like the transactions between fur and wampum, the profits come not from expended labor or some objective increase in use value, but rather from the extortionary dynamics of exchange value. One person controls a necessary commodity or service, yielding the individual power to demand a higher price. Profit is borne of individual power.

As New York has expanded its hinterland over greater and greater areas, it has been able to further centralize economic functions into the city. (In fact, into Manhattan; see Harris, 1991). In manufacturing, banking and finance, food processing—an entire range of industries—New York-based corporations were able to utilize the advantages afforded them by the city's economies of scale and buy competitors, both within the city and the region as a whole. The communities in which those companies were headquartered often lost the best jobs (i.e., executive and managerial-professional positions) as they were transferred over time to headquarters in New York. Increasingly, it is these companies that are networked with other global cities, and New York City retains its privileged position of trade. The community left behind might maintain a small regional headquarters or back office employment.

The case of HSBC provides an interesting and typical example. Based today in London and maintaining its American headquarters in New York City as HSBC USA Incorporated, the corporation was originally founded in Hong Kong in 1875 as the Hong Kong and Shanghai Banking Corporation. By the end of the century, it had opened branches in San Francisco and New York. But it is not HSBC that is specifically interesting in this case. Rather, it is HSBC Bank USA, a wholly owned subsidiary of HSBC USA Incorporated.

HSBC Bank USA was actually founded in Buffalo as Marine Trust Company, later to be known as Marine Midland bank. It was meant to service the burgeoning Erie Canal-Great Lakes trade that was booming in the port city. It was one of many banks founded during this time period, including Williamsburgh Savings Institution in what is today Brooklyn, Metropolitan Savings Bank and Citizens Savings Bank in New York City, and Union Trust

Company in Rochester. All are today part of HSBC. Marine Midland grew during the early and mid-twentieth century by expanding its local branches, but particularly by buying other local banks. In 1925, it merged with Buffalo Trust Company; the merger was followed by those with banks in other western New York towns, such as Tonawanda, North Tonawanda, Lockport, Albion, Medina and Niagara Falls. Other urban banks in upstate New York were pursuing similar policies of growth through merger (see Thomas, 2003), and Marine Midland purchased these as well. Some of the mergers, such as that with Syracuse Trust Company in 1951 and First Bank and Trust of Utica in 1954, spread Marine Midland into competing metropolitan areas and transformed it into a major statewide bank (HSBC, 2003). Similar concentration in banking was occurring in New York as well, such as the purchase of Manhattan Saving Bank and Citizens Savings bank by Metropolitan Savings Bank, both in 1942. In 1980, HSBC bought a 51 percent share of Marine Midland. In 1987, Marine Midland became a wholly owned subsidiary of New York-based HSBC USA Incorporated, itself owned by the parent company now headquartered not in Hong Kong or Shanghai, but in London. The consolidation of the local banks transformed their home communities from headquarter cities to mere branches. In some cases, larger cities, such as Syracuse and Utica, maintained regional headquarters, but in time most major administrative functions and the good-paying jobs they fostered were moved primarily to Buffalo and New York. The fact that the American headquarters is in New York means that it is New York City that deals with other global cities, and not Buffalo. Figure 12-1 shows a partial list of such communities in upstate New York.

Table 12.1: Upstate Communities Left Behind in HSBC's Rise

Bank Acquired	Headquarters City
Union Trust Company	Rochester
Elmira Trust Company	Elmira
Manufacturer's National Bank	Troy
Power City Trust Company	Niagara Falls
First Commercial Trust	Tonawanda
Union Trust Company	Jamestown
Worker's Trust Company	Binghamton
1st & 2nd national Bank	Oswego
Syracuse Trust Company	Syracuse
First Bank & Trust	Utica

SOURCE: HSBC, 2003.

Similar trends were occurring in other industries, with the eventual result in many communities that production was moved elsewhere. In textiles, for instance, Utica was home to two of the largest companies in the world by the end of World War I. By 1960, however, nearly all of the textile industry in the

Utica metropolitan area had been merged with non-local, and in many cases New York City, companies and production moved elsewhere (Thomas, 2003). There were similar results in industry after industry, from aerospace to computers.

In agriculture, the increased reliance of rural communities on selling to the urban market resulted first in the decline of subsistence agriculture and later the decline of agriculture for profit. The first collapse occurred in the 1880s as communities heavily dependent on the production of Hops, including Schoharie County, found increasing competition from producers in the west, in particular Washington. During the twentieth century, competition from other states in markets for fruits and vegetables, dairy products, and even maple syrup resulted in increased concentration of agriculture in the hands of fewer but larger farms. Coupled with the mechanization of agriculture, the results for farm laborers were devastating.

In both cases, shifts in the economy were the result of the fact that New York had expanded its sphere of influence—its hinterland, so to speak—far beyond the confines of its home state to encompass large swaths of the world. If Wisconsin cheese costs less, then New York farmers lose. If Nebraska corn costs less, then New York farmers lose. If Guatemalan labor is less, then New York workers lose. If California labor is more skilled in a particular industry, then New York workers lose.

As New York grew, much of the infrastructure that might have been spread throughout the state tended to concentrate in the city instead. Education is a good example. On paper, New York State appears to have an impressive list of major universities. Some of the best in the nation, such as Columbia University, are located in the state. But the development of such institutions has been very uneven: all but eight of the state's major (graduate degree-granting) research universities are located in the New York metropolitan area, two of which are technology rather than general education universities. Of the remaining eight, four are located within ten miles of one another. The Albany metropolitan area, for example, is home to two: the State University of New York at Albany and Rensselaer Polytechnic Institute; Rochester is home to the University of Rochester and Rochester Institute of Technology. Albany and Rochester are home to the only two metropolitan areas in upstate New York to not lose population between 1990 and 2000[1]. Three of the other four—State University of New York at Buffalo, State University of New York at Binghamton, and Syracuse University -- are found in metropolitan areas. Only Cornell University, in Ithaca, is not found in a metropolitan center—and Cornell maintains its medical school in New York City. In short, upstate New York was woefully unprepared for an economy based on information and advanced education, whereas the metropolitan area has developed into a leader of such industries and

---

1. A third metropolitan area, Glens Falls, also exhibited modest growth, but this is more likely due to its proximity to the Albany metropolitan area with which it shares suburbs.

bills itself as "Silicon Alley." Curiously, a number of the technology firms had upstate origins, such as General Electric (Schenectady), IBM (Binghamton), and Unisys (Utica).

. Where did the expansion of New York's hinterland leave upstate New York? As the hinterland expanded and flowed through upstate, workers and small businesses found they were competing against those who could produce more for less cost. Increasingly, even many New York City companies could not be found in the region. There is a Saks Fifth Avenue in Birmingham, Alabama, about the size of Syracuse, but none north of the Tappan Zee Bridge in New York State. There are Tower Records stores across the country and the world, but none in upstate New York. As New York's business elite found new opportunities around the world, investment in their immediate neighbors slowed. Upstate is no longer the hot spot for investment that it once was, and many local residents know it.

Knowing Your Place

Within the complex system of the world political economy is the remains of Gilboa, its population spread throughout the state. In the aftermath of the building of the dam, the remaining local residents still attend school at the Depression-era school built for the community but live, of necessity, elsewhere. In such a rural area, local residents have a keen assessment of the role of Gilboa in the world economy.

In a township once characterized by self-sufficient farmers, it is interesting that in the 2000 census only nine people claimed to be involved in farming, fishing, or forestry occupations (USBC, 2003). The major industry today in Gilboa is Education, Health and Social Services, in which 23 percent of the working population is employed. Transportation and utilities is the next largest employer with 12 percent of the population working in those industries, and 11 percent in retail trade. An additional 10 percent works in construction. Most often, however, local residents do not work in Gilboa, with the average commuting time of 32 minutes spent in a car driving somewhere else. This is not the profile of an economy at the center of global capitalism, but rather the profile of an economy generated by the simple fact of the population's existence. Increasingly, many local residents do not work at all, having moved to the area, primarily from metropolitan New York, to retire. In addition, the local economy is increasingly dominated by tourism.

At first glance, Gilboa appears very similar to national trends. The percentage of residents who graduated high school is only slightly below the national average and well above that for New York City. However, only 13.9 percent of residents held four-year college degrees. This is due in part to the fact that the average age of residents is considerably higher than the national

Table 12.2: Selected Social Characteristics, 2000

	United States	New York CMSA*	New York City	Gilboa
Percent completed High School	80.4	79.4	72.3	78.5
Percent earned Bachelor's Degree	24.4	30.5	27.4	13.9
Percent Divorced	9.7	7.4	7.7	8.0
Percent who are Veterans	12.7	8.6	5.7	18.1
Percent of Women in Labor Force	57.5	55.2	51.9	47.6
Median Age	35.3	35.9	34.2	42.6

* Includes New York City
SOURCE: U. S. Census Bureau, 2003

average, in particular because of the use of Gilboa as a retirement community. Another reason for the lower percentage of residents with bachelor's degrees is that those residents who receive them are also more likely to leave the area upon completion of their education. A survey of high school juniors and seniors (see chapter 11) found that 61 percent intended to earn a bachelor's degree (or higher). As a local adult commented:

> Kids here, they wanna leave. That's why they go to college—get a degree and move somewhere else more exciting. . .But a lot of times it just works out that way. A kid leaves to go to college and they get a job somewhere else. They have to really want to come back to come back.

Indeed, the survey found no correlation between educational goals and the desirability to live in the local area, implying that local children leave town as a result of finding employment elsewhere.

Table 12.3: Selected Economic Characteristics, 2000

	United States	New York CMSA	New York City	Gilboa
Percent in Labor Force	63.9	61.9	57.8	50.6
Percent of Labor Force Unemployed	3.7	4.1	5.5	2.6
Mean Commute Time (in Minutes)	25.5	34.0	40.0	32.1
Median Household Income	41,994	50,795	38,293	35,156
Percent living in Poverty	12.4	12.9	21.2	11.9

SOURCE: U. S. Census Bureau, 2003

The effect of the burgeoning retirement population in the Catskills is evident in Gilboa where only 51 percent of residents are in the labor force (see Table 12.2). Between the retired population and a comparatively less educated workforce, its median household income is lower than the national and state averages, and is more similar to that of New York City itself. There is a sizeable population of working poor, with only 2.6 percent of the workforce unemployed and a lower-than-average poverty rate. Only one percent of the population received public assistance. The population is not the "surplus labor force" found in the inner city, but rather it is living on the margins of the global economy (see Table 12.3).

Table 12.4: Percent Collecting Various Types of Income, 2000

	United States	New York CMSA	New York City	Gilboa
Earnings	80.5	79.7	76.3	69.5
Social Security	25.7	25.2	22.3	42.4
Supplemental Security Income (SSI)	4.4	5.0	7.5	5.1
Public Assistance	3.4	4.5	7.5	1.0
Retirement	16.7	15.6	12.4	31.7

SOURCE: U. S. Census Bureau, 2003

With a high percentage of retirees, Gilboa has a lower than average percentage of households receiving income through earnings and a higher than average percentage gaining income through social security and retirement (see Table 12.4).

Tourism and retirement is evident in the area's housing stock. Over half of the town's 996 housing units are vacant, nearly all as the result of them being for recreational use (see Table 12.5). The area's largest source of tourists is the New York metropolitan area, although there are day-trippers from upstate communities as well. The reliance on tourism is also a major source of the retired population as people buy (or build) vacation properties earlier in life and then move there upon retirement. But while tourism is an effective supplement to a community's economy, providing additional shoppers in local stores, it is not a replacement for an economy rooted in either rural or urban production. It is highly dependent upon economic conditions and fads in other communities, in this case New York, while offering little in actual wealth creation in the local area itself. In many cases local residents are forced to contend with property values that are in accord with those found in the other source community, thus driving local prices up. In many cases, local residents are forced to move elsewhere (Ringholz & Muscolino, 1992). In addition, conflicts can arise between the generally upper-middle to upper class clientele and the poorer local residents (Thomas, 2003).

Table 12.5: Selected Housing Characteristics, 2000

	United States	New York CMSA	New York City	Gilboa
Housing Vacancy Rate	9.0	5.8	5.6	51.8
Percent Housing for Recreational Use	3.1	1.9	0.9	47.5
Mobile Homes as Percent of Housing	7.6	0.5	0.1	15.0
Median Housing Value	119,600	203,100	211,900	85,600
Median Mortgage Payment	1,088	1,679	1,535	802
Median Rent	602	740	705	525

SOURCE: U. S. Census Bureau, 2003

Partly as a result of the reservoir and partly of the tourism economy, many local residents have expressed latent resentment toward the city. For instance, 81 percent of high school students surveyed agreed with the statement, "New York City cares little for local's feelings" (see Chapter 11). When asked, some students indicated the historical precedent of destroying the town in order to build the reservoir, but far more suggested current conflicts. Many students commented about the regulations regarding the watershed:

> The regulations are ridiculous. In Prattsville you can swim in the creek on the upper side of the bridge but not the other. . .That's right, if you swim on one side you're fine but if you swim under the bridge then they (New York City authorities) will give you a ticket.

Another student commented:

> You gotta have a permit if you want to do anything down by the reservoir. I guess sometimes they're worse than others about the tickets. Used to be you could get away with it, but now, you know, after 9-11, they'll chuck you in jail if you get caught. . .You gotta make sure you don't get caught.

Others comment about the tourists:

> They've got major money and they have the nice houses around. You know, lots of us live in shacks and they got these $200,000 homes that they only stay in once in a while. And they're rude: they act all "look at me" and treat us like we're dirt.

The resentment is not simply a matter of historical legacy, but rather of ongoing perceived snubs.

Gilboa residents have had to contend with a bubble in real estate values that are in line with the real estate bubble in the metropolitan area despite the fact that there is little productive wealth (and thus little to drive increased property values) in the local area itself. In addition, many of the newcomers exhibit different (urban) customs and values that some in the local area find irritating. But the attraction of the Gilboa area to metropolitan residents for retirement is readily apparent: the median housing value of $85,600 is less than half that found in the metropolitan area. And median housing values in some suburban communities are higher yet: $460,000 in Garden City, Long Island; 399,000 in North Caldwell, New Jersey; and 283,800 in Mount Kisko, New York (USBC, 2003).

The local economy has thus experienced a similar trend as that found in upstate New York as a whole. Competing farming communities in other parts of the United States and increasingly the world have by and large replaced the productive function that was performed by the area in terms of agricultural output. The avant-garde technologies of the world economy are found elsewhere, and as such Gilboa's population is not utilized for either its ability to grow food (rural productive capacity) or its ability to produce finished goods to be traded in New York (urban production). In fact, the area is today used primarily as a playground for those who wish to escape the city; the locals themselves are increasingly unnecessary for this function.

Local residents comprehend such a position in the global economy but respond to it in differing ways. Some residents view their remoteness as positive:

> Why the hell would you want to live in New York anyway? You got people in your backyard and there's nowhere to walk in the woods. People are rude and don't know each other. There are just too many people there and that's why I live here.

Others do not:

> I wish there was a place where you could buy a soda after 9:00 (PM). You gotta drive all the way to Middleburgh or Stamford. And there's no jobs here—I wish there was more here.

For many residents, their feelings combine some of both sentiments.

Gilboa is highly influenced by the dominant urban culture. Bombarded by media influences from major cities, including television, radio, internet, and other forms of popular culture, the tastes of area residents is dominated by urban interests. When students at the local high school were asked about their favorite activities, many students responded "shopping," normally in the Albany metropolitan area nearly an hour away. In terms of music, 39 percent indicated their favorite music as "hip hop" and an additional 33 percent indicated "rock." Only 18 percent indicated country, although it is worth noting that country music is not indigenous to the northeast but rather a popularization of southern musical styles.

Table 12.6: High School Students Preferences for Future Residence, 2003

Type of Environment in which to Reside in Future	Number who Preferred	Percent
Within 15 miles of home	8	20.5
A different rural area	11	28.2
Small city	2	5.1
Medium size city	9	23.1
Large city	8	20.5
Foreign Country	1	2.6
Total	**39**	**100.0**

Table 12.6 shows students' preference in terms of a place to reside in the future. It is notable that only 21 percent perceived the Gilboa area as a desirable place for their future, but not necessarily an indication that 80 percent will leave the area. In all, nearly half of respondents indicated a desire to live in an area like Gilboa, and it is very likely that the majority of those students will remain in close proximity to the school district after graduation. Equally as interesting is the fact that 46 percent preferred to move to an area very different from the community of their youth, with a roughly equal split between large and medium size cities as preferable.

As a group, respondents rated Gilboa positively as a place to live, with only New York City and Albany scoring higher (4.6 and 4.7, respectively). The major upstate cities besides Albany received an average rating of 3.7, meaning that students had a slightly negative impression of upstate New York cities. Of these, Buffalo and Rochester, both with metropolitan areas of over one million, scored best (4.0 and 3.8 respectively). The smaller upstate cities of Syracuse, Utica, and Binghamton scored worse (3.8, 3.6, and 3.7, respectively). In contrast, both Boston and Washington (4.1 each) were rated slightly above average. This was not entirely due to familiarity or lack thereof as students indicated very good familiarity with both Oneonta and Kingston but rated the two small cities differently (4.3 and 3.8 respectively). Rather, it is an indication that students are aware of the favored cities in the global economy, and upstate New York cities do not fare well. If they cannot find a job in a familiar location, they would prefer to go to the favored global cities. It is based in part on perceived opportunities in these cities, but also on an overall image as portrayed in the media and in day-to-day social interaction. As one student commented:

> You know, you think of Binghamton and you think of a bunch of old factories and closed-up stores. I don't know, it just seems dirty to me—old, gross. Everything has that dingy feel. But you go to Albany and they got new buildings and glass and a good mall. It's just different, you know. People don't talk shit about Albany, but nobody wants to go to Binghamton.

In fact, both cities have suffered deindustrialization, but Albany still holds a more positive image for that student and others like her.

Gilboa and the Bronx

Much can be made of the role of Gilboa and of inner city neighborhoods. Statistically, of course, Gilboa fares better, although there is a skew introduced into area statistics because of former metropolitan area retirees. What is important to understand, however, is the role that these two populations hold in the global economy.

As illustrated by many scholars (e.g., Sassen, 1991, 1994; Wilson, 1987), the population of inner city poor functions as a reserve pool of labor for capitalist enterprises. Living geographically in close proximity to business, they can be easily brought in and out of the labor force depending on the business cycle. If times are good, they can find employment; if not, they may be unemployed. In a capitalist society, such a reserve pool of labor is an important component of urban production. It is not, however, necessarily relevant in rural production.

It may be tempting to compare the population of rural areas to the reserve pool of industrial labor, but it is more accurate to consider the land itself as being in reserve. Rural populations throughout upstate New York have been in decline, but the land is what is in reserve. Rural land can be used as recreational property, but its primary purpose is still as a potential source of raw materials. To the degree to which a workforce is necessary to aid in rural production then there is a reserve pool of labor, but rural production is more heavily dependent upon natural processes of transformation than on labor itself. It is the land that must be safeguarded against encroachment or held in trust in case it is ever necessary for food production.

The population of the northern Catskills can thus not be understood as a reserve pool of labor: they often live too far from major sites of industrial activity to be effective in this regard. Instead, they are overlooked by the global economy as their local economy is dominated by basic functions generated by the simple existence of the population: education, health care, retail sales. To the degree to which the community has something to offer urban consumers wealth can be brought into the area. In Gilboa, this most often is the land itself, not for farming or as a site for manufacturing, but as a place to escape the global economy for a weekend or a lifetime. The local economy thus produces a degree of wealth but not the spectacular holdings characterized by capitalist development. In essence, as food production and manufacturing for New York's daily needs is increasingly handled by other communities in other parts of the world, Gilboa and similar communities have been left to their own economies, generating enough wealth to continue in their role as consumers but essentially left the scraps as arranged by tourism. Indeed, as urban consumers often consider conservation a positive feature of the Catskills by preserving their own escape from the city, tourism is based to some degree on the area's economic marginalization. That some locals perceive environmentalism as a self-serving urban interest group is not surprising, and ultimately points to the need to better understand the problems affecting rural areas as central to the environmentalist agenda.

Gilboa is not, and likely will never be, as independent as it was in the days of the Anti-Rent Wars. Characterized by subsistence farming on leased lands, it is unlikely that anyone in the area would glorify the social arrangements found in those times anyway. But Gilboa is increasingly left to its own devices, to fend for itself, as there is little actual production for the benefit of the global political economy that occurs there. The population no longer benefits from the favored position of being in New York's hinterland as that now includes so much of the world. Like the rest of upstate New York, Gilboa must compete against Honduran farmers and Chinese manufacturers, and given the disparities in wage levels and taxes it is doubtful that the competition will go well.

13 Urban Dependency Revisited

On April 5, 1987, the bridge carrying the New York State Thruway (Interstate 90) over Schoharie Creek collapsed, killing ten people as the vehicles were propelled off the pavement and into the chasm below. The incident was an hour north of Gilboa, where the Schoharie meets the Mohawk River at its full force. It was a tragic reminder of nature's ability to reassert herself over would-be human masters. Nevertheless, the bridge was quickly rebuilt for commuters heading to Albany and the trucks for New York. For all its human-made objects, the urban system is itself a product of nature, just as humans are themselves of the natural world. As social scientists, we should be careful not to separate our human endeavors from nature's laws. If we appear to rule the world, it is only because we have insulated ourselves in urban cocoons from which we cannot see the world's supremacy over us.

The Urban Fallacy

To understand the city—any city, and thus urban society itself—as dependent upon its rural hinterland strikes a severe psychological blow to imagery of an independent metropolis. Quite the contrary, the image is of an immense population dependent upon their weaker cousins in the country. So sophisticated, so civilized, the city must of necessity find a way to control the products of the hinterland. Such dependency requires a myth of urban self-sufficiency. In fact, supremacy. There are two seemingly contradictory values that accompany such a myth.

A myth of urban self-sufficiency requires that the culture define urban areas as unique from rural. The cognitive emphasis is thus on the built environment— the settlement space—rather than on the system as a whole. Urban comes to be defined as "settled" or "developed," and as such it defines all areas not immediately developed as "non-urban," and thus acceptable places for exploitation. Not surprisingly, many of those interviewed for this work—in Gilboa and among New Yorkers—referred to the watershed as "in the middle of nowhere." Such an image allows people to dismiss the area as "there's nothing there." But as one Gilboa resident asked, "why does something need to be there?" The answer, unfortunate though it is for residents of rural communities, is that an urban society defines it so.

If the myth of urban self-sufficiency defines "urban" strictly in terms of settlement space, the next obvious step is to define cities—in particular in cultural terms—as superior to rural areas (and, by extension, rural people). Cities are thus seen as the harbingers of civilization, and not agriculture nor trade—both of which were conducted by rural societies long before the advent of cities. From such a perspective, cities do not so much exploit rural resources as they bring civilization to them. In Gilboa, the act of condemning and destroying the village was overshadowed by the technological innovations, the building of paved roads in an otherwise unpaved wilderness, and the jobs created at the dam site. That there were victims of the project was downplayed as an unfortunate side effect of an otherwise brilliant project.

A second condition associated with the myth of urban self-sufficiency is the perception and portrayal of peoples with whom the city comes in contact. The general perception of those people and territories outside the city is best described as exoticism, with all of its attendant schizotypal stereotypes. Stereotypes of necessity must both ingratiate the urbanite to rural areas and justify the exploitation of the hinterland. The result is a set of stereotypes that emphasize the natural beauty and pastoral simplicity of the countryside while simultaneously portraying the population as somehow different from the mainstream urban culture found in the city.

In upstate New York, not surprisingly, much of the emphasis for tourism and other economic activity stresses, to a historically inaccurate degree, the rural countryside. A perusal of the New York State Museum in Albany, for example, leads one through a fascinating exhibit about New York City, a reconstruction of an Iroquoian longhouse, and a large area devoted to logging in the Adirondack Mountains. There are smaller exhibits devoted to the Holocaust and the contributions of African-Americans. There are large collections of wildlife and some mention of the geologic history of the region. All are necessary components of such a museum, but there is shockingly little about the Erie Canal and the cities spawned along its route. Given the centrality of the canal in creating the economic dominance of both the city and the state, this omission stands as an academic lesion in the portrayal of New York's history, the neglect of the other major cities further stains against an otherwise outstanding institution. Curiously, there have been few complaints about this lack of attention to the remainder of the state. Similarly, the state license plate shows pictures of the Manhattan skyline and Niagara Falls with mountains in between. Tourist literature typically shows urban imagery of New York City and rural countryside, with little if any mention of upstate cities and other urbanized places.

If the countryside receives good reviews, the population that inhabits that countryside receives a mixed bag of opinions directed their way. Rural life is frequently portrayed as more simple and uncomplicated than urban life. Thus, such television shows as *Greenacres* and *Northern Exposure* portrayed rural residents as being literally more simple—even dumb—than might be found in a metropolitan area. Other cultural productions, such as the film *Deliverance*, posit such simplicity in a more ominous tone, as the plot revolved around a group of "normal" metropolitan men being accosted by deviant hillbillies. "Redneck" jokes are founded on such stereotypes and are acceptable in polite company where similar jokes about other oppressed groups would not be tolerated.

Attempts are also made to incorporate such cultural difference into the urban culture, and diversity is at times embraced by the elite classes. Such inclusiveness, however, is most often in regard to the cultural artifacts of a subject population, such as American Folk Art, Thai cuisine, and African-American musical forms, even as the population itself is not embraced. Further, such an embrace of diversity is often treated as other cultural objects and thus subject to fads: during the early twenty-first century, many residents of New York City and other major cities proclaimed a great love of the cultural artifacts of some groups, such as Latin American-inspired "peasant" blouses and jewelry, but abhorred the diversity found among the working classes of their own hinterland and inner city, such as Country music and Buffalo Chicken wings, as hopelessly parochial. Indeed, an acceptance of "diversity" is necessary for a global economy built on post-colonial relationships, whereas acceptance of internal colonists helps one little in the boardroom or the storefront. It is the drive for the exotic that aids capitalist expansion, not the continued courting of those already in the system.

Such cultural manifestations of urbanization—the myth of urban superiority, a taste for exotic cultural artifacts, and a reluctance to perceive those living at some distance from the city as equals—are easily adaptable. Perceiving the immediate hinterland as a place for exploitation, it takes little beyond population growth, or even individual ambition, to view nearby cities as exploitable hinterland as well. Does urbanization explain violence and greed? No—war has been documented in hunting and gathering societies as well (see, for example, Johnson & Earle, 1987; Maryanski & Turner, 1992). But certainly it has changed in character, focused as it is on the acquisition and control of resources. As the state is the manifestation of the urban system—the network of various political-economic elites—it should not be surprising that it, too, conducts wars and other functions in the name of the urban elite. And hence, war was committed for the city of Athens, the empire of Rome, and the vast global empire of the British.

Urban Waves

New York City had begun as a trading center and it has continued as such for hundreds of years. It was the development of modern capitalism that made the city what it is today. The city's elite turned its attention to industrial production as a way of creating items for trade. In order to power the factories workers from throughout the world flocked to the city, not only producing trade items, but creating the market for them as well. Thus, the city's population growth created both the market for products and the ability to make them. New York's settlement space expanded and absorbed outlying areas—hinterlands—such as the Bronx and Brooklyn. Residents sought refuge in the hinterlands of Westchester County, first as tourists but eventually moving there and absorbing the county into the metropolitan area. New York City's settlement space today extends dozens of miles from the legal boundaries of the city itself, with new housing and businesses developing as far north as Orange County and commanding commuters from as far away as Ulster and Sullivan Counties in the Catskills—not to the city itself but to the edge cities far removed from the high peaks of Manhattan. Formerly independent cities such as Newburgh, Middletown, and Poughkeepsie are now considered part of the metropolitan area. But the settlement space, expanding as a wave from the heart of the city, is only one of several that have worked through the region and now extend far beyond.

Gilboa was once relatively autonomous. As the urban system developed in the nineteenth century, the economic integration with the city in the form of the money economy was the first wave of urbanization to overcome the village. Today, money has become such a worldwide phenomenon that many economists (but not all) consider it a natural extension of the human condition, willfully ignorant of the millions of years of human history spent in money-free hunting and gathering societies. The significance of money was in its utility in trading agricultural and other rural goods for urban products. Money allowed for the distortions in exchange values that created profit for urban merchants. More importantly, money fostered the appearance of equality in trade relations—the city looked neither dependent on its hinterland nor all-powerful over it. New York's reliance on the hinterland for food was thus concealed, but continued growth in the city necessitated expansion of the hinterland to both meet demand and keep prices low. Eventually, the Great Lakes basin was supplying much of New York City's food. As transportation and refrigeration technology improved, even foods such as dairy could be produced at greater distances, taking advantage of the lower cost of living away from the city and its accompanying low labor costs as well as superior farmland in the Great Plains.

The city next emanated a wave of industrialization. Industrialization not only produced trade goods in the city, but throughout the trade corridors of New York State as well. The companies upstate were typically independent of New

York corporations, but nevertheless they depended upon city merchants to bring their products to market. Early on, such companies in upstate cities relied on the built-in markets of their home regions, but introduction to the global economy through New York City allowed them to grow far beyond the scale proffered by their hometowns. In time, the advantages of economies of scale encouraged corporate concentration, with those companies located in larger markets—in larger cities—benefiting. Upstate factories became locations where labor was bought for production, and as more area was subsumed into the urban system populations willing to work for less could easily replace the comparatively well-paid New Yorkers. Those jobs eventually went to the southern United States, to Mexico, and now increasingly to even lower wage areas in Asia.

Various service industries, such as finance, insurance, and retail sales, have taken the place of manufacturing by selling urban products to the hinterland. Increasingly, metropolitan areas function as outlets for the sale of products produced by the urban system in faraway lands. At the top of the services hierarchy are cities that have headquarters for such companies, often enveloping the administrative and creative functions of the economy. Smaller cities and towns, however, often rely on lower wage-scale activities in these companies, such as customer service call centers and retail sales. Tourism, too, is such an industry, as communities clamor for monthly scraps in the family budget to be used for entertainment. Many rural communities, Gilboa included, are left with only this option.

As these waves have emanated from the city, communities have changed accordingly. Much of Brooklyn was once farmland to support the cities, then became the frontline of temporary escape from the city only to become the city itself. Many of the suburbs of Westchester County were autonomous farming villages, then tourist or resort communities, and finally suburbs. Some communities missed a stage as it went further a field—many Westchester County towns had little industry as manufacturing went further upstate. Like Gilboa, more distant locales had advantages not matched by the more proximate rural communities. In time, the urban system rediscovered them and turned them into suburbs—their relative lack of development the basis of their appeal.

Gilboa has missed stages. As part of the agricultural hinterland, the community failed to develop the industrial base due to its remote location and lack of population. Indeed, many Gilboans of the time would have questioned the necessity for Gilboa to develop in such a way. Upstate New York's time at the forefront of the global economy arrived and passed through the region with barely a noticeable effect on Gilboa. The state's economy has matured, and the forefront of economic innovation has continued its march toward the frontiers, financed by the money in Manhattan but bypassing the hinterland that created the city. Gilboa today has a service economy based on tourism, based as it is on the relative lack of development. It is helpful for some, but with little actual economic production in the region there is little homegrown wealth.

As each wave has passed through upstate New York, communities have experienced increases and declines in prosperity: increasing prosperity with agricultural trade and then decline as more efficient producers are found elsewhere. Increasing prosperity as manufacturing grows followed by decline as cheaper labor is found elsewhere. Even the suburbs of the city itself have experienced such patterns as real estate development is new and then ages—attracting the poor as the middle class go further abroad. Such waves should not, however, be confused with the regular advance suggested by concentric zone theory (see Burgess, 1925); such waves are chaotic in their advance, hyper-developing some places and ignoring others.

What is striking about the case of Gilboa is the exercise of raw power on display. A social system is most stable when its members agree on basic norms, values, and needs. That is, the stability of a social system is greatly enhanced by the exercise of hegemonic power. Conflict is, however, inevitable and the use of coercive means is often found in such cases. Conflicts vary, and the level of diametric opposition of interests not surprisingly is related to the use of power. Gilboa residents' interests were in direct opposition to those of the city, and a more spirited defense of the community was necessary to halt the project. Such a fight was, of course, unwinnable. New York City had considerable power. In terms of political power, city interests dominated state government. The city had immense economic resources. And ultimately, military power—in the form of the National Guard or, more likely, the police powers as exercised by the Albany County Sheriff during the Anti-Rent Wars—could have stopped anyone who dared challenge the city's supremacy. With so many residents knowing this, hegemonic power was enough—you can't fight City Hall.

Like the people of Gilboa so many years ago, we long for epistemological security. We seek out stories of the disadvantaged defeating their supposed superiors, whether in the form of David killing Goliath or Tweety outsmarting Sylvester. Myths exist in Gilboa, as in countless other defeated places, as to the final bursts of resistance against an outside intruder. Countless books have been written about such resistance, expressing the satisfaction of watching the downtrodden suddenly gain the upper hand. Such stories inspire hope and goodwill in looking to our own situations, reinforcing for each of us a sense of justice in the world. Like so many, I hoped for the victory of the victims or, knowing the outcome, a noble campaign of resistance to the city's plans. A longer string of lawsuits, perhaps, or human barricades in front of condemned houses, or even a cultural legacy of poetry, song, or story in opposition to the community's condemnation. It is my fear that Gilboa is all too typical. I, too, looked for David in the waters of the Schoharie Reservoir, but I found Spartacus instead.

Bibliography

Albion, R. G. 1984. *The Rise of New York Port, 1815—1860*. Boston: Northeastern University Press.

Allen, O. E. 1990. *New York, New York: A History of the World's Most Exhilarating and Challenging City*. New York: Atheneum.

___. 1993. *The Tiger–The Rise and Fall of Tammany Hall*. New York: Addison—Wesley Publishing Company.

Alleyne, E. P. 1980. *A History of Conflict on the Waters of Schoharie Creek: The Gilboa Dam*. Cornell Agricultural Economics Staff Paper, No. 80—18.

Allswang, John M. 1977. *Bosses, Machines, and Urban Voters*. New York: Kennikat Press.

Aquila, R. 1977. *The Iroquois Restoration: A Study of Iroquois Power, Politics, and Relations with Indians and Whites*. Ph.D. Dissertation, Ohio State University.

Bachman, V. C. 1969. *Peltries or Plantations*. Baltimore: John Hopkins U. Press.

Bean, P. A. 1994. The Irish, the Italians, and Machine Politics. *Journal of Urban History, 20, 2, 205—239*.

Bedstuyonline. 2003. *History*. <http://www.bedstuyonline.com; accessed 5 May 2003.

Berger, P. L. & Luckmann, T. 1968. *The Social Construction of Reality*. New York: Anchor Books.

Bluestone, B. & Harrison, B. 1982. *The Deindustrialization of America*. New York: Basic Books.

Blumer, H. 1990. *Symbolic Interactionism: Perspective and Method*. Berkeley, Ca.: U. California Press.

Bohls, C. 1991. *Industrial Order in Leatherstocking Country: Textile Mills and Mill Workers in Otsego County, New York*. M.A. Thesis, State University of New York College at Oneonta.

Bourdieu, P. 1972. *Outline of a Theory of Practice*. New York: Cambridge U. Press.

Burgess, E. W. 1925. The Growth of the City. *Publications of the American Sociological Society, 18, 85—97*.

Burns, R. 2001. *New York*. PBS Home Video.

Burrows, E. G. & Wallace, M. 1999. *Gotham: A History of New York City to 1898*. New York: Oxford U. Press.

Business Week. 22 Oct. 2001. *The Center Must Hold*. Business Week.

BWS. . .see New York City Board of water Supply.

Cannon, J. & Griffiths, R. 2000. *The Oxford Illustrated History of the British Monarchy*. New York: Oxford U. Press.

Castells, M. 1977. *The Urban Question: A Marxist Approach*. Cambridge, Ma.: MIT Press.

Cauvin, J. 2000. *The Birth of the Gods and the Origins of Agriculture*. Trevor Watkins, Translator. New York: Cambridge U. Press.

Cheyney, E. P. 1887. *The Anti-Rent Agitation in the state of New York, 1839—1846*. Philadelphia: U. Pennsylvania Press.

Christman, H. 1945. *Tin Horns and Calico: A Decisive Episode in the Emergence of Democracy*. New York: Henry Holt & Company.

Clarke, T. W. 1952. *Utica, for a Century and a Half*. Utica, N. Y., Widtman Press.

Collins, R. 1975. *Conflict Sociology: Toward an Explanatory Science*. New York: Academic Press.

___. 1982. *The Credential Society: An Historical Society of Education and Stratification*. New York: Academic Press.

Connolly, P. & Dodge, H. 2000. *The Ancient City: Life in Classical Athens and Rome*. New York: Oxford U. Press.

Cornog, E. 2000. *The Birth of Empire: DeWitt Clinton and the American Experience, 1769—1828*. New York: Oxford U. Press.

Crane, S. 1997. *The Red Badge of Courage*. New York: Tor Books.

Daniels, J. 2000. *Discovering the Forgotten History of African-Americans in Schoharie County*. Cobleskill, N. Y.: Times-Journal Press.

Duell, D. H. (ed.). 1986. *On the Road in Schoharie*. Cobleskill, N. Y.: State University of New York at Cobleskill.

Duffy, J. 1968. *A History of Public Health in New York City 1625—1866*. New York: Russell Sage Foundation.

Durkheim, E. 1997. *The Division of Labor in Society*. New York: Free Press.

Ellis, D. M. 1946. *Landlords and Farmers in the Hudson-Mohawk Region, 1790—1850*. Ithaca, N. Y.: Cornell U. Press.

Ellis, D. M., Frost, J. A., Syrett, H. C., & Carman, H. J. 1957. *A Short History of New York State*. Ithaca, N. Y.: Cornell U. Press.

Ellis, D. M. & Preston, D. M. 1982. *The Upper Mohawk Country: An Illustrated History of Greater Utica*. Woodland Hills, Ca.: Windsor Publications.

Environmental Protection Agency. 1996. *Watershed Progress: New York City Watershed Agreement*. Paper: EPA840-F-96-005.

EPA...see Environmental Protection Agency.

Fagan, B. M. 2000. *Ancient North America*. Third Edition. New York: Thames & Hudson.

Fainstein, S. 1993. *The City Builders*. New York: Blackwell.

Fischer, J. R. 1997. *A Well-Executed Failure: The Sullivan Campaign against the Iroquois, July-September 1779*. Columbia, S. C.: U. South Carolina Press.

Fitchen, J. M. 1991. *Endangered Spaces, Enduring Places*. San Francisco, Ca.: Westview Press.

Fleming, T. 1999. *The Duel: Alexander Hamilton, Aaron Burr, and the Future of America*. New York: Perseus.

Ganshof, F. L. 1996. *Feudalism*. Translated by Philip Grierson. Toronto: U. Toronto Press.

Garreau, J. 1981. *The Nine Nations of North America*. New York: Avon Books.

Galusha, D. 1999. *Liquid Assets: A History of New York's Water System*. Fleischmanns, N. Y.: Purple Mountain Press.

Gibson, C. (United States Bureau of the Census). 1998. *Population of the 100 Largest Cities and other Urban Places in the United States: 1790 to 1990*. United States Census Bureau Population Division Working Paper No. 27. Washington, D.C.: United States Census Bureau.

Giddens, A. 1991. *Modernity and Self-Identity: Self and Society in the Late Modern Age*. Stanford, Ca.: Stanford U. Press.

Gilman, L. 1971. *The Development of a Neighborhood: Bedford, 1850—1880: A Case Study*. M.A. Thesis: Columbia University.

Goffman, E. 1959. *The Presentation of Self in Everyday Life*. New York: Doubleday.

Granovetter, M. 1985. Economic Action and Social Structure: The Problem of Embeddedness. *American Journal of Sociology, 91, 481-510*.

Graymont, B. 1990. *The Iroquois in the American Revolution*. Syracuse, N. Y.: Syracuse University Press.

Hall, P. 1998. *Cities in Civilization*. New York: Fromm International.

Hamilton, A., Madison, J., & Jay, J. 2003. *The Federalist Papers*. Edited by C. Rossiter. New York: Signet Classic.

Harris, R. 1991. "The Geography of Employment and Residence in New York since 1950." In Mollenkopf, J. & Castells, M (eds.), *Dual City: Restructuring New York*. New York: Russell Sage Foundation.

Hartmann, T. 2002. *Unequal Protection: The Rise of Corporate Dominance and the Theft of Human Rights*. New York: Rodale.

Harvey, D. 1999. *The Limits to Capital*. New Edition. New York: Verso.

Heilbroner, R. L. & Milberg, W. 1998. *The Making of Economic Society*. New York: Pearson.

Hendrix, L. E. & Hendrix, A. W. (eds.). 1995. *The Sloughters' History of Schoharie County 1795—1995*. Bicentennial Edition. Schoharie, N. Y.: The Tryon Press.

Herman, E. S. & Chomsky, N. 1988. *Manufacturing Consent: The Political Economy of the Mass Media*. New York: Pantheon.

Hicks, M. A. 1995. *Bastard Feudalism*. New York: Longman.

Hooker, M. T. 1999. *The History of Holland*. New York: Greenwood Press.

HSBC. 2003. *Web Site*. <http://www.hsbc.com; accessed 15 June 2003>.

Israel, J. 1998. *The Dutch Republic: Its Rise, Greatness, and Fall 1477—1806*. New York: Oxford U. Press.

Jackson, K. T. 1985. *Crabgrass Frontier: The Suburbanization of the United States*. New York: Oxford U. Press.

Johnson, A. W. & Earle, T. 1987. *The Evolution of Human Societies: From Foraging Group to Agrarian State*. Stanford, Ca.: Stanford U. Press.

Johnstone, R. L. 2001. *Religion in Society*. Sixth Edition. New York: Prentice Hall.

Kay, J. H. 1998. *Asphalt Nation: How the Automobile took over America and How we can take it Back*. Berkeley, Ca.: U. California Press.

Kehoe, A. B. 1992. *North American Indians: A Comprehensive Account*. Second Edition. Englewood Cliffs, N. J.: Prentice Hall.

Keller, S. 2003. *Community: Pursuing the Dream, Living the Reality*. Princeton, N. J.: Princeton U. Press.

Kennedy, P. 1989. *The Rise and Fall of the Great Powers: Economic Change and Military Conflict from 1500 to 2000*. New York: Random House.

Klein, D. B. & Majewski, J. 1992. Economy, Community, and Law: The Turnpike Movement in New York, 1797—1845. *Law & Society Review, 26, 3, 469—512*.

Koeppel, G. T. 2000. *Water for Gotham: A History*. Princeton, N. J.: Princeton U. Press.

Larkin, F. D. 1990. *John B. Jervis: An American Engineering Pioneer*. Iowa City, Ia.: Iowa U. Press.

____. 1998. *New York State Canals: A Short History*. Fleischmanns, N. Y.: Purple Mountain Press.

Linden, E. 1992. A Curious Kinship: Apes and Humans. *National Geographic, March, 2-45*.

Logan, J. R. & Molotch, H. 1987. *Urban Fortunes: The Political Economy of Place*. Berkeley, Ca.: U. California Press .

Magnusson, M. 1965. *Vinland Sagas: Norse Discovery of America*. New York: Viking Press.

Mann, M. 1986. *The Sources of Social Power*. New York: Cambridge U. Press.

Maryanski, A. & Turner, J. H. 1992. *The Social Cage: Human Nature and the Evolution of Society*. Stanford, Ca.: Stanford U. Press.

Martien, J. 1996. *Shell Game: A True Account of Beads and Money in North America*. New York: Mercury house.

Marx, K. 1985 (1848). *The Communist Manifesto*. New York: Penguin Books.

___. 1990 (1867). *Capital; Volumes One through Three*. New York: Penguin Books.

Maslow, A. H. 1968. *Toward a Psychology of Being*. New York: Van Nostrand Reinhold.

Mayham, A. C. *The Anti-Rent War on Blenheim Hill: An Episode of the 40s*. Jefferson, N. Y.: Frederick L. Frazee.

McCarthy, J. D. & Zald, M. N. 1977. Resource Mobilization and Social Movements: A Partial Theory. *American Journal of Sociology, 82, 1212-41*.

Melton, B. F. Jr. 2001. *Aaron Burr: Conspiracy to Treason*. New York: John Wiley & Sons.

Milgram, S. 1969. *Obedience to Authority*. New York: Harper.

Morey, S. K. 1991. *Mat Hooks in Black Hands: African-Americans in Schoharie County, New York*. M.A. Thesis, State University of New York College at Oneonta.

Morley, N. 2002. *Metropolis and Hinterland: The City of Rome and the Italian Economy, 200 B.C. to 200 A.D.* New York: Cambridge U. Press.

Nash, B. B. 1999. *Red, White, and Black: The Peoples of Early North America*. Fourth Edition. New York: Prentice-Hall.

Nash, J. C. 1989. *From Tank Town to High Tech: The Clash of Community and Industrial Cycles*. Albany, N. Y.: State University of New York Press.

National Archives. 1998. Fort Stanwix Boundary Line Treaty. *National Archives Microfilm Publication No. 668: Ratified Indian Treaties; 1722-1868, No. 7 frame Nos. m=0138-142, pgs. M-5*. Washington, D. C.: National Archives & Records Administration.

New York City Board of Water Supply. 1914. *Eighth Annual Report of the Board of Water Supply of the City of New York*. New York: Author.

___. 1915. *Ninth Annual Report of the Board of Water Supply of the City of New York*. New York: Author.

___. 1916. *Tenth Annual Report of the Board of Water Supply of the City of New York*. New York: Author.

___. 1917. *Eleventh Annual Report of the Board of Water Supply of the City of New York*. New York: Author.

___. 1918. *Twelfth Annual Report of the Board of Water Supply of the City of New York*. New York: Author.

___. 1919. *Thirteenth Annual Report of the Board of Water Supply of the City of New York*. New York: Author.

___. 1920. *Fourteenth Annual Report of the Board of Water Supply of the City of New York*. New York: Author.

___. 1921. *Fifteenth Annual Report of the Board of Water Supply of the City of New York*. New York: Author.

___. 1922. *Sixteenth Annual Report of the Board of Water Supply of the City of New York*. New York: Author.

___. 1923. *Seventeenth Annual Report of the Board of Water Supply of the City of New York*. New York: Author.

___. 1924. *Eighteenth Annual Report of the Board of Water Supply of the City of New York*. New York: Author.

___. 1925. *Nineteenth Annual Report of the Board of Water Supply of the City of New York*. New York: Author.

___. 1926. *Twentieth Annual Report of the Board of Water Supply of the City of New York*. New York: Author.

___. 1927. *Twenty-first Annual Report of the Board of Water Supply of the City of New York*. New York: Author.

___. 1928. *Twenty-second Annual Report of the Board of Water Supply of the City of New York*. New York: Author.

___. 1929. *Twenty-third Annual Report of the Board of Water Supply of the City of New York*. New York: Author.

___. 1930. *Twenty-fourth Annual Report of the Board of Water Supply of the City of New York*. New York: Author.

___. 1931. *Twenty-fifth Annual Report of the Board of Water Supply of the City of New York*. New York: Author.

New York State Department of Economic Development. 2000. *New York State Data Center*. <http://www.nylovesbiz.com/nysdc/default.asp; accessed 17 March 2003>.

Noyes, M. F. (ed.). 1964. *A History of Schoharie County*. Richmondville, N. Y.: Richmondville Phoenix.

O'Connor, J. 1998. *Natural Causes: Essays in Ecological Marxism*. New York: Guilford.

Ormerod, P. 1994. *The Death of Economics*. New York: St. Martins.

Parsons, T. 1951. *The Social System*. New York: Free Press.

PASNY…see Power Authority of the State of New York.

Pena, E. S. 2001. The Role of Wampum Production at the Albany Almshouse. *Historical Arcehology, 5, 2, 155—74.*

Phillips, K. 2002. *Wealth and Democracy*. New York: Broadway Books.

Plunkitt, G. W. 1995 [1905]. *Plunkitt of Tammany Hall*. New York: Penguin Putnam.

Power Authority of the State of New York. 2003. *Blenheim-Gilboa Power Project*. <http://www.nypa.gov/facilities/blengil.htm; accessed 14 march 2003>.

Rabrenovic, G. 1996. *Community Builders*. Philadelphia, Pa.: Temple U. Press.

Reynolds, S. 1996. *Fiefs & Vassals*. New York: Oxford U. Press.

Ringholz, R. C. & Muscolino, K. C. 1992. *Little Town Blues: Voices from the Changing American West*. Salt Lake City, Ut.: Gibbs-Smith Books.

Rosenberg, C. E. 1962. *The Cholera Years: The U. S. in 1832, 1849, and 1866*. Chicago: U. Chicago Press.

Roscoe, W. 1882. *History of Schoharie County*. <http://www.rootsweb.com/~nyschoha/chap7.html>.

Ryan, M. P. 1981. *Cradle of the Middle Class*. New York: Cambridge U. Press.

Sassen, S. 1991. *The Global City*. Princeton, N. J.: Princeton U. Press.

___. 1994. *Cities in a World Economy*. Thousand Oaks, Ca.: Pine Forge Press.

Shaw, R. 1966. *Erie Water West: A History of the Erie Canal, 1792—1854*. Lexington, Ky.: U. Press of Kentucky.

Sheriff, C. 1997. *The Artificial River: The Erie Canal and the Paradox of Progress, 1817—1862*. New York: Hill & Wang.

Shupe, B., Steins, J., & Pandit, J. 1987. *New York State Population: 1790—1980*. New York: Neal-Schuman Publishers.

Smith, H. 1989. *The Religions of Man*. New York: Harper-Collins.

Steuding, B. 1985. *The Last of the Handmade Dams: The Story of the Ashokan Reservoir*. Fleischmanns, N. Y.: Purple Mountain Press.

Stratigos, L. T. 1998. *Sesquicentennial: Gilboa, New York 1848—1998*. Gilboa, N. Y.: Gilboa Historical Society.

Tauxe, C. S. 1993. *Farms, Mines, and Main Streets: Uneven Development in a Dakota County*. Philadelphia: Temple U. Press.

Taylor, A. 1995. *William Cooper's Town*. New York: Knopf.

Thomas, A. R. 1998. *Economic and Social Restructuring in a Rural Community*. Ph.D. Dissertation: Northeastern University.

___. 2003. *In Gotham's Shadow: Globalization and Community Change in Central New York*. Albany: SUNY Press.

Toennies, F. 2001. *Community and Civil Society*. New York: Cambridge U. Press.

United States Bureau of the Census. 2000. *Decennial Census of Population*. <http://www.census.gov; accessed 11 Dec. 2002>.

___. 2003. *American Factfinder*. <http://www.census.gov/factfinder; accessed 4 May 2003>.

United States Library of Congress. 31 May 1779. George Washington Papers at the Library of Congress, 1741—1799: Series 4. General Correspondence. 1697—1799. *Letter from George Washington to John Sullivan, May 31, 1779*. <http://memory.loc.gov/ammem/gwhtml/gwhome.html>; (accessed 30 Jan. 2001).

Vanema, J. 1999. Poverty and Charity in Seventeenth Century Beverwijck/Albany, 1652—1700. *New York History, 80, 382-405*.

Weber, M. 1986. *Economy and Society*. Volumes 1 & 2. Berkeley, Ca.: U. California Press.

___. 1992 [1930]. *The Protestant Ethic and the Spirit of Capitalism*. New York: Routledge.

Weidner, C. H. 1974. *Water for a City: A History of New York's Problem from the Beginning to the Delaware River System, 1897—1966*. New Brunswick, N. J.: Rutgers U. Press.

Wilson, W. J. 1987. *The Truly Disadvantaged*. Chicago: U. Chicago Press.

Wirth, L. 1938. Urbanism as a Way of Life. *American Journal of Sociology, 44,* *1-24.*

Witt, S. K. 1963. *The Democratic Party in Utica*. M.A. Thesis: Syracuse University.

Zinn, H. 2003. *A People's History of the United States, 1492—Present*. New York: Perennial Classics.

Index